SAME-SEX PAR
BEST INTERI

This book is written for academics, and non-governmental organisatior LGBT+ parenting. The book prese recognition of gay and lesbian famil the best interests of the child. In this reference to children's rights and to manner, it is argued that the best i demand that same-sex parenting recognition and protection. Suggest most appropriate manner of providir of parental responsibility, adoption, These suggestions are drawn from con England and Wales, Ireland and Soutl assessment of the best interests princip

LYDIA BRACKEN is an Assistant Dean, (AHSS) and a Lecturer in Law, Univer a former Department of Children and Yo author of numerous publications on chi for her research from the Irish Researcl funding bodies.

SAME-SEX PARENTING AND THE BEST INTERESTS PRINCIPLE

LYDIA BRACKEN
University of Limerick

CAMBRIDGE
UNIVERSITY PRESS

CAMBRIDGE
UNIVERSITY PRESS

University Printing House, Cambridge CB2 8BS, United Kingdom

One Liberty Plaza, 20th Floor, New York, NY 10006, USA

477 Williamstown Road, Port Melbourne, VIC 3207, Australia

314–321, 3rd Floor, Plot 3, Splendor Forum, Jasola District Centre, New Delhi – 110025, India

79 Anson Road, #06–04/06, Singapore 079906

Cambridge University Press is part of the University of Cambridge.

It furthers the University's mission by disseminating knowledge in the pursuit of education, learning, and research at the highest international levels of excellence.

www.cambridge.org
Information on this title: www.cambridge.org/9781108497190
DOI: 10.1017/9781108684460

First published 2020

Printed in the United Kingdom by TJ International Ltd. Padstow Cornwall

A catalogue record for this publication is available from the British Library.

Library of Congress Cataloging-in-Publication Data
Names: Bracken, Lydia, author.
Title: Same-sex parenting and the best interests principle / Lydia Bracken, University of Limerick.
Description: Cambridge, United Kingdom ; New York, NY, USA : Cambridge University Press, 2020. | Includes bibliographical references and index.
Identifiers: LCCN 2019037319 (print) | LCCN 2019037320 (ebook) | ISBN 9781108497190 (hardback) | ISBN 9781108684460 (ebook)
Subjects: LCSH: Gay-parent families – Law and legislation. | Parent and child (Law)
Classification: LCC K700 .B73 2020 (print) | LCC K700 (ebook) | DDC 346.01/7–dc23
LC record available at https://lccn.loc.gov/2019037319
LC ebook record available at https://lccn.loc.gov/2019037320

ISBN 978-1-108-49719-0 Hardback

For my wonderfully 'non-traditional' family, with love and thanks

CONTENTS

TABLE OF CASES

AB and Surrogacy Advisory Group v. *the Minister of Social Development (Centre for Child Law as Amicus Curiae)* [2016] ZACC 43
AB (Surrogacy: Consent) [2016] EWHC 2643 (Fam)
AD and Another v. *DW and Others (Centre for Child Law as Amicus Curiae; Department of Social Development as Intervening Party)* 2008 (3) SA 183 (CC)
BVerfG, Judgment of the First Senate of 19 February 2013 – 1 BvL 1/11
Case XII ZB 463/13 (10 December 2014)
Centre for Child Law v. *Minister of Social Development* 2014 (1) SA 577 (GSJ)
Charron and Merle-Montet v. *France*, app. no. 22612/15, 16 January 2018
City View Press Ltd v. *An CO* [1980] IR 381
CM v. *NG* 2012 (4) S.A. 452 (WCC)
Cour de Cassation, Ruling no. 619 (3 July 2015)
D and L (Surrogacy) [2012] EWHC 2631 (Fam)
De Reuck v. *Director of Public Prosecutions (Withwatersrand Local Division)* 2004 (1) SA 406 (CC)
Dickson v. *United Kingdom*, app. no. 44362/04, 4 December 2007
Du Toit and Another v. *Minister of Welfare and Population Development and Others* 2001 (12) BCLR 1225
Du Toit and De Vos v. *Minister of Welfare and Others* (CCT 40/01) [2002] ZACC 20
EB v. *France*, app. no. 43546/02, 22 January 2008
Evans v. *United Kingdom*, app. no. 6339/05, 10 April 2004
Ex Parte MS and Others 2014 (3) SA 415 (GP)
Farnell and Another v. *Chanbua* [2016] FCWA 17
FN and EB v. *CO* [2004] 4 IR 311
Gas and Dubois v. *France*, app. no. 25951/07, 15 March 2012
Gaskin v. *United Kingdom*, app. no. 10454/83, 7 July 1989
In the Matter of an Application by the Northern Ireland Human Rights Commission [2013] NICA 37
In the Matter of Z (A Child) (No. 2) [2016] EWHC 1191 (Fam)
J and B v. *Director-General, Department of Home Affairs* (2003) (5) BCLR 463
JMcD v. *PL and BM* [2010] 2 IR 199
Johnston v. *Ireland*, app. no. 9697/92, 18 December 1986

J v. *National Director of Public Prosecutions and Another* 2014 (2) SACR 1 (CC)
Karner v. *Austria*, app. no. 40016/98, 24 July 2003
Labassee v. *France*, app. no. 65941/11, 26 September 2014
Marckx v. *Belgium*, app. no. 6833/74, 13 June 1979
Mennesson v. *France*, app. no. 65192/11, 26 September 2014
Minister of Welfare and Population Development v. *Fitzpatrick and Others* 2000 (3) SA 422 (CC)
MR v. *An tArd Chláraitheoir* [2014] 3 IR 533
M v. *The State* [2007] ZACC 18
North Western Health Board v. *HW* [2001] 3 IR 622
N v. *Health Service Executive* [2006] 4 IR 374
Oliari and Others v. *Italy*, app. nos. 18766/11 and 36030/11, 21 July 2015
Paradiso and Campanelli v. *Italy*, app. no. 25358/12, 27 January 2015
PW v. *AW* (21 April 1980, unreported), High Court
Re B (A Child) [2009] UKSC 5
Re B (Role of Biological Father) [2007] EWHC 1952 (Fam), [2008] 1 FLR 855 (CA)
Re E-R (A Child) [2015] EWCA Civ 405
Re D (Contact and Parental Responsibility: Lesbian Mothers and Known Father) [2006] EWHC 2 (Fam), [2006] 1 FCR 556
Re G (Children) (Residence: Same-Sex Partner) [2006] UKHL 43
Re H (Parental Responsibility) [1998] 1 FLR 855
Re JH [1985] IR 375
Re KD (a Minor) (Ward: Termination of Access) [1988] 1 ALL ER 577
Re K (a Minor) (Ward: Care and Control) [1990] 3 All ER 795
Re K (a Minor) (Wardship: Adoption) [1991] 1 FLR 57
Re L (A Child) (2010) 3146 (Fam)
Re N (2007) EWCA Civ 1053
Re P (Adoption: Unmarried Couple) [2008] UKHL 38
Re PC (Change of Surname) [1997] 2 FLR 730
Re T and M (Adoption) [2010] EWHC 964 (Fam), [2011] 1 FLR 1487
Re T (Change of Surname) [1998] 2 FLR 620
Re X (A Child) (Surrogacy: Time limit) [2014] EWHC 3135 (Fam)
Re X and Y (Foreign Surrogacy) [2008] EWHC 3030 (Fam)
Rose v. *Secretary of State* [2002] EWHC 1593
R v. *E and F (Female Parents: Known Father)* [2010] EWHC 417 (Fam), [2010] FLR 383
Salgueiro Da Silva Mouta v. *Portugal*, app. no. 33290/96, 21 December 1999
Saucedo Gomez v. *Spain*, app. no. 37784/97, 26 January 1999
Schalk & Kopf v. *Austria*, app. no. 30141/04, 24 June 2010
Sonderup v. *Tondelli* 2001 (1) SA 1171 (CC)
S v. *M (Centre for Child law as Amicus Curiae)* 2008 (3) SA 232
Supreme Court of Germany decision XII ZR 201/13, BGH, Urteil vom 28. January 2015 – XII ZR 201/13
The Northern Ireland Human Rights Commission's Application [2012] NIQB 77

Van der Linde v. *Van der Linde* 1996(3) SA 509 (O)
WH and Others [2011] ZAGPPHC 185
X and Others v. *Austria*, app. no. 19010/07, 19 February 2013
X, Y and Z v. *United Kingdom*, app. no. 21830/93, 22 April 1997
Yousef v. *Netherlands*, app. no. 33711/96, 5 November 2002
Zappone and Gilligan v. *Revenue Commissioners* [2008] 2 IR 417

TABLE OF INSTRUMENTS

British Columbia

Family Law Act 2011

Denmark

Danish Act on Registered Partnerships

Iceland

Icelandic Act on Registered Partnerships

International

Council of Europe, Recommendation No. R(84)4

European Convention on Human Rights, Strasbourg, 4 November 1950, in force 3 September 1953

European Tissues and Cells Directive (Directive 2004/23/EC)

Hague Convention on Protection of Children and Co-operation in Respect of Intercountry Adoption, 29 May 1993, in force 1 May 1995

Optional Protocol to the Convention on the Rights of the Child on the Sale of Children, Child Prostitution and Child Pornography, New York, 25 May 2000, in force 18 January 2002

United Nations Convention on the Rights of the Child, New York, 20 November 1989, in force 2 September 1990

Ireland

Adoption Act 2010

Adoption (Amendment) Act 2017

Bunreacht na hÉireann

Children Act 1997

Children and Family Relationships Act 2015

Children and Family Relationships (Amendment) Act 2018

Criminal Justice (Forensic Evidence and DNA Database System) Act 2014

Criminal Justice (Mutual Assistance) Act 2008

Firearms Act 1925

General Scheme of the Assisted Human Reproduction Bill 2017

General Scheme of the Children and Family Relationships Bill 2014

Guardianship of Infants Act 1964

International Criminal Court Act 2006

Marriage Act 2015
Passports Act 2008
Protection of Young Persons (Employment) Act 1996
Status of Children Act 1987
Thirty-Fourth Amendment of the Constitution (Marriage Equality) Act 2015

New Zealand

Care of Children Act 2004

Norway

Norwegian Act on Registered Partnerships

South Africa

Children's Act 38 of 2005
Children's Status Act 82 of 1987
Civil Union Act 17 of 2006
Constitution of the Republic of South Africa
National Health Act 61 of 2003
Regulations Relating to Artificial Fertilisation of Persons 2012

Sweden

Swedish Law of Artificial Insemination 1984 (SFS 1984 1140)

United Kingdom

Adoption and Children Act 2002
Children Act 1989
Children and Families Act 2014
Civil Partnership Act 2004
Human Fertilisation and Embryology Act 1990
Human Fertilisation and Embryology Act 2008
Human Fertilisation and Embryology Act 2008 (Remedial) Order 2018, SI 1413/2018
Human Fertilisation and Embryology Authority (Disclosure of Donor Information Regulations) 2004, SI 2004/1511
Marriage (Same Sex Couples) Act 2013
Surrogacy Arrangements Act 1985

Victoria, Australia

Assisted Reproductive Treatment Act 2008

Introduction

I.1 Introduction

> The decision to have a child of one's own has for thousands of years formed a central part of the lives of human beings. It is a blessing that is for the most part taken for granted. The effects of an inability to carry out that decision have, for so many of us, been nothing short of devastating.[1]

Gay and lesbian people have been having children for millennia. Yet, the legal recognition and social acceptance of gay and lesbian couples as parents are relatively recent developments in many countries. The quote from Khampepe J above illustrates the profound effect that an inability to have a child can have on an individual. In this book, it is argued that the inability to have the relationship between parent and child legally recognised is just as profound and that the 'devastating' consequences of that decision are felt most forcefully by the child.

Although many countries have adopted measures to legally recognise gay and lesbian families in recent years, many others have moved in the opposite direction and have taken active steps to impede the legal recognition of 'new' and 'non-traditional' families. States including Hungary, Croatia, Romania and Slovakia, have introduced explicit prohibitions on same-sex marriage through legislation or constitutional amendment within the past ten years. As marriage is tied to many important parenting rights, these are notable developments. It is evident that society is increasingly polarised as regards family recognition: restrictive marriage and parenting laws have become tighter while liberal laws have seemingly become more permissive. This 'contrapuntal pattern' of regulation is

[1] Khampepe J in *AB and Surrogacy Advisory Group* v. *the Minister of Social Development (Centre for Child Law as Amicus Curiae)* [2016] ZACC 43, para. 1.

based on diverse political, moral and cultural factors causing States to move 'one by one in opposite directions'.[2]

Where any legal regulation is considered, the rights and interests of children should be instrumental in provoking change. Yet, as the quote from Khampepe J above demonstrates, discussions about parenting are often framed in an adult perspective. Traditionally, arguments in favour of the legal recognition of same-sex parenting have followed a similar pattern, presented in terms of non-discrimination and equality concerning the adults, rather than the children involved. By contrast, the rights and interests of children are frequently invoked by those who are *opposed* to the legal recognition of gay and lesbian families. It is often claimed that gay and lesbian parents cannot secure the best interests of children, and so legal recognition should not be forthcoming.[3] The dichotomy in the use of the best interests principle highlights the malleability of the principle and the inherently subjective nature of the concept. This book addresses the question of subjectivity and seeks to find an objective approach to applying the best interests principle in the context of parenting. Arguably, the subjectivity of the principle can never be entirely eliminated, but it can, at least, be minimised using the conceptual framework identified in this book, that is through reliance on the guidance of the Committee on the Rights of the Child and by applying social science literature to guide otherwise subjective ideas.

This book adopts an essential perspective – the best interests of the child – through which to examine the legal recognition of same-sex parenting arrangements. This perspective is necessary due to the fact that the children of same-sex couples are the group who are most affected by the law's failure to recognise their family relationships. Therefore, given that under the United Nations Convention on the Rights of the Child (UNCRC)[4] the best interests principle is to be the paramount (Article 21), or at least a primary (Article 3), consideration in decisions as to their upbringing, it is necessary to examine the legal recognition of these families through the lens of children's rights and interests.

Applying the best interests principle in the manner described above, the book addresses the overarching question of *whether* the law should

[2] Tim Amos and Joe Rainer, 'Parenthood for same-sex couples in the EU' in Katharina Boele-Woelki and Angelika Fuchs (eds.), *Same-Sex Relationships and Beyond*, 3 ed. (Cambridge: Intersentia, 2017), p. 83.

[3] See Chapter 2.

[4] United Nations Convention on the Rights of the Child, New York, 20 November 1989, in force 2 September 1990.

offer legal recognition and protection to gay and lesbian families and the more discrete matter of *how* legal protection should be provided. It is argued that the best interests principle can be used to demand that same-sex parenting arrangements are afforded legal recognition and protection. Suggestions are also presented as to the most appropriate manner of providing for this recognition. These suggestions are drawn from comparative case studies that are used to facilitate assessment of the best interests principle. Ultimately, it is hoped that the arguments presented in each chapter provide a persuasive 'advocacy toolkit' to argue for reform of laws in jurisdictions that do not currently recognise LGBT+ parenting arrangements or that provide restrictions on same.

This Introduction sets out the central themes that arise in the chapters that follow. These themes form a common thread throughout the later chapters, providing a consistent structure for the arguments that are presented. The Introduction will also provide an explanation of the terminology that is used throughout the book to describe various family forms. Parenting is multifaceted, and so this book does not attempt to address all aspects. Instead, the focus is on common pathways to parentage that are available to same-sex couples and on applying the best interests principle in each context. The final section of the Introduction provides an overview of the chapter structure, which demonstrates the parameters of the research.

I.2 Central Themes

I.2.1 The Best Interests Principle

The best interests principle provides the theoretical foundation for the arguments advanced in this book. It is applied to address the questions of *whether* the law should offer legal recognition to gay and lesbian families and *how* legal protection should be provided. Following consideration of some of the perceived deficiencies of the best interests principle, Chapter 1 identifies a theoretical framework for applying the principle. Later chapters subsequently draw on this framework to present suggestions for the most appropriate manner of providing for legal recognition.

The book does not attempt to formulate a 'universal' definition of best interests. A universal definition is simply not possible because the definition will depend on the constitutional, political, social and cultural contexts in which the principle is applied. The comparative case studies serve to highlight this. Through analysis of the selected jurisdictions, the need for a conceptual framework to benchmark progress becomes apparent and the suitability of the identified framework is revealed.

I.2.2 Comparative Case Studies

Comparative case studies are used in the book to assess, compare and contrast the current laws of selected jurisdictions in order to identify best practice in the protection of the interests of children who are raised by same-sex couples. England and Wales, Ireland and South Africa are selected as comparator jurisdictions. In each of the selected jurisdictions, the best interests or welfare of the child determines how decisions concerning children are made. Notably, despite their common reference point, each jurisdiction takes a different approach to assessing best interests or welfare. It is necessary, therefore, to benchmark the conflicting approaches that are adopted against the UNCRC and against relevant sociological and psychological data to understand how decisions should be made with respect to children and to identify an appropriate legal response to gay and lesbian parenting.

England and Wales has had comprehensive legislation in place for a number of years dealing with adoption, parental responsibility and assisted reproductive technologies with specific provisions relating to gay and lesbian parents.[5] This legislation is purportedly grounded upon consideration of the welfare of the child, but, nonetheless, failings are identified. For instance, the English laws on surrogacy have come under increasing scrutiny in recent years and many commentators have called for reform of the law due to perceived inadequacies in the legal regulation. Indeed, such are the calls for reform that the area is currently under review by the Law Commissions for England and Wales and Scotland.[6] Hence, those and other laws must be assessed against the best interests principle to ensure that the English law operates in the best interests of children born through this process. The English approach must be systematically benchmarked against the best interests principle and contrasted with the other comparator jurisdictions in order to identify best practice and child-centred suggestions for reform.

[5] For example: Adoption and Children Act 2002; Children Act 1989; Civil Partnership Act 2004; Human Fertilisation and Embryology Act 1990; Human Fertilisation and Embryology Act 2008.

[6] Law Commission and Scottish Law Commission, *Building Families through Surrogacy: A New Law* (Law Commission Consultation Paper No. 244; Scottish Law Commission Discussion Paper No. 167, 2019).

Ireland is chosen as a case study because the legal recognition of gay and lesbian parenting is a relatively new development in that country. Prior to 2015, there was no legal mechanism in place to recognise same-sex couples as joint legal parents in Ireland. Since 2015, Irish family law has evolved considerably: the Marriage Equality Referendum was passed in that year to allow for civil marriages to take place between couples of the same sex and the Children and Family Relationships Act 2015 was enacted (though, at the time of writing, many important parts of the Act have yet to be commenced), thereby improving the position of children who are raised by gay and lesbian couples in many respects. Ireland has become a world leader in advancing LGBT+ rights. The international community acknowledged this in 2019 when Ireland was presented with an award at the World Pride festival in recognition of commitments made to protect LGBT+ citizens' rights.[7] Since these are recent developments, the impact of law reform as regards the best interests of children raised by gay and lesbian couples has yet to be comprehensively reviewed in academic literature. As such, one of the objectives of the book is to inspect and appraise the current Irish regulation to ensure compliance with the best interests principle. This analysis is particularly relevant given that there are some significant shortcomings at present. For example, the area of surrogacy is not regulated under Irish law. As such, suggestions are presented on how the law could or should regulate this contentious area in Ireland.

South African legislation recognises a diverse range of pathways to parentage for gay and lesbian couples.[8] In addition, section 28(2) of the South African Constitution expressly recognises that '[a] child's best interests are of paramount importance in every matter concerning the child'. As a result of this provision, the South African legislation is framed in a manner that seeks to ensure that the best interests of the child are protected. The South African approach to the best interests principle closely mirrors the approach endorsed by the Committee on the Rights of the Child. Therefore, the South African approach, in echoing that which is recommended by the Committee, shows that the Committee's vision of the best interests principle is realistic and practically achievable. This approach to best interests is grounded in realistic standards and, therefore, helps to guide the identification of best practice in this area. Despite

[7] Cormac McQuinn, 'Ireland set for award for support of LGBTI community at World Pride event', *Irish Independent*, 15 May 2019.

[8] Children's Act 38 of 2005.

the advantages of the South African application of the best interests principle, some areas of South African law arguably fall short of the requirements of the principle and must also, therefore, be assessed against the approaches of the other jurisdictions to identify that best practice.

Comparison of the laws of the selected jurisdictions provides guidance on how the best interests principle is to be applied in the context of same-sex parenting. Both the advantages and disadvantages of particular laws are examined. The political, social, economic and cultural differences between the countries are also identified and addressed. These considerations are particularly important in the context of research that pertains to same-sex parenting, and also to the best interests of the child, given that these issues are highly dependent upon political, cultural and social attitudes.

In each comparative case study, the book assesses the laws relating to the most common pathways to parentage that are available to gay and lesbian parents, namely parental responsibility, adoption, donor conception and surrogacy. These laws are assessed against the best interests principle as described above. Where failings are identified, suggestions for reform of the individual laws are presented.

I.2.3 Social Reality

Although the issues advanced in this book are discussed and evaluated with a primary applicability and relevance to same-sex parenting, the arguments that are advanced are relevant to many other family contexts. This serves to underline the normality of LGBT+ families: that issues concerning legal recognition and family acceptance affect adults and children regardless of sexuality, marital or other status. It is hoped that same-sex parenting will one day be so unremarkable that it can simply be termed 'parenting'. By highlighting issues that are as relevant to opposite-sex parents as they are to same-sex parents, this book aims to take another step towards that goal.

For now, specific terminology is required to effectively discuss the nuances of different parenting arrangements, discussed further below. A common thread running through this book is a need to recognise social reality for families and a need for the legislature to depart from the sexual family norm in order to regulate effectively for diverse family forms. In each chapter, it is shown that the reluctance of law makers to embrace 'non-traditional' and 'new' family forms has frustrating effects for all types of families, whether they are headed by same-sex, opposite-sex, transgender, gender-diverse or single parents. It is argued that love makes a family, not heteronormative ideals, and that, in many cases, the law needs to catch up with this reality.

I.3 Terminology

As is discussed in Chapter 3, the choice of terminology is very important in child and family law because language can serve to shape social perceptions. Thus, specific terminology has been chosen in this book to reflect the underlying ethos of the suggested legal reforms that are advanced in each chapter. This section provides an explanation of some of the common terms that are used.

New and Non-traditional Families

The term 'non-traditional' has been used for many years to describe a variety of family forms that depart from the normative ideal of one heterosexual mother and one heterosexual father living with genetically related offspring. This might encompass, for example, a single mother or unmarried cohabiting adults with a child. Many people would also place gay and lesbian families in this 'non-traditional' descriptor, while others think that further nuance is required. Golombok, for example, distinguishes between 'non-traditional' and 'new' families. Golombok contends that non-traditional families 'result largely from parental separation or divorce and the formation of new cohabiting or marital relationships'.[9] By contrast, 'new' family forms are those 'that either did not exist or were hidden from society until the latter part of the twentieth century, and that represent a more fundamental shift away from traditional family structures than do non-traditional families'.[10] These 'new' families include lesbian mother families, gay father families, families headed by single mothers by choice and families created by assisted reproductive technologies. However, in Golombok's view, the terms 'new' and 'non-traditional' are 'not mutually exclusive'; new families can also be non-traditional.

[9] Susan Golombok, *Modern Families: Parents and Children in New Family Forms* (Cambridge: Cambridge University Press, 2015), p. 3.

[10] Above.

This distinction in terminology is useful. The 'non-traditional' moniker, although increasingly celebrated as an emblem of difference, often has unconscious negative connotations. After all, the 'traditional' family remains the celebrated social unit. Hence, deviation from that 'gold standard' conjures up undesirable associations, especially when used as a branding device. 'New' gleams with positivity. It conveys modernism and innovation without any non-conforming baggage. Language can influence social attitudes, and so it is submitted that advocates for legal recognition of same-sex parenting arrangements should adopt affirmative language when discussing diverse family forms. For this reason, this book will primarily describe gay and lesbian families as 'new' families. However, it is acknowledged that this term will not accurately reflect all situations. Thus, 'non-traditional' is also used where necessary to avoid a situation where all families that deviate from the heteronormative model are shoehorned into a single category.

Parentage, Parenthood and Parents

This book discusses aspects of same-sex parenting from the perspective of the best interests principle. The concept of 'parenting' may be broken down into three distinct parts, namely 'parentage', 'parenthood' and 'parental responsibility'.[11] These terms are used throughout this book.

Traditionally, the concept of 'parentage' has been most closely associated with genetic parentage. Hence, some commentators, such as Bainham and Herring, suggest that only those persons who are genetically related to the child should be regarded as having 'parentage'.[12] Where a person is not genetically related to the child but is regarded by the law as a legal parent, Bainham and Herring suggest that the phrase 'parenthood' more accurately describes that person's role.[13] Therefore, a distinction is sometimes created between the idea of genetic parentage and that of legal parenthood. At the same time, the terms 'parentage' and 'parenthood' are often used interchangeably and, perhaps most notably, 'the law does not

[11] Andrew Bainham, 'Parentage, parenthood and parental responsibility: subtle, elusive yet important distinctions' in Andrew Bainham, Shelly Day Sclater and Martin Richards (eds.), *What Is a Parent? A Socio-Legal Analysis* (Oxford: Hart Publishing, 1999).

[12] Bainham, above, 28–30; Jonathan Herring, *Family Law*, 5 ed. (Harlow: Pearson Education Limited, 2011), p. 324.

[13] Bainham, above; Herring, above.

distinguish between the two and legislation instead usually refers to *parents* or, occasionally, to *mothers* and *fathers*'.[14]

This book uses the term 'parentage' to describe those persons who are the *legal parents* of the child. This shift in terminology is necessary to tackle the heteronormative bias that has become ingrained in the law. It is submitted that it would be inappropriate to focus exclusively on the genetic relationship as the determinant of parentage when discussing same-sex parenting given that both members of a same-sex couple can never have a genetic connection to the child. The use of the phrase 'parentage' to mean 'legal parentage', therefore, allows for parity in the law's treatment of these 'new' families. The phrase 'parenthood' is used periodically where this has been adopted in academic commentary.

In discussing the 'parents' of the child in this book, it is necessary to distinguish between different categories of 'parent', namely the 'legal' parent, the 'genetic' or 'biological' parent, the 'gestational' parent, the 'birth' parent and the 'social' parent. This necessity arises due to the fact that the law continues to ascribe certain rights and responsibilities on the basis of genetics or gestation.[15] As such, in order to fully describe the current legal framework governing same-sex parenting, it is necessary to refer to the different categories of parent.

The 'legal' parent of a child is taken to mean the person who is recognised, by law, as the parent. This person will have been registered as a legal parent and their name will appear on the child's birth certificate or adoption certificate.

The term 'genetic' or 'biological' parent is used to refer to the person whose gametes were used to enable the conception of the child. These terms are used to highlight the way in which the law distinguishes between genetic and non-genetic parents. It is also, at times, necessary to refer to the 'natural' parents of a child to describe the genetic parents. This terminology is not favoured as the necessary implication of using this term is that, if some children are 'natural', then others must be 'unnatural'. This term is adopted only where it has been used in case law or in academic commentary.

The term 'birth' parent is also used. Primarily, this term is employed in the context of adoption so as to describe the person or persons who were legally recognised as parents at the time of the child's birth.

[14] Bainham, above, 28 (emphasis in original).

[15] For example, Irish law currently ascribes maternity on the basis of gestation, whereas paternity is determined by reference to genetics.

Finally, the term 'social parent' is used to refer to the person who carries out the same duties as the legal parent but who does not enjoy a legal or genetic connection to the child. Throughout the book, the objective is to assess whether this social parent should be afforded the opportunity to acquire legal responsibilities and rights in respect of the child and how the law should facilitate this.

I.4 Chapter Structure

Each of the chapters in this book build upon one another to construct a cohesive argument and to examine the impact and demands of the best interests principle in the context of same-sex parenting.

Chapter 1 examines the theoretical basis of the best interests principle. This chapter examines the implications and demands of the principle and it explores how the principle is to be applied. In line with the guidance provided by the Committee on the Rights of the Child, the best interests principle is understood to be a right, the content of which is guided by reference to the other rights contained in the UNCRC. The advantage of this approach is that it allows the best interests principle to be realised in a structured manner, namely one that is guided by the UNCRC. The chapter provides further nuance to the best interests principle by identifying a new conceptual framework for its application. This framework is designed to overcome the perceived deficiencies of the principle. The framework is largely based on the guidance of the Committee, but also suggests that social science literature should be incorporated into the best interests assessment to provide broader guidance about what is 'best' for children in particular situations.

Chapter 1 begins with a discussion of the foundational development of the UNCRC to provide greater context to the differing interpretations of the best interests principle adopted in the comparator jurisdictions, discussed later in the chapter. Thereafter, the chapter justifies the use of the best interests principle as the guiding principle in legal and policy decisions relating to children in light of those criticisms. It is argued that the criticisms against the principle are myopic in that they do not appreciate the principle's full potential and further that the apparent deficiencies of the principle can be overcome through identification of an appropriate conceptual framework. In this regard, it is argued that the best interests principle represents the most suitable mechanism through which to promote children's rights and interests.

Chapter 2 analyses sociological and psychological research pertaining to same-sex parenting. This chapter builds on Chapter 1 as it uses the relevant research to guide the application of the best interests principle. This research is used to inform the demands of the principle and to reduce the indeterminacy and subjectivity of decision-making as it relates to the children of gay and lesbian families. Existing sociological and psychological studies are assessed to determine whether children's best interests can be served by same-sex parents and, consequently, whether legal recognition of these family relationships is desirable. This approach is also used to assess the application of specific laws in terms of their impact on the best interests of the child.

Chapters 3 to 6 subsequently apply the findings of Chapters 1 and 2 to assess the demands of the best interests principle in the context of specific pathways to parentage that might be available to gay and lesbian couples. Chapter 3 addresses the question of extending parental responsibility to social parents. Parental responsibility is an important mechanism through which to confer responsibilities and rights upon social parents. It is particularly useful in the context of same-sex parenting given that it is quite common for gay and lesbian couples to become parents in situations where the child was born to one of them as part of a previous heterosexual relationship. The extension of parental responsibility provides a mechanism whereby the partner or spouse of the parent can acquire responsibilities and rights towards the child in a manner that does not affect the status of the legal parents. In this respect, parental responsibility can be regarded as an important aspect of the best interests principle as it gives the social parent the necessary legal tools to properly care for the child. This chapter considers whether the extension of parental responsibility is appropriate and, if so, examines the manner in which it may be extended. The concepts of parental responsibility, guardianship and parental responsibilities and rights are also addressed and the differences between the concepts as they apply in England and Wales, Ireland and South Africa are examined to consider whether any particular type of parental role is preferable to the others.

Chapter 4 examines the area of adoption law. Adoption is a mechanism that extinguishes the parental responsibilities and rights of the birth parents and transfers these to the adoptive family. It is a child-centred process and one in which the best interests of the child must be to the fore. This premise is recognised at an international level by Article 21 UNCRC, which provides that State Parties that recognise and/or permit a system of adoption 'shall ensure that the best interests of the child shall be the paramount consideration'. As a result of this provision, it is acknowledged that the child's best interests are to be the paramount focus in any decision concerning the adoption of a child. This chapter argues that, from a children's rights perspective, there is no logical basis for refusing to allow same-sex couples to access joint adoption and further that the best interests of the child may in fact demand that such access is made available.

The suitability of adoption as a means to secure existing family relationships (so-called second-parent adoption) is also considered. Second-parent adoption is somewhat controversial given that the effect of this type of adoption order is to extinguish the child's legal relationship with the 'other' birth parent (i.e. that parent who is not in a relationship with the step-parent) and extended family. Thus, where the child has an ongoing relationship with the other parent, second-parent adoption would not be appropriate and, instead, it may be preferable to extend parental responsibility to the social parent. It must be recalled, however, that adoption creates secure and life-long family relationships, and it allows the child to be fully integrated into their family. Therefore, while the extension of parental responsibility may improve the position of the family in many respects, it is not a panacea, nor will it be the most appropriate solution for every child. As such, given that the best interests of the child must be assessed on a case-by-case basis, it is submitted that the widest range of options should be available so that the best individual solution can be found for each individual child.

Chapter 5 addresses the regulation of donor conception. This chapter examines how parentage should be allocated in situations where this procedure is used. The aim of the chapter is to identify a means of allocating parentage that is most in keeping with the best interests principle. The chapter examines the allocation of parentage in cases where donor conception is used in each of the comparator jurisdictions. This analysis reveals that a distinction is typically created between children conceived through this process in clinical and non-clinical settings. The chapter assesses the demands of the best interests principle in this context so as to understand whether it is legitimate that different rules of parentage apply in these situations. The child's right to identity and safeguards required to vindicate this right in cases of donor conception are also considered, as is the issue of access to services for gay and lesbian couples.

Chapter 6 examines the allocation of parentage in cases of surrogacy. Surrogacy is a process that is fraught with legal and ethical issues, leading many to criticise its use as a method of family formation. It must be acknowledged, however, that prohibiting surrogacy in one country will not stop its use in another. Therefore, the children who are born, and who will continue to be born, in this way must be legally recognised and protected. The chapter seeks to identify a way to regulate surrogacy that adheres to the best interests principle and balances the interests and needs of all stakeholders in the process. It is suggested that an intention-based model of surrogacy, which is facilitated through a preconception allocation of parentage, satisfies the requirements of the best interests principle. The child's right to identity is also examined in this chapter.

The Conclusion reviews the main arguments raised in the chapters, and it provides suggestions for future reform of the law in each of the comparator jurisdictions. The conclusions of the individual chapters are assessed to identify best practice in terms of the legal recognition and regulation of same-sex parenting which is not only of relevance to the countries under examination but to any of the 196 countries that have ratified the UNCRC.

While every effort has been made to ensure that this book reflects the most recent legal developments in the field, the law stated is as it stood in October 2019.

1

The Best Interests Principle

Theoretical Understanding

1.1 Introduction

The best interests principle is widely acknowledged as a means through which to promote the rights and interests of children. The principle is expressly recognised in Article 3(1) of the United Nations Convention on the Rights of the Child (UNCRC), which provides:

> In all actions concerning children, whether undertaken by public or private social welfare institutions, courts of law, administrative authorities or legislative bodies, the best interests of the child shall be a primary consideration.[1]

This Article expresses one of the fundamental values of the UNCRC and is regarded as one of the four general principles of the Convention for interpreting and implementing all of the rights of the child contained therein. Reference is also made to the principle in Article 9 UNCRC (separation from parents), Article 18 (parental responsibilities), Article 20 (deprivation of family environment and alternative care), Article 21 (adoption), Article 37(c) (separation from adults in detention) and Article 40 (juvenile justice).

Most domestic legal systems also acknowledge and protect the best interests of the child in some form. These systems afford different weight to the best interests principle in domestic laws, and this weight varies depending on the specific context. Despite this divergence, it is clear that '[t]he idea that society should respect the *best interests of the child* is seen as fundamental in all cultures'.[2]

[1] United Nations Convention on the Rights of the Child, New York, 20 November 1989, in force 2 September 1990, Art. 3.

[2] Thomas Hammarberg, 'The principle of the best interests of the child: What it means and what it demands from adults' (lecture by Thomas Hammarberg, Commissioner for Human Rights, Council of Europe, Warsaw, 30 May 2008) [emphasis in original].

The best interests principle underpins the theoretical framework of this monograph. It is applied throughout the book to argue that legal recognition should be given to same-sex parenting arrangements. The principle is examined to assess what is 'best' for the children raised by such couples in order to identify exemplary approaches to the legal regulation of various pathways to parentage. It is shown that the principle is a malleable concept that is invoked by both advocates and opponents of same-sex parenting. Thus, a fundamental aim of each chapter is to examine the implications of the principle in the context of specific aspects of parenting so as to assess the validity of arguments in favour of and against the legal recognition of same-sex parenting.

It is also necessary to consider the suitability of the best interests principle as an appropriate central theme for the analysis of parenting. After all, despite the widespread acceptance of the principle, it has also become the subject of widespread criticism. Primarily, the concept of the child's best interests is criticised for its vague and indeterminate nature. It is unclear what is meant by 'best interests', and, in most jurisdictions, the concept is not defined in legislation. As such, a significant amount of discretion is left to the decision-maker who is likely to be influenced by their own subjective views on the matter.

The aim of this chapter is to identify a conceptual framework for the application of the best interests principle and to locate best practice using that framework. The objective is to move away from subjective or moral conceptions of the best interests principle to an understanding that is informed by relevant sociological and psychological data and that is guided by reference to the rights contained in the UNCRC. Although subjective views of best interests can never fully be eliminated, the validity of subjective arguments as a means to argue against the legal recognition of gay and lesbian families can be challenged by reference to the objective criteria.

This chapter does not propose to identify a 'universal' definition of best interests. A universal definition is simply not possible because the definition will depend on the constitutional, political, social and cultural contexts in which the principle is applied. Instead, the chapter seeks to identify a universal *process* or conceptual framework for determining the best interests of the child. The analysis focuses on best practice in the application of the principle as a right, interpretive principle and procedural tool to vindicate the rights and interests of children. From this analysis, broad insights are gleaned that must be adapted on a case-by-case basis. These insights form the basis of situation-specific discussions in later chapters. These discussions demonstrate that the suggested conceptual framework for the best interests principle advanced in this chapter is applicable to a range of countries but must be adapted according to the political, social and cultural norms of that jurisdiction.

The chapter begins with a brief examination of the foundational development of the UNCRC. In total, 196 State Parties have ratified the UNCRC to date and thus accepted the Article 3(1) best interests principle. As such, it is necessary to briefly chart the development of Article 3(1) to understand its contemporary context. Thereafter, the chapter addresses the criticisms that have been levied against the best interests principle and questions whether it is appropriate to maintain the indeterminate standard in the face of such negative appraisal. The chapter engages with the ongoing debate of whether a purely rights-based approach, rather than one that is based on an assessment of the child's best interests, is preferable when determining issues relating to children or whether, in fact, the best interests principle already incorporates and complements existing rights. In this regard, the guidance provided by the Committee on the Rights of the Child in relation to the best interests principle[3] is assessed. Ultimately, it is argued that the criticisms of the principle are myopic in that they do not appreciate the principle's full potential and further that the apparent deficiencies of the principle can be overcome, or at least reduced, through identification of an appropriate conceptual framework that is in line with the guidance of the Committee on the Rights of the Child.

Having identified an appropriate conceptual framework, the chapter examines the application of the best interests principle in three comparator jurisdictions: England and Wales, Ireland and South Africa. This analysis shows that the application of the best interests principle at the domestic level does not always align with the identified conceptual framework. It serves to highlight the strengths of the conceptual framework as a means to overcome perceived deficiencies in the domestic application of the principle. It also underlines the role of cultural, social and political factors in the application of the best interests principle.

[3] Committee on the Rights of the Child, *General comment No. 14 (2013) on the right of the child to have his or her best interests taken as a primary consideration (art. 3, para. 1)* CRC/C/GC/14.

1.2 Foundational Development of the UNCRC

The UNCRC is a comprehensive, international agreement on the rights of children, adopted by the United Nations General Assembly in 1989. To date, 196 countries have ratified the Convention, making it the most widely ratified human rights treaty in history. The rights protected by the UNCRC are comprehensive and address all areas of relevance to the child.[4]

Prior to the adoption of the UNCRC, children's rights were recognised in other international conventions, including the Geneva Declaration on the Rights of the Child (1924), the Declaration on the Rights of the Child (1948) and the Declaration of the Rights of the Child (1959). These instruments were largely directed at the care and protection of children. The 1959 Declaration also contained one of the first references, at the international level, to the best interests principle. Principle 2 of the 1959 Declaration provided, inter alia, that 'the best interests of the child shall be the paramount consideration', while Principle 7 provided that '[t]he best interests of the child shall be the guiding principle of those responsible for [the child's] education and guidance'. These principles would become forebears of the modern standard.

The initial impetus for the creation of the UNCRC came from Poland in 1978. In that year, Poland submitted a draft convention to the United Nations Commission on Human Rights. This submission coincided with the twentieth anniversary of the Declaration of the Rights of the Child as well as the celebration (in 1979) of the International Year of the Child. The aim was to create an internationally binding instrument, in the form of a convention, to protect the rights of children. The proposed convention was essentially a duplicate of the 1959 Declaration with the addition of an implementation mechanism. This first draft was rejected by the Commission. Most representatives felt that it would not be appropriate to simply incorporate the provisions of the 1959 Declaration, which was concluded twenty years earlier, and felt that the new proposed convention should take into account broader matters and contemporary issues.[5] Poland subsequently tendered a revised proposal. The second proposal was a more detailed document that was more rights-focused in nature. Notably, the second draft also included a provision giving the child 'who

4 Thomas Hammarberg, 'The UN Convention on the Rights of the Child – and how to make it work' (1990) 12 *Human Rights Quarterly* 97.

5 Sharon Detrick (ed.), *The United Nations Convention on the Rights of the Child: A Guide to the 'Travaux Preparatoires'* (The Hague: Martinus Nijhoff, 1992), p. 89.

is capable of forming his own views the right to express his opinion in matters concerning his own person'.[6] Many authors regard the inclusion of this Article as a turning point in the development of children's rights.[7] Previously, children's rights had been expressed and understood almost exclusively in terms of care and protection. By contrast, the UNCRC established that children are themselves rights-holders and are entitled to exercise a broader catalogue of children's rights. This understanding was developed throughout the drafting process and is seen to have its origins in this original provision.

After Poland submitted the second draft, a ten-year drafting process followed. During this time, an open-ended working group of approximately eighty countries participated in the drafting of the text of the UNCRC. The Convention was drafted on consensus, and so the countries often had to reconcile their differing cultural beliefs and traditions to reach a compromise on the content of the rights that should be protected by the Convention. Non-governmental organisations (NGOs) also played a significant role in the drafting process. Importantly, as Price Cohen notes, the NGOs 'provided a critical buffer between the East and West' as the drafting progressed during the divisive Cold War period.[8] The NGOs had been involved since the first proposal was submitted, but it was not until 1983 that the NGO Ad Hoc Group was formed.[9] The NGOs submitted annual reports to the Working Group, held briefing sessions for government representatives and organised meetings concerning the future of the Convention.[10] The NGOs also encouraged and facilitated the input and participation of developing countries in the drafting process. Alston notes that this 'enhanced the eventual acceptability of the draft to those countries' and 'laid the foundations for the extraordinarily widespread support which was to be accorded to the Convention in the early 1990s'.[11] The political climate at the time thus had a significant impact on the content and subsequent endorsement of the UNCRC.

[6] Article 7 of the Revised Draft Convention on the Rights of the Child.

[7] Cynthia Price Cohen, 'The role of the United States in the drafting of the Convention on the Rights of the Child' 20 (2006) *Emory International Law Review* 185, p. 189; Nigel Thomas, *Children's Rights: Policy into Practice* (Lismore: Centre for Children and Young People, 2011), p. 7.

[8] Price Cohen, above, 192.

[9] Detrick, above n. 5, 24.

[10] Detrick, above n. 5, 24–25.

[11] Philip Alston, 'Best interests principle: Towards a reconciliation of culture and human rights' (1994) 8 *International Journal of Law, Policy and the Family* 1, p. 7.

During the drafting process, all members of the Working Group seem to have agreed on the desirability of including the best interests principle, but there was some debate as to the weight to be afforded to it. As noted above, the original Polish proposal was essentially a duplicate of the 1959 Declaration, and so it included the full text of the best interests principle as provided for in Principle 2 of the Declaration. Principle 2 read as follows:

> The child shall enjoy special protection, and shall be given opportunities and facilities, by law and by other means, to enable him to develop physically, mentally, morally, spiritually and socially in a healthy and normal manner and in conditions of freedom and dignity. In the enactment of laws for this purpose, the best interests of the child shall be the paramount consideration.

The revised Polish submission contained a paired-down version of the best interests principle. Article 3(1) of the revised Polish draft read:

> In all actions concerning children, whether undertaken by their parents, guardians, social or State institutions, and in particular courts of law and administrative authorities, the best interests of the child shall be the paramount consideration.[12]

The United States subsequently put forward an alternative wording during the 1981 session of the Working Group. Paragraph 1 of this revised Article 3(1) read:

> In all official actions concerning children, whether undertaken by public or private social welfare institutions, courts of law, or administrative authorities, the best interests of the child shall be a primary consideration.[13]

Although a number of delegates felt that the broader Polish text was preferable and better protected the child, in order to achieve a compromise, it was agreed that the US wording would form the basis of the subsequent discussions. When this provision was considered by the Working Group, the debate centred on whether the best interests principle should be 'a primary' or 'the paramount' consideration. The former wording was preferred as the latter was felt to be too broad. The Working Group also subsequently deleted the word 'official' from the proposed text and added the phrase 'legislative bodies'.[14] Alston notes

[12] Detrick, above n. 5, 132.
[13] Detrick, above n. 5, 133.
[14] Detrick, above n. 5, 137.

that this amendment represented a compromise between those delegates who wanted private actors to be covered by the provision but who did not want to impose explicit obligations on parents.[15]

There was, however, no real analysis of the meaning of 'best interests' at the drafting stage. Alston notes that 'its meaning seems either to have been taken for granted or to have been considered unimportant'.[16] During the second reading of the Convention, the representative of Venezuela expressed concern about the subjectivity of the term 'best interests' and about the fact that, without any other guidance in the Convention, the interpretation of the principle would be left to the person making the decision. In the debate that followed, most other delegates expressed satisfaction with the phrase as it stood, and so the representative from Venezuela withdrew her suggestion.[17] Thus, the meaning of the phrase was not considered during the drafting process, nor was there any specific discussion of the inclusion of the phrase in Article 3(1) rather than elsewhere in the Convention.

In this context, it would seem that Article 3(1) had a relatively straightforward path to implementation. Even before the adoption of the UNCRC, the best interests principle occupied a unique position in the legal landscape that it retains to this day: it is a principle that is widely accepted and fits comfortably into most legal systems around the world, yet it has no universal meaning, nor is there any consensus on how it is to be applied.

As will be discussed below, the Committee on the Rights of the Child, the body that monitors States Parties' compliance with the UNCRC, has now provided guidance on the interpretation of the best interests principle. Nonetheless, it must be acknowledged that the principle is indeterminate and that it will always be influenced by cultural, social and political values. The UNCRC does not provide a definite statement of what is best for a child in a particular situation, nor does the Committee prescribe what is best for a child at any point in time. Instead, the Committee presents a framework for assessing and determining the child's best interests which provides an element of objectivity by clarifying each element of Article 3(1). These clarifications form the basis of the discussions later in this chapter.

15 Alston, above n. 11, 14. Although Article 3(1) UNCRC does not explicitly mention parents, it should be noted that under Article 18(1) the best interests of the child are stated to be the 'basic concern' of parents and legal guardians.

16 Alston, above n. 11, 11.

17 Detrick, above n. 5, 137.

1.3 Widespread Acceptance

The best interests principle acknowledges that children are in a special situation of dependency, maturity and legal status and that it is more difficult for them to assert their rights than it is for adults.[18] As Eekelaar notes, the virtue of the principle is that

> it requires a decision made with respect to a child to be justified from the point of view of a judgment about the child's interests. Put another way: it would be inconsistent with the welfare principle to make a decision that is *overtly* justified by reference to the way the outcome benefitted some *other* interest or interests.[19]

As noted above, the child's best interests are expressly protected under a number of provisions of the UNCRC, including Article 3(1). The ambit of Article 3(1) is generally broader than other configurations of the best interests principle since it applies in 'all actions' concerning children and is not confined to specific applications. However, given that Article 3(1) is a general principle of the UNCRC that is applicable in a wide range of situations, it is a weaker formulation than others, protecting the best interests of the child as 'a primary consideration'. The use of the indefinite article 'a' in the Article demonstrates that the child's best interests are not the only factor to be considered, and the use of the word 'primary' indicates that the child's interests will not necessarily be the prevailing factor. In other provisions of the UNCRC (and in domestic laws), the best interests principle is expressed in stronger terms. For example, in the specific context of adoption, Article 21 UNCRC provides that the best interests of the child 'shall be the paramount consideration'. This stronger wording is justified as the Article is directed at a particular situation.

According to the Committee on the Rights of the Child, where the best interests of the child are expressed as a 'primary consideration', those interests have 'high priority' and 'a larger weight must be attached to what serves the child best'.[20] Where best interests are described as the 'paramount consideration', they are to be 'the determining factor when taking a decision'.[21]

The widespread acceptance of the UNCRC partly explains the widespread acceptance of the best interests principle. However, as noted

[18] Committee on the Rights of the Child, above n. 3, para. 37.

[19] John Eekelaar, 'Beyond the welfare principle' (2002) 14 *Child and Family Law Quarterly* 237, p. 240 [emphasis in original].

[20] Committee on the Rights of the Child, above n. 3, para. 39.

[21] Committee on the Rights of the Child, above n. 3, para. 38.

above, many countries included some reference to the principle prior to the adoption of Article 3(1).[22] Hence, the principle was widely established before the UNCRC ever came to be.

The best interests principle has also gained popularity in the political sphere. In South Africa, for example, during the debates on the post-apartheid Constitution, there was a strong consensus as to the desirability of including children's rights in the Constitution along with a specific provision protecting the best interests of the child at a constitutional level.[23] Sloth-Nielsen has explained this as occurring due to the fact that the promotion of children's rights is both 'a "vote winning" and a "non-vote alienating" cause to espouse: children's rights do not offend any known political constituency'.[24] In Ireland, an equivalent consensus was seen during the Children's Rights Referendum of 2012 when all of the major political parties supported the insertion of a specific children's rights clause into the Constitution.[25] Similarly, in England and Wales, the paramountcy principle is noted to have passed through the legislative process without dissent.[26]

The widespread acceptance of the best interests principle could be due to ignorance, or indeed laziness, about what the principle entails. Worse still, the proliferation of the principle might be driven by a desire to manipulate its use. The concept of 'best interests' is vague and indeterminate, which allows for discretion on the part of the decision-maker. In this way, it has been argued that the principle could be used to justify almost any outcome.[27] This is because the indeterminacy of the principle allows for unarticulated assumptions and external factors to creep into the decision-making process, creating a 'smokescreen' around the actual reasons for the decision.[28]

[22] Alston, above n. 11, 11.

[23] Julia Sloth-Nielsen, 'The contribution of children's rights to the reconstruction of society: Some implications of the constitutionalism of children's rights in South Africa' in Michael Freeman (ed.), *Children's Rights. Volume II* (Dartmouth: Ashgate Publishing Limited, 2005), p. 326.

[24] Above.

[25] It should be noted that a small number of campaign groups were opposed to this amendment. Mary Minihan, 'Who opposes children's referendum?' *Irish Times*, 30 October 2012.

[26] Helen Reece, 'The paramountcy principle: Consensus or construct?' (1996) 49 *Current Legal Problems* 267, p. 269.

[27] Above, 298.

[28] Jonathan Herring, *Family Law*, 5th ed. (Harlow: Pearson Education Company, 2011), p. 431.

It is also notable that the best interests principle, as enunciated in Article 3(1) UNCRC, does not include the word 'right'. Notwithstanding that the Committee on the Rights of the Child has emphasised that the principle is a substantive right,[29] some authors question this status.[30] Kilkelly opines that the absence of rights language in Article 3(1) renders the best interests principle more acceptable to policymakers and others who want to protect children but who are wary of extending rights to children.[31] The softer and more malleable language of best interests seems non-threatening when compared to child-specific rights and may therefore explain the enthusiasm for the best interests principle.

All of these factors culminate in a principle that seemingly allows adults to pay lip service to the interests of children, while at the same time justifying whatever decision *they* want to make. This is a rather cynical view of the best interests principle, but the factors mentioned above may certainly have contributed to the consensus surrounding the desirability of including the best interests principle in most domestic legal systems around the world.

The next section considers three common criticisms raised against the use of the best interests principle, namely indeterminacy, the 'smoke-screen' concern and the lack of a rights focus. It is argued that the criticisms levied against the principle can be addressed through the application of objective criteria to guide the application of the best interests principle. In line with the guidance of the Committee on the Rights of the Child, the best interests principle is presented as a threefold concept: it is a substantive right, a fundamental interpretive legal principle and a rule of procedure.[32] This understanding of best interests is employed to add an element of objectivity and to challenge the perception that the best interests principle is a subjective, adult-centred concept. It is argued that the principle cannot be used to justify any decision; it can only uphold a decision that is child-centred, transparent and supported by reference to other rights protected by the UNCRC. Although the seemingly nebulous characteristics of the principle likely supported its initial widespread adoption, those shaky foundations must be stabilised

[29] Committee on the Rights of the Child, above n. 3.

[30] Ursula Kilkelly, 'The best interests of the child: A gateway to children's rights?' in Elaine Sutherland and Lesley-Anne Barnes Mcfarlane (eds.), *Implementing Article 3 of the United Nations Convention on the Rights of the Child: Best Interests, Welfare and Well-Being* (Cambridge: Cambridge University Press, 2017), pp. 56–59.

[31] Above, 65.

[32] Committee on the Rights of the Child, above n. 3, para. 6.

to ensure the full and effective enjoyment of all the rights recognised in the UNCRC.

1.4 Criticisms of the Best Interests Principle

1.4.1 Indeterminacy

One of the main criticisms of the best interests principle is that it is a vague and indeterminate standard. While there is broad consensus as to the value of protecting children's interests, there is no agreement about what those interests are or how they are to be determined.[33] As a result, the determination of the child's best interests becomes value-laden and will turn on the decision-maker's own preferences and ideals. As Mnookin famously wrote in 1975:

> Deciding what is best for a child poses a question no less ultimate than the purposes and values of life itself. Should the judge be primarily concerned with the child's happiness? Or with the child's spiritual and religious training? Should the judge be concerned with the economic 'productivity' of the child when he grows up? Are the primary values of life in warm, interpersonal relationships, or in discipline and self-sacrifice? Is stability and security for a child more desirable than intellectual stimulation? These questions could be elaborated endlessly. And yet, where is the judge to look for the set of values that should inform the choice of what is best for the child?[34]

Alston has suggested that the UNCRC itself represents 'the broad ethical or value framework' that provides a greater degree of certainty to the best interests principle.[35] For him, the UNCRC provides 'a number of sign-posts capable of guiding those seeking to identify what is in the best interests of the child, and excludes from the equation, by implication, various other elements'.[36] Similarly, the former Commissioner for Human Rights of the Council of Europe, Thomas Hammarberg, has opined that '[t]he definition of what is indeed in the best interests of the child is rooted in the substantive articles of the Convention itself'.[37]

[33] Reece, above n. 26, 271.

[34] Robert Mnookin, 'Child-custody adjudication: Judicial functions in the face of indeterminacy' (1975) 39 *Law and Contemporary Problems* 226, p. 260.

[35] Philip Alston, 'The best interests principle: Towards a reconciliation of culture and human rights' in Philip Alston (ed.), *The Best Interests Principle: Reconciling Culture and Human Rights* (Oxford: Oxford University Press, 1994), p. 19.

[36] Above.

[37] Hammarberg, above n. 2.

This approach mirrors that recommended by the Committee on the Rights of the Child. In its General Comment on Article 3 of the UNCRC, the Committee notes that '[i]t is through the interpretation and implementation of article 3, paragraph 1, *in line with the other provisions of the Convention*, that the legislator, judge, administrative, social or educational authority will be able to clarify the concept and make concrete use thereof'.[38] The Committee emphasises that '[t]he full application of the concept of the child's best interests requires the development of a rights-based approach'[39] and further that, when the best interests principle is applied as an interpretive principle, '[t]he rights enshrined in the Convention and its Optional Protocols provide the framework for interpretation'.[40] These statements indicate that the rights contained in the UNCRC itself should be used to determine the child's best interests.

In addition, the Committee has formulated 'a non-exhaustive and non-hierarchical list of elements that could be included in a best-interests assessment by any decision-maker having to determine a child's best interests'.[41] All of the suggested elements are derived from rights contained in the UNCRC. The Committee recommends that the following elements be taken into consideration in determining the child's best interests:

(a) The child's views,
(b) The child's identity,
(c) Preservation of the family environment and maintaining relations,
(d) Care, protection and safety of the child,
(e) Situation of vulnerability,
(f) The child's right to health,
(g) The child's right to education.[42]

The Committee presents these elements as part of a non-exhaustive list and emphasises that it is possible to consider other factors relevant to the specific circumstances of the individual child or group of children.[43] Furthermore, the Committee does not attempt to strictly define the proposed elements. Instead, it recommends that the content of each

[38] Committee on the Rights of the Child, above n. 3, para. 32 [emphasis added].
[39] Committee on the Rights of the Child, above n. 3, para. 5.
[40] Committee on the Rights of the Child, above n. 3, para. 6.
[41] Committee on the Rights of the Child, above n. 3, para. 50.
[42] Committee on the Rights of the Child, above n. 3, paras. 53–79.
[43] Committee on the Rights of the Child, above n. 3, para. 50.

element should vary from case to case, as should the weight to be afforded to each element in the overall evaluation.[44] As such, although the list of proposed elements provides a useful guide to determining best interests, it does not solve the indeterminacy issue, because the application of the suggested elements (and identification of any additional relevant factors) will still require subjective values to be incorporated into the decision – a point that is expressly recognised by the Committee.

By way of example, consider factor (c) on the list: the preservation of the family environment and maintaining relations. As the Committee explains in relation to this issue,

> shared parental responsibilities are generally in the child's best interests. However, in decisions regarding parental responsibilities, the only criterion shall be what is in the best interests of the particular child ... In assessing the child's best interests, the judge must take into consideration the right of the child to preserve his or her relationship with both parents, together with the other elements relevant to the case.[45]

Thus, the Committee acknowledges that the decision-maker should weigh up various factors when assessing the child's best interests. The suggested elements (a) to (g) above should be incorporated into this balancing exercise, but the ultimate decision will entail a value judgement, meaning that different adjudicators may still reach very different conclusions when presented with the same scenario.

Problems may also arise in situations where the rights contained in the discrete subheadings clash. In such a situation, which right is to be accorded priority? For instance, in relation to the child's right to identity, a situation might arise where a child has been adopted from a foreign country by a gay or lesbian person as a single applicant. That parent may subsequently enter into a relationship and their new partner may, after some years, seek to become that child's second legal parent. The country of the child's origin may allow for single adoptions by gay or lesbian persons but not joint adoptions by same-sex couples. Thus, a second-parent adoption in this case would not adhere to the child's cultural background and may cause problems in later years if the child was to return to their country of origin alongside both adoptive parents.[46] Yet, the child's present needs, that is, their right to family life with the social

[44] Committee on the Rights of the Child, above n. 3, para. 80.

[45] Committee on the Rights of the Child, above n. 3, para. 67.

[46] Mia Dambach, 'The international legal context governing intercountry adoptions by gay men and lesbians' (2011) 35 *Adoption and Fostering* 65, p. 67.

parent, may require that the adoption should take place. In such circumstances, should the child's immediate needs take precedence, or should their future situation be the determining factor?[47] Once more, this decision will ultimately require a value judgement, which does little to remove the indeterminacy of the best interests principle. Hence, while the rights contained in the UNCRC can provide broad guidance as to what is in a child's best interests, it is apparent that using the Convention as a 'signpost' does not remove subjectivity and individual values from the ultimate decision.

Some jurisdictions have attempted to overcome the indeterminacy of the best interests principle through the use of 'checklists' that are designed to guide the application of the principle.[48] In South Africa, for example, the decision-maker is required to consider twenty-two factors that may affect the child when coming to a decision as to best interests.[49] In England and Wales, section 1(3) of the Children Act 1989 sets out a similar, but less comprehensive, list of factors to which the courts must have regard when determining the welfare of the child. In Ireland, the Children and Family Relationships Act 2015 introduced a 'best interests checklist' into Irish law for the first time.[50]

These checklists ensure that decision-making follows a rational and transparent process. It is submitted, however, that the use of such checklists gives rise to the same difficulties outlined above, that is, that a value judgment is still ultimately required to determine the best course of action for a particular child or group of children. In each jurisdiction, similar to the Committee's list of suggested elements, there is no indication of the weight to be afforded to each factor on the checklist, and so the decision-maker retains a measure of discretion in making the decision. Thus, the checklist does not eliminate indeterminacy in the best interests assessment.

It would seem, therefore, that indeterminacy is inherent in the application of the best interests principle. However, this is not necessarily disadvantageous. The indeterminate nature of the principle may, in fact,

47 The appropriateness of second-parent adoption following an intercountry adoption is discussed in Chapter 4.

48 See, for example, South Africa: Children's Act 38 of 2005, s 7; England and Wales: Children Act 1989, s 1(3); and Ireland: Guardianship of Infants Act 1964, s 31(2), as inserted by Children and Family Relationships Act 2015, s 63.

49 Children's Act 38 of 2005, s 7.

50 Guardianship of Infants Act 1964, s 31(2) as inserted by Children and Family Relationships Act 2015, s 63.

be a positive attribute. As the Committee on the Rights of the Child has explained:

> [T]he concept of the child's best interests is flexible and adaptable. It should be adjusted and defined on an individual basis, according to the specific situation of the child or children concerned, taking into consideration their personal context, situation and needs.[51]

In this light, the unfixed nature of the best interests principle is actually its strength. The absence of a strict definition permits flexibility in the application of the principle, which allows for individualised assessments of what is best for a particular child or group of children. Children are not a homogenous group, and so the determination of best interests will vary from case to case. As such, it would not be appropriate to apply the same strict definition of best interests in every situation. As Eekelaar notes:

> It does not matter that [the best interests principle] does not point to determinate results in all, or even in most, cases. It would be alarming if it did, because that would suggest that relationships involving children and children's interests needed constantly to conform to community rules. The best interests principle, which incorporates the need to have regard to the child's perspective, opens the way for evaluating the effects of social rules on particular children and for creative solutions that go beyond such rules.[52]

Notwithstanding the above, it is suggested that objective criteria can be applied to guide the application of the best interests principle to ensure consistency of process. In this work, sociological and psychological research is used to demystify and inform the application of the principle by providing an objective statement about what is indeed best for children in the context of parenting. Although subjective determinations of best interests can never be fully eliminated, the accepted research provides solid guidance about what is best for children, significantly reducing the scope for discretion on the part of the decision-maker. This approach can be used to guide best interests determinations about individual children by judges or others as well as the development of policy decisions and legislation. For example, the evidence of sociologists and psychologists was heavily relied upon in the drafting of the Human Fertilisation and

[51] Committee on the Rights of the Child, above n. 3, para. 32.

[52] John Eekelaar, 'The role of the best interests principle in decisions affecting children and decisions about children' (2015) 23 *International Journal of Children's Rights* 3, pp. 25–26.

Embryology Act 2008 in the United Kingdom.[53] This legislation regulates the use of assisted reproductive technologies – an area that is fraught with social and ethical concerns. By drawing on social science data in developing this legislation, this socially sensitive area arguably became more socially acceptable given that it was guided by accepted research.

Reliance on sociological and psychological evidence can vastly reduce the indeterminacy of the best interests principle by providing a clear statement of how the law should be structured so as to benefit children. In the context of same-sex parenting, there is a growing body of sociological and psychological research on the outcomes for children who are raised by gay and lesbian couples that can act as a guide in determining the best interests of those children. This literature is discussed in Chapter 2 and will thereafter form the basis for the evaluation of various pathways to parentage available to same-sex couples in later chapters.

Overall, it is suggested that the indeterminacy of the best interests principle can be reduced by adopting a holistic, rights-based approach to the determination of best interests and through reliance on established sociological and psychological research to guide decision-making. This approach to determining the best interests of a particular child or group of children will not completely remove the potential for indeterminacy, and it would not be appropriate if it did. The best interests principle must remain flexible and adaptable, and so strict definitions and rigid procedures are to be avoided. The framework for the principle that is endorsed in this chapter injects an element of objectivity into the decision-making process, while still allowing for individualised decisions to be made.

1.4.2 'Smokescreen' Argument

The concerns surrounding the indeterminacy of the best interests principle are linked to another criticism of the principle: the 'smokescreen' concern. Essentially, this argument is premised on the contention that the uncertainty surrounding the best interests principle allows for other considerations (and potentially subjective biases) to be 'smuggled' into the decision-making process, thereby concealing the real basis for the decision. Others argue that the indeterminacy of the principle has permitted determinate policies to take precedence and that such policies

53 See, for example: *Joint Committee on the Human Tissue and Embryos (Draft) Bill Volume 1: Report*, HL Paper 169-I, HC Paper 630-I (2007).

may involve subjective, and perhaps unconfirmed, assumptions about what is best for a particular child or group of children.[54] Reece, for example, points to the traditional preference shown by the courts for heterosexual parents over gay or lesbian parents in legal disputes about residence. In these situations, Reece opines that 'a policy [had] usurped the role of the paramountcy principle, the policy being that the child should live in the unit which [was] closest to the nuclear family'.[55] Somewhat similarly, Freeman has suggested that the best interests principle 'can cloak prejudices, for example anti-gay sentiments'.[56] Furthermore, he suggests that the principle 'can also be merely a reflection of "dominant meanings"'.[57]

Freeman's latter suggestion, namely that the best interests principle is simply a reflection of dominant meanings, is arguably inescapable given that the question of what is 'best' for a certain child will depend on the child's social, economic and cultural circumstances. These circumstances will have a significant impact on the 'dominant meanings' within that culture. But, of course, dominant meanings can and do evolve, and this is squarely demonstrated by the evolution in attitudes towards gay and lesbian parents. Whereas thirty years ago, the 'dominant understanding' was that gay and lesbian persons were not fit to act as parents, causing them to lose custody of their children in many cases, today it is widely acknowledged that children who are raised by same-sex couples have broadly the same outcomes as those who are raised by opposite-sex couples.[58] Psychological and sociological research can also be influential in ascertaining the 'dominant meaning' as this can provide an accepted statement of scientific consensus regarding the suitability of gay and lesbian parents. The use of this research will be particularly important in jurisdictions where the 'dominant meaning' within the domestic

[54] Eekelaar, above n. 19, 237; Reece, above n. 26, 295.

[55] Reece, above, 294.

[56] Michael Freeman, 'Article 3: The best interests of the child' in André Alen, Johan Vande Lanotte, Eugène Verhellen, Fiona Ang, Eva Berghmans and Mieke Verheyde (eds.), *A Commentary on the United Nations Convention on the Rights of the Child* (Leiden: Martinus Nijhoff Publishers, 2007), p. 3.

[57] Above.

[58] The evolution in attitudes towards gay and lesbian parents can also be seen in the approach of the European Court of Human Rights. Indeed, the 'dominant meanings' discourse is particularly relevant in this example due to the reliance which the European Court places on the existence or non-existence of a European consensus on a certain issue. For a discussion of the evolution in attitudes of the English and South African courts towards same-sex parents, see: Ivan Schäfer, *The Law of Access to Children* (Cape Town: LexisNexis, 2007), p. 93.

culture cannot be reconciled with the child's rights. Psychological and sociological research is discussed in Chapter 2 and, as that discussion will demonstrate, the current state of the art could certainly be used to challenge the application of presumptions against same-sex parents.

Furthermore, it is suggested that the 'smokescreen' concern can be reduced by reference to the guidance provided by the Committee on the Rights of the Child on the best interests principle. The Committee has indicated that the best interests principle is not only a right but also an interpretive principle and a rule of procedure. As a rule of procedure, the Committee has emphasised that the best interests principle imposes an obligation on States 'to demonstrate how the interests of the child have been examined and assessed, and what weight has been ascribed to them in the decision'.[59] States must

> explain how the [best interests] right has been respected in the decision, that is, what has been considered to be in the child's best interests; what criteria it is based on; and how the child's interests have been weighed against other considerations, be they broad issues of policy or individual cases.[60]

The approach endorsed by the Committee has the potential to significantly reduce the risk that 'smokescreen' considerations will determine the outcome of the best interests assessment. Requiring States to enunciate how a certain conclusion has been reached minimises the possibility that unfounded or unarticulated assumptions about what is best for children will govern decision-making. As such, the guidance provided by the Committee can help to moderate the smokescreen concerns.

The framework advanced by the Committee for determining the best interests of the child offers an expedient means for promoting children's rights and interests. When combined with consideration of sociological and psychological research, it represents a logical structure for determining best interests that addresses the issues of indeterminacy and transparency. However, as will be discussed later in this chapter, it is questionable as to whether the best interests principle is currently applied at the domestic level in the manner recommended by the Committee. This point is considered through examination of the domestic framework for best interests in the jurisdictions of England and Wales, Ireland and South Africa. Before engaging in this analysis, it is necessary to consider two final, interrelated criticisms of the best interests principle: that it

[59] Committee on the Rights of the Child, above n. 3, para. 14.

[60] Committee on the Rights of the Child, above n. 3, para. 6.

lacks a rights-focus and that it is a paternalistic standard that should be replaced by a purely rights-based approach.

1.4.3 *Paternalism and Rights-Based Determinations*

The Committee on the Rights of the Child has stated that Article 3(1) of the UNCRC gives children the *right* to have their best interests assessed and taken as a primary consideration.[61] Furthermore, as discussed above, the Committee advocates for a rights-based approach to the determination of best interests. Nonetheless, the best interests principle is often presented as a paternalistic standard that lacks a child-rights focus.[62] Indeed, Eekelaar has opined that the right of a child to have their best interests considered by an adult, according to their own conception of best interests, is 'really no right at all'.[63] That said, elsewhere Eekelaar has argued that 'treating the application of the "best interests" principle as a child's right and not merely as a way of acting beneficially towards the child should reduce the risk that it will be applied entirely from an adult point of view'.[64]

When the best interests principle is applied, the adult decision-maker decides what is best for the child, and so it is sometimes argued that the child is treated more as an object of rights rather than a holder of rights.[65] This 'rights-less' view of the principle has led some authors to call for the introduction of a purely rights-based approach to replace the best interests principle. As Fortin notes, there is a view that the 'welfare' approach and the 'rights' approach are 'diametrically opposed' and require different approaches to decision-making.[66] It has also been suggested that a purely rights-based approach would better address the issues of indeterminacy and transparency discussed above.[67]

[61] Committee on the Rights of the Child, above n. 3, para. 1.
[62] Kilkelly, above n. 30, 56–57
[63] John Eekelaar, 'Families and children: From Welfarism to rights' in Christopher McCrudden and Gerald Chambers (eds.), *Individual Rights and the Law in Britain* (Oxford: Clarendon Press, 1994), p. 301
[64] John Eekelaar, *Family Law and Personal Life*, 2 ed. (Oxford: Oxford University Press, 2017), p. 60.
[65] Kilkelly, above n. 30, 56–57.
[66] Jane Fortin, *Children's Rights and the Developing Law*, 3 ed. (Cambridge: Cambridge University Press, 2009), p. 25.
[67] For example: Sonia Harris-Short, 'Family law and the Human Rights Act 1998: Judicial restraint or revolution?' (2005) 17 *Child and Family Law Quarterly* 329, p. 359.

This section addresses arguments concerning the rights credentials of the best interests principle and considers whether a purely rights-based approach would be preferable. Overall, it is suggested that rights-based adjudication is no more determinate than decision-making using the best interests principle. Furthermore, it is argued that the best interests principle is itself a right and that a rights-based approach must be adopted when determining best interests. In this context, it is argued that the criticisms of the principle are misplaced and, in fact, the best interests principle offers an expedient means to promote both children's rights and their interests.

1.4.3.1 Indeterminacy, Values and Rights

If value judgments and indeterminacy are regarded as the main disadvantages of the best interests principle, then it seems quite unlikely that a move to a purely rights-based approach will satisfy its critics. As Bainham notes, while the best interests principle is indeterminate, indeterminacy 'is also a problem with rights'.[68] The meaning of best interests must be determined by the decision-maker, but equally the meaning and content of children's rights must be determined and applied.[69] Indeed, in discussing children's rights under the European Convention on Human Rights in England and Wales, Bainham contends that there is 'no appreciable judicial awareness that there may even be a distinction between applying the welfare principle and upholding children's Convention rights'.[70]

According to Bainham, welfare and rights-based approaches are 'both grounded in value judgments and require the courts to adjudicate between competing values'.[71] By way of example, he references the child's right to know their identity. He notes that while it is the child's right to have such information, revelation of the child's true genetic origins may, in some cases, conflict with the mother's desire for confidentiality. In such situations, Bainham opines that revealing to the child their origins, against the mother's wishes, could destabilise the child's security with the mother. In such a case, the court will have to decide whether to attach more weight to truth or to stability – which is essentially a value

[68] Andrew Bainham, 'Can we protect children and protect their rights?' (2002) 32 *Family Law* 279, p. 280.

[69] Above.

[70] Above.

[71] Above.

judgment.[72] As such, he concludes that 'just as there might be competing and conflicting values at play in defining a child's best interests, so there may be these competitions and conflicts in defining the content of children's rights'.[73] A similar conclusion was reached earlier in this chapter in the initial discussion of indeterminacy. It was argued that the rights contained in the UNCRC should be applied to guide the best interests principle, but, in some cases, these rights will clash. In this situation, a value judgment will be required to determine what is in the best interests of the child.

1.4.3.2 The Best Interests Principle Is a Right that Complements Other Rights

Another criticism of the best interests principle is that it lacks a rights-focus. This claim is countered by reference to the guidance provided by the Committee on the Rights of the Child. The Committee has emphasised that children have a right to have their best interests treated as a primary consideration. The Committee has stated that the best interests principle is a substantive right that 'creates an intrinsic obligation for States, is directly applicable (self-executing) and can be invoked before a court'.[74] The advantage of this approach is that it makes the principle justiciable and means that it be litigated if required. Furthermore, the recognition of the principle as a right places obligations on others to secure it. As Thomas notes, '[a] right is not just any old statement about what is desirable or ought to happen. A statement of right is a claim that demands a response.'[75]

Consideration of the child's right to have their best interests taken as a primary consideration should incorporate rights-based reasoning. As discussed above, the rights contained in the UNCRC should be applied to guide the application of the best interests principle. This type of decision-making helps to contextualise the child's specific rights and strengthens those rights by providing clarity and depth.[76] Thus, the best interests principle does not exclude the consideration of children's rights but is intended to sit alongside and complement such rights.

It is also important to recall the critical role played by the principle – without it, decisions could be made about children without any reference

[72] Above, 283.
[73] Above, 288.
[74] Committee on the Rights of the Child, above n. 3, para. 6(a)
[75] Thomas, above n. 7, 2.
[76] Trevor Buck, *International Child Law* (London: Cavendish Publishing, 2005), pp. 59–60.

to their interests. As the Committee has noted, '[i]f the interests of children are not highlighted, they tend to be overlooked'.[77] The principle is justified by reference to the vulnerability, dependency and inferior legal status of children. As such, the principle plays an essential role in ensuring that decision-makers consider the interests of children. The principle does not exclude consideration of children's rights – it requires that such rights are examined. By contrast, a move to a purely rights-based approach would abolish the best interests principle and, in doing so, would not respect the child's position of vulnerability which justifies the use of the principle in the first place. Under the rights-based approach, the rights of children would have to be considered on the same level as those of adults. Consequently, the removal of the best interests principle would also remove the priority afforded to children's rights and interests.

1.4.3.3 Paternalism

The best interests principle is also criticised on the basis that it is a paternalistic standard, and it has been argued that a purely rights-based approach would provide a more child-centred method of decision-making with greater opportunity to hear the voice of the child.[78] The problem with this contention is that it ignores the fact that the child's right to express their views is an inherent part of the best interests assessment. The Committee on the Rights of the Child has made it clear that the best interests of the child *cannot* be ascertained without first hearing the child's views. As the Committee has stated:

> Assessment of a child's best interests must include respect for the child's right to express his or her views freely and due weight given to said views in all matters affecting the child. This is clearly set out in the Committee's general comment No. 12 which also highlights the inextricable links between articles 3, paragraph 1, and 12 [the right of the child to express their views]. The two articles have complementary roles: the first aims to realize the child's best interests, and the second provides the methodology for hearing the views of the child or children and their inclusion in all matters affecting the child, including the assessment of his or her best interests. Article 3, paragraph 1, cannot be correctly applied if the requirements of article 12 are not met.[79]

Therefore, the 'correct' application of the best interests principle *requires* that the child's right to express their views is respected. Those views will

[77] Committee on the Rights of the Child, above n. 3, para. 37.
[78] Fortin, above n. 66, 23.
[79] Committee on the Rights of the Child, above n. 3, para. 43.

not necessarily be conclusive, but they must be taken into consideration by the decision-maker when adjudicating upon the best interests of the child.

It must be acknowledged that, even if a purely rights-based approach was introduced, the child's wishes would not be determinative of the outcome of every case. Indeed, most proponents of the rights-based approach accept that the child's decisions should still be restricted in certain circumstances, namely where their choices would be contrary to their self-interests.[80] Therefore, even in the rights-based model, paternalism is evident given that the courts, in curtailing the child's decision-making powers, are essentially using a value judgment to determine what is 'best' for that child.

In this context, there would seem to be little advantage in promoting the rights-based approach over the best interests principle so as to allow for increased participation by the child in the decision-making process. Application of the best interests principle should respect the child's right to express their views. As Herring explains, '[a] child welfarist can, therefore readily accept that children should be able to make decisions for themselves, and a children's rights proponent can readily accept that children's choices should be restricted in order to protect their welfare'.[81] Thus, it has been suggested that the same result would likely be achieved regardless of whether a rights-based approach or a best interests approach is adopted.[82]

Overall, therefore, it is submitted that there would be no discernible advantage in abolishing the best interests principle and utilising a purely rights-based approach in its place. Firstly, the use of a purely rights-based approach would still require value judgments to be made, and so it is unlikely that this means of decision-making would produce more predictable results than the best interests approach. Secondly, consideration of the best interests of the child incorporates consideration of children's rights. Further, there seems to be little difference between the rights-based approach and the best interests approach in terms of the child's ability to participate in the decision-making process. Finally, it is submitted that children's rights and interests need to be prioritised so that they can be properly evaluated. A move to a purely rights-based approach would remove the priority that is afforded to children's rights by the best

[80] For a useful discussion of this point, see: Herring, above n. 28, 446.
[81] Herring, above n. 28, 446.
[82] Herring, above n. 28, 446.

interests principle. Without such priority, it would be more difficult for those rights to be realised. Consequently, it is submitted that the best interests principle should not be abandoned. The principle plays an important role in terms of guiding, clarifying and strengthening children's rights. It is used to complement those rights and so must be maintained in order to protect children.

When applied in the manner suggested by the Committee, guided by the other rights recognised in the UNCRC, the best interests right is a powerful tool to promote both children's rights and interests. This approach can be seen in the South African legal system, where the best interests principle is recognised as a constitutional right and has been instrumental in achieving the advancement of children's rights in that jurisdiction. Yet this approach does not eliminate subjectivity in the application of the principle, and so objective guidance in the form of social science literature remains important. It must also be noted that most countries do not recognise a substantive 'right' to best interests in domestic law. This is evident through examination of the domestic application of the best interests principle in England and Wales and Ireland later in the chapter. The purpose of this examination is to demonstrate the extent to which the application of the best interests principle is variable according to the constitutional, political, cultural and social contexts in which it is invoked.

1.5 A Conceptual Framework for the Best Interests Principle

From the preceding sections, a broad conceptual framework for the application of the best interests principle is identified, drawing primarily on the guidance of the Committee on the Rights of the Child.[83] This framework allows the principle to be applied in a way that overcomes the perceived deficiencies in the application of the principle and allows it to achieve its full potential as an effective mechanism to promote the rights and interests of children:

(1) The best interests principle is a threefold concept. It is a substantive right, a fundamental interpretive legal principle and a rule of procedure.
(2) The determination of best interests must be guided by the other rights contained in the UNCRC. Those rights provide broad guidance as to what is in a child's best interests. Consideration of the

[83] Committee on the Rights of the Child, above n. 3.

other UNCRC rights allows for a holistic, rights-based approach to the determination of best interests.

(3) The best interests principle must remain flexible, and must not be strictly defined, so that it can be applied on an individualised basis to assess what is 'best' for a particular child or group of children.
(4) Sociological and psychological research data should be applied to guide the application of the principle. Consideration of these data provides objective evidence to inform the decision-making process.
(5) Decision-making must be transparent and should explain how the best interests right has been respected in the decision.
(6) The views of the child should inform the best interests assessment.

This framework provides an effective process for determining the best interests of the child. It allows for consistency in the application of the principle and injects an element of objectivity into the decision-making process, while still allowing for individualised decisions to be made.

The following sections examine the domestic application of the best interests principle in England and Wales, Ireland and South Africa. This analysis shows that the application of the best interests principle at the domestic level does not always align with the conceptual framework for the principle endorsed above. This discussion reveals the difficulties that are created where the principle diverges from this framework and serves to underline the importance of establishing a robust framework for the application of the principle. It is argued that the framework above can address shortcomings in the domestic application of the principle, which highlights the suitability of this framework as a central theme for the analysis in later chapters.

1.6 Domestic Application of the Best Interests Principle

1.6.1 England and Wales: The Welfare Principle

In England and Wales, section 1 of the Children Act 1989 provides that

> When a court determines any question with respect to –
> (a) the upbringing of a child; or
> (b) the administration of a child's property or the application of any income arising from it,
>
> the child's welfare shall be the court's paramount consideration.[84]

[84] Children Act 1989, s 1.

This section evaluates the application of the welfare principle in England and Wales to consider whether it aligns with the conceptual framework for the determination of best interests endorsed above. The discussion centres on the approach of the English courts to the application of the principle. It demonstrates that indeterminacy and smokescreen concerns arise in the application of the English welfare principle and that, traditionally, these issues were exacerbated by presumptions developed by the courts. However, in recent years, the courts have moved away from applying such presumptions and now adopt an approach that is more in line with the framework for best interests discussed above.

1.6.1.1 Application of the Welfare Principle in England and Wales

In determining the best interests or welfare of a particular child, the English judiciary is obliged to consider a 'welfare checklist' set out in section 1(3) of the Children Act 1989. As part of this checklist, the courts must consider a range of factors, including the wishes of the child; physical, emotional and educational needs; the likely effect of any change in the child's circumstances; and any risk of harm to the child. This checklist helps to guide decision-making, but, of course, it does not remove subjectivity from the decision. This is because there is no indication as to how much weight is to be afforded to each factor, and so the decision-maker retains a considerable amount of discretion. As a result, it has been noted that there is great disparity in the exact use of the checklist.[85]

Furthermore, although a failure to consider an item on the checklist could constitute a ground of appeal,[86] the English courts are under no obligation to expressly enunciate their consideration of the factors set out on the checklist. As Baroness Hale of Richmond noted in *Re G (Children) (Residence: Same-Sex Partner)*, 'any experienced family judge is well aware of the contents of the statutory checklist and can be assumed to have had regard to it whether or not this is spelled out in a judgment'.[87] This stance is contrary to the advice of the Committee on the Rights of the Child and does not align with the conceptual framework for best interests endorsed earlier. As a rule of procedure, the Committee has emphasised that the principle requires decision-makers to set out

[85] Herring, above n. 28, 497.
[86] Herring, above n. 28, 497.
[87] *Re G (Children) (Residence: Same-Sex Partner)* [2006] UKHL 43, para. 40.

precisely *how* the decision as to best interests has been reached and what criteria that decision is based upon.[88] In failing to expressly refer to each item on the welfare checklist, the approach of the English judiciary falls short of what is required. The approach adopted could also be criticised on the basis that it opens up the possibility that unarticulated biases might creep into the decision-making. In order to comply with the guidance provided by the Committee, the English judiciary should explain how each factor on the checklist has been considered and evaluated.

The application of the welfare principle in England and Wales is also, at times, influenced by extraneous presumptions and policies that obscure individualised assessment of the child's best interests. For example, the courts have traditionally shown a preference for 'natural parents' over social parents or other carers.[89] In cases concerning gay and lesbian families, the English courts' deference to the position of natural parents has meant that there has sometimes been a failure to properly consider the important role played by the social parent in the child's life. Consequently, the assessment of the child's best interests may be hindered as all circumstances relevant to this assessment may not be appropriately taken into account.

This approach can be seen in the judgment of the House of Lords in *Re G (Children) (Residence: Same-Sex Partner)*.[90] In this case, two women had lived together in a committed relationship for almost seven years. During the course of that relationship, one of the partners, CG, gave birth to two children by way of artificial insemination. Under the law at the time, only the woman who gave birth was regarded as the legal mother of the children, and so the birth mother's partner, CW, did not have any parental status. The relationship between the couple ultimately broke down and CW applied for contact and shared residence orders.

At first instance, CW was refused her application for the shared residence order, but the application as to contact was granted. She then successfully appealed to the Court of Appeal against the refusal of the shared residence order. Just one month after the Court of Appeal ruling, however, CG removed the children to Cornwall in an attempt to prevent contact and in breach of court orders. The Court of Appeal this time held

[88] Committee on the Rights of the Child, above n. 3, para. 6.

[89] See, for example, *Re KD (a minor) (ward: termination of access)* [1988] 1 ALL ER 577; *Re K (a minor) (ward: care and control)* [1990] 3 All ER 795; *Re K (a minor) (wardship: adoption)* [1991] 1 FLR 57.

[90] *Re G (Children) (Residence: Same-Sex Partner)* [2006] UKHL 43.

that the shared residence order should continue, but the times spent under it were reversed so that the children spent the majority of term-time with CW. CG subsequently appealed this decision to the Court of Appeal, but this application was dismissed.

Upon appeal to the House of Lords, the importance of biological parentage was emphasised. The Lords noted:

> In reaching its decision the court should always have in mind that in the ordinary way the rearing of a child by his or her biological parent can be expected to be in the child's best interests, both in the short term and also, and importantly, in the longer term. I decry any tendency to diminish the significance of this factor. A child should not be removed from the primary care of his or her biological parents without compelling reason.[91]

The Lords concluded that 'the fact that CG is the natural mother of these children in every sense of that term, while raising no presumption in her favour, is undoubtedly an important and significant factor in determining what will be best for them now and in the future'.[92] According to the Lords, the lower courts had failed to give this factor sufficient attention. Baroness Hale did acknowledge the important role that CW played in the children's lives,[93] but, ultimately, the decision of the Court of Appeal was reversed and the terms of the original shared residence order were reinstated.

The dicta in *Re G* show great deference to the position of 'natural' parents. As Baroness Hale noted, 'the natural mother ... is the genetic, gestational and psychological parent. Her contribution to the welfare of the child is unique.'[94] As a result, more weight was given to the birth mother's role. By contrast, the absence of a biological connection between CW and the child was highlighted.[95] Thus, notwithstanding the fact that the children had been conceived on foot of a conscious decision by both of the women, and had been jointly raised by them for a number of years, the position of the birth mother was emphasised and prioritised throughout the judgment due to her genetic and gestational connection to the children. As Bainham has noted, 'the speeches in *Re*

[91] Above, para. 2.

[92] Above, para. 44.

[93] Baroness Hale noted that, as a social or psychological parent, CW made an 'important contribution' to the children's welfare and further that CW's 'importance in these children's lives has been stressed by both the professionals and all the judges who have decided this case'. *Re G*, above, paras. 37 and 45.

[94] Above, para. 36.

[95] Above, paras. 37–38.

G indicate a clear preference for natural parents unless there is a good and demonstrable reason for preferring alternative carers'.[96] Although the Lords emphasised that there was no presumption in favour of natural parents, as Bainham ponders, '[w]hat is this if not a presumption?'[97]

In subsequent cases, the English courts moved away from the natural parent presumption, acknowledging that the paramount consideration in cases of upbringing must be the welfare of the child. *Re B (A Child)*,[98] for example, concerned a four-year-old boy, B, who had lived with his maternal grandparents since birth. In March 2009, a residence order was made in favour of the child's grandmother but which allowed for contact by the child's parents. The father successfully appealed this decision to the Family Division and residence was transferred to him. This decision was upheld by the Court of Appeal, but the Supreme Court allowed the grandmother's appeal and affirmed the original residence order in her favour.

According to the Supreme Court, Richards J sitting in the Family Division had misunderstood the precedent set by *Re G*. Richards J had quoted with approval the House of Lords' finding that 'the rearing of a child by his or her biological parents can be expected to be in the child's best interests',[99] and he referred to the 'right of the child to be brought up in the home of his or her natural parent'.[100] The Supreme Court found that this reasoning betrayed 'a failure on the part of the judge to concentrate on the factor of overwhelming – indeed, paramount – importance which is, of course, the welfare of the child'.[101] Furthermore, the Supreme Court found that Richards J had erred in suggesting that as long as the parenting that the father could provide was 'good enough', it was of no consequence that that which the grandmother could provide would be better.[102] The Court emphasised that '[t]he court's quest is to determine what is in the best interests of the child, not what might constitute a second best but supposedly adequate alternative'.[103]

96 Andrew Bainham, 'Rowing back from Re G? Natural parents in the supreme court' [2010] *Family Law* 394, p. 401.

97 Above.

98 *Re B (A Child)* [2009] UKSC 5.

99 Above, para. 18.

100 Above, para. 19.

101 Above.

102 Above, para. 20.

103 Above.

The Supreme Court accepted that '[i]n the ordinary way one *can* expect that children will do best with their biological parents'.[104] However, it was emphasised that

> many disputes about residence and contact do not follow the ordinary way. Therefore, although one should keep in mind the common experience . . . one must not be slow to recognise those cases where that common experience does not provide a reliable guide.[105]

According to the Supreme Court, '[i]t is only as a contributor to the child's welfare that parenthood assumes any significance'.[106]

In *Re E-R (A Child),*[107] the Court of Appeal considered an appeal by the mother of a child (who was terminally ill) and her friends against a child arrangements order providing for the child to live with the father following the mother's death. The trial judge held that there was 'a broad natural parent presumption in existence under our law', which justified the making of the order.[108] The Court of Appeal held that the trial judge had wrongly conducted his analysis of the child's best interests and clarified that there is no presumption in favour of a natural parent in English law.[109] The Court noted that 'the fact that a person is a natural parent does not in itself create a presumption in favour of that person in the proceedings',[110] but equally there is no presumption in favour of a person with whom the child has been living for a significant period of time. Rather, each factor has to be considered and given appropriate weight depending on the particular facts of the case. Thus, the Court acknowledged that the assessment of the child's best interests must be considered in light of all relevant circumstances and no factor is automatically determinative of the case.

The case law discussed above shows a clear move away from the natural parent presumption. The decline of the use of the presumption is to be welcomed. The current approach is in keeping with the framework for best interests identified above in so far as it allows for the evaluation and balancing of all elements relevant to the child's situation. Furthermore, it is evident that prioritising the position and decisions of biological parents fails to appreciate and recognise the structure of gay and lesbian families.

104 Above, para. 35 [emphasis in original].
105 Above.
106 Above, para. 37.
107 *Re E-R (A Child)* [2015] EWCA Civ 405.
108 Above, para. 2.
109 Above, para. 32.
110 Above, para. 35.

In situations where the child has an existing relationship with both a genetic parent and a social parent, their relationship with the latter should not be disregarded or treated as secondary to the relationship with the former. The best interests of the child should not be obscured by automatically presuming that those best interests are to be met by a genetic parent – the importance to the child of maintaining a relationship with the social parent must also be taken into account.

The final point of note in this discussion of the welfare principle is that it is never expressed as a 'right' of the child under English law. Instead, the judicial dicta typically refer to the *rights of parents* and the *interests of children*. Children are recognised as rights-holders, but rights seem to be very much separate from the consideration of welfare. As the Supreme Court noted in *Re B (A Child)*:

> To talk in terms of a child's rights – as opposed to his or her best interests – diverts from the focus that the child's welfare should occupy in the minds of those called on to make decisions as to their residence.[111]

Thus, contrary to the advice of the Committee on the Rights of the Child, and in contrast to the best interests framework suggested above, rights and welfare seem to be separate and distinct matters for the English courts.

1.6.2 Ireland: The Best Interests Principle

In 2012, the Irish public voted in favour of the Thirty-First Amendment of the Constitution to insert a new Article 42A into the Irish Constitution (Bunreacht na hÉireann). This amendment was signed into law on 28 April 2015,[112] and the new Article 42A now provides for express constitutional recognition of the rights of the child. In addition, the amendment acknowledges the best interests principle. Article 42A.4.1 provides that provision shall be made by law that in all proceedings 'brought by the State ... for the purpose of preventing the safety and welfare of any child from being prejudicially affected' or 'concerning the adoption, guardianship or custody of, or access to, any child', 'the best interests of the child shall be the paramount consideration'.[113] This constitutional mandate has been implemented by various legislative

[111] *Re B (A Child)* [2009] UKSC 5, para. 19.

[112] The result of the referendum campaign was subsequently challenged before the High Court and Supreme Court which delayed the insertion of the amendment.

[113] Bunreacht na hÉireann, Art. 42A.4.1.

provisions, including section 3 of the Guardianship of Infants Act 1964, as amended by section 45 of the Children and Family Relationships Act 2015. The new section 3 of the 1964 Act sets out that in any proceedings where the 'guardianship, custody or upbringing of, or access to, a child' or the 'administration of any property belonging to or held on trust for a child or the application of the income thereof' is in question, 'the court, in deciding that question, shall regard the best interests of the child as the paramount consideration'.[114]

This section assesses the application of the best interests principle in Ireland. It is noted that the application of the principle in Ireland falls short of the recommendations of the Committee on the Rights of the Child in many respects and that Article 42A of the Irish Constitution has not significantly enhanced the status of the principle in Irish law.

1.6.2.1 Application of the Best Interests Principle in Ireland: Compliance with the Recommendations of the Committee on the Rights of the Child

Article 42A.4.1 does not enshrine the best interests principle as a free-standing right or as a free-standing principle in the Irish Constitution. It merely creates a constitutional requirement that legislation is enacted so as to give effect to the principle as 'the paramount consideration' in certain legal proceedings.[115] The obligation does not extend to policy decisions. The Committee on the Rights of the Child has specifically recommended that Ireland should ensure that the best interests principle is applied 'in all political, judicial and administrative decisions, as well as projects, programmes and services that have an impact on children'.[116] Ireland's legislative response clearly falls short of this recommendation.

It should also be recalled that the Committee has emphasised that the best interests principle is itself a right, the content of which is determined by reference to other rights contained in the UNCRC.[117] In the past, the Irish courts have suggested that the best interests principle could be recognised as a constitutional right, but this case law is limited. In *PW*

[114] Guardianship of Infants Act 1964, s 3, as amended by Children and Family Relationships Act 2015, s 45.

[115] Pre-existing statutes require the courts to regard the 'welfare' of children as the first and paramount consideration in certain legal proceedings.

[116] Committee on the Rights of the Child, *Consideration of Reports submitted by States parties under Article 44 of the Convention on the Rights of the Child. Concluding Observations: Ireland* (Committee on the Rights of the Child, 2006), para. 23.

[117] Committee on the Rights of the Child, above n. 3, paras. 6 and 32.

v. *AW*, Ellis J found that 'the child has the personal *right* to have its welfare regarded as the paramount consideration in any such dispute as to its custody'.[118] Similarly, in the later case of *FN and EB* v. *CO*, the High Court held that 'the personal rights of a child referred to in Article 40.3 [of the Constitution] include a *right* to have a decision in relation to his/her custody taken in the interests of his/her welfare'.[119]

The contention that the welfare of the child should be regarded as a constitutional right has not, however, been raised or examined in any other case law. Furthermore, it is notable that Article 42A.4.1 of the Irish Constitution does not express the principle as a constitutional right – the principle is expressed as a consideration (albeit the paramount one) which is to be protected through legislation. A previous proposed version of the constitutional amendment relating to children had expressly set out that children should have a *right* to have their welfare regarded as a primary consideration.[120] This wording was changed in 2012 to instead express the best interests of the child as 'the paramount consideration', and this is the wording that is now adopted in Article 42A.4.1. This suggests that the best interests principle was not intended to be recognised as a constitutional right in the new Article.

In Ireland, there is also a constitutional presumption that the welfare of the child will be met by the marital family. The courts have established that the welfare of the child is presumed to be found within the marital family unless there are compelling reasons as to why this cannot be achieved or the case is an exceptional one where the parents are found to have failed in their moral duty towards their child or children.[121] Thus, as Shannon explains, in cases concerning the marital family, 'the court will assume, without investigation, that the welfare of the child is being properly protected within the marital family unit unless evidence is produced to the contrary'.[122]

On the one hand, this presumption could be seen to minimise the indeterminacy of the best interests principle as it is clear that in cases of conflict between marital parents and non-parents, the court will find that the child's best interests will be served by the marital parents in all but the

118 *PW* v. *AW* (21 April 1980, unreported), High Court, pp. 73–74 [emphasis added].

119 *FN and EB* v. *CO* [2004] 4 IR 311, para. 44 [emphasis added].

120 Joint Committee on the Constitutional Amendment on Children, *Final Report* (Dublin: Joint Committee on the Constitutional Amendment on Children, 2010), p. 11.

121 *Re JH* [1985] IR 375.

122 Geoffrey Shannon, *Child Law*, 2 ed. (Dublin: Thomson Reuters, 2010), p. 12.

most exceptional of cases.[123] However, in line with the arguments made in the previous section, it is submitted that the application of the presumption impedes the assessment of the best interests of the child as all of the circumstances relevant to the child's best interests will not be taken into account unless the threshold for rebutting the presumption is met, that is, that 'where the parents, regardless of their marital status, fail in their duty towards their children to such extent that the safety or welfare of any of their children is likely to be prejudicially affected'.[124]

The Committee on the Rights of the Child has indicated that the best interests principle must be applied on an individual basis, 'according to the specific situation of the child or children concerned, taking into consideration their personal context, situation and needs'.[125] It is argued that this individualised assessment is impeded in Ireland in cases concerning the marital family as all circumstances relevant to the child's best interests are not taken into account unless the threshold for rebutting the presumption is met. Furthermore, it should be noted that the constitutional presumption as to welfare does not apply to non-marital children.[126] Therefore, in relation to non-marital children, 'the courts can ensure that the welfare of the child is the paramount consideration as there is no automatic presumption that such welfare will be found with the parents'.[127] There is a clear difference in the application of the best interests principle in cases concerning marital and non-marital children. Once more, this situation is at odds with the recommendations of the Committee on the Rights of the Child. The Committee has explained that Article 3 UNCRC imposes an obligation on States to 'ensure that the child's best interests are *appropriately integrated and consistently applied* in every action . . . and judicial proceedings which directly or indirectly impact on children'.[128] It is evident, however, that the best interests

[123] See, for example: *Re JH* [1985] IR 375; *North Western Health Board* v. *HW* [2001] 3 IR 622; *N* v. *Health Service Executive* [2006] 4 IR 374.

[124] Bunreacht na hÉireann, Art 42A.2.1.

[125] Committee on the Rights of the Child, above n. 3, para. 32.

[126] The rights of marital parents stem from Articles 41 and 42 of the Irish Constitution. Article 41.1 recognises the family as 'the natural primary and fundamental unit group of Society' and Article 41.3 pledges 'to guard with special care the institution of Marriage, on which the Family is founded, and to protect it against attack'. Furthermore, Article 42.1 acknowledges that 'the primary and natural educator of the child is the Family'. By contrast, the rights of non-marital parents derive from Article 40.3 of the Irish Constitution. See: Shannon, above n. 122, 14.

[127] Shannon, above n. 122, 14.

[128] Committee on the Rights of the Child, above n. 3, para. 14 [emphasis in original].

principle is not 'consistently applied' by the Irish courts as per the Committee's guidance as the principle is treated differently depending on the marital status of the parents. It is evident that, in many respects, the application of the best interests principle in Ireland does not align with the guidance of the Committee or with the framework for best interests endorsed earlier.

A significant recent development in Ireland was the introduction of same-sex marriage in 2015, following a successful marriage equality referendum. As a result of this referendum, gay and lesbian couples may enter into civil marriages, thereby acquiring protection under Articles 41 and 42 of the Constitution.[129] Where children are brought into such families, the constitutional presumption as to welfare will apply to them: their welfare will be deemed to be best met by their married gay or lesbian parents. This situation represents a seismic shift in the Irish constitutional position regarding gay and lesbian families, and it demonstrates an evolution in attitudes. As recently as 2008, Dunne J, giving judgment in *Zappone and Gilligan* v. *Revenue Commissioners*, was unsure as to whether the welfare of children could be met by same-sex couples and felt that there was 'simply not enough evidence from the research done to date that could allow firm conclusions to be drawn as to the consequences of same sex marriage, particularly in the area of the welfare of children'.[130] As such, Dunne J held that the exclusion of same-sex couples from marriage was justifiable to ensure the welfare of children.[131] Now, there is a constitutional presumption in Ireland that the welfare of children is *best* served by their married gay or lesbian parents. In light of the above, the utility of this presumption may be questioned in terms of its impact on the best interests assessment, but the extension of the presumption to gay and lesbian families is nonetheless a momentous change for Irish law.

1.6.3 South Africa: The Best Interests Principle

The preceding sections have argued that the Irish and English courts fail, in certain situations, to afford the requisite paramountcy to the best interests principle and that ancillary principles and policies have influenced the determination of what is meant by the best interests of the

[129] See note 126 above.
[130] *Zappone and Gilligan* v. *Revenue Commissioners* [2008] 2 IR 417, p. 500.
[131] Above, 499–500.

child. In this regard, it has been suggested that the Irish and English approaches fail to adhere to the recommendations of the Committee on the Rights of the Child in relation to how the best interests principle should be applied and fail to align with the conceptual framework for best interests that is endorsed in this chapter. By contrast, it is submitted that the application of the best interests principle in South Africa is more closely aligned with the conceptual framework and guidance of the Committee. Section 28(2) of the Constitution of the Republic of South Africa provides that '[a] child's best interests are of paramount importance in every matter concerning the child'.[132] As a result of this provision, the best interests principle has a high status in South African law. The South African courts have acknowledged that the best interests principle is not only a fundamental constitutional right but also a legal rule, a value and a principle of interpretation.[133] Furthermore, for the most part, the South African courts avoid allowing extraneous considerations to dictate the application of the principle. Instead, it is recognised that legal presumptions can hinder the application of the principle. As Sachs J stated in *AD and Another* v. *DW and Others*, 'child law is an area that abhors maximalist legal propositions that preclude or diminish the possibilities of looking at and evaluating the specific circumstances of each case'.[134]

This section evaluates the application of the best interests principle in South Africa. It is suggested that the South African approach aligns with the conceptual framework for best interests above and that this approach offers an expedient means of protecting children's rights and interests. It has, however, been argued that the South African courts do not treat the best interests principle in the same manner that they treat other constitutional rights.[135] As such, it is necessary to first consider the status of the principle in South African law before examining its application.

1.6.3.1 A Constitutional Right

Section 28 of the Constitution of the Republic of South Africa is titled 'Children'. Section 28(1) sets out a list of specific rights that are afforded to every child, while section 28(2) provides that '[a] child's best interests

[132] The Constitution of the Republic of South Africa, s 28(2).

[133] Elsje Bonthuys, 'The best interests of children in the South African constitution' (2006) 20 *International Journal of Law, Policy and the Family* 23.

[134] *AD and Another* v. *DW and Others (Centre for Child Law as Amicus Curiae; Department of Social Development as Intervening Party)* 2008 (3) SA 183 (CC), para. 55.

[135] Bonthuys, above n. 133.

are of paramount importance in every matter concerning the child'. Thus, the best interests principle is not included under the heading of 'rights' in the text of section 28. Nonetheless, the Constitutional Court has held that the principle is a constitutional right. In *Minister of Welfare and Population Development* v. *Fitzpatrick and Others*,[136] for example, the Court expressly found that section 28(2) of the Constitution 'creates a right that is independent of those specified in s.28(1)'.[137]

The recognition of the best interests principle as a right is further supported by the objects clause of the Children's Act 2005, which expressly refers to the best interests of the child as 'a constitutional right'. This clause sets out that one of the objects of the Act is 'to give effect to the following *constitutional rights* of children', including '(iv) that the best interests of the child are of paramount importance in every matter concerning the child'.[138]

Thus, there is both judicial and legislative authority for regarding the best interests principle as a constitutional right in South African law. The value in recognising the principle as a free-standing right, rather than simply as a principle of interpretation, is that this approach makes the principle justiciable. As such, there is scope to challenge actions and policies that do not operate in the best interests of a particular child or group of children. As will be seen below, the best interests principle has been effectively utilised as an advocacy tool in cases before the South African courts to secure and promote children's rights and interests.

Of the three jurisdictions discussed in this chapter, the South African approach to the best interests principle most closely aligns with the identified conceptual framework for best interests. As noted above, the principle is itself a right. Moreover, in line with the recommendations of the Committee on the Rights of the Child,[139] the content of the best interests principle in South Africa is determined by reference to other children's rights. As such, it is possible to bring a claim based on the best interests principle to the South African courts and the judiciary will then resolve that dispute by reference to the child's other rights and interests. This approach was adopted in *J* v. *National Director of Public Prosecutions and Another*,[140] which concerned the constitutionality of

[136] *Minister of Welfare and Population Development* v. *Fitzpatrick and Others* 2000 (3) SA 422 (CC).

[137] Above, para. 17.

[138] Children's Act 38 of 2005, s 2(b)(iv) [emphasis added].

[139] Committee on the Rights of the Child, above n. 3, para. 32.

[140] *J* v. *National Director of Public Prosecutions and Another* 2014 (2) SACR 1 (CC).

legislation that required the names of child offenders to be automatically included on the National Register for Sex Offenders. In that case, the *only* argument put forward by the *amici curiae* was that this legislation was contrary to the best interests principle.[141] This argument was embraced by the Constitutional Court, which then elaborated upon the implications of the best interests principle in the context of child offenders. According to the Court, the best interests principle 'encapsulate[s] the idea that the child is a developing being, capable of change and in need of appropriate nurturing to enable her to determine herself to the fullest extent and to develop her moral compass'.[142] In line with this 'developmental impetus of the best-interests principle',[143] the Court went on to consider a number of other issues that are of relevance to the child offender, such as the need for an individualised approach (which also respects the flexibility of the best interests principle);[144] the child's right to be heard;[145] and the reformative aims of child justice.[146] The Court found that each of these factors had been infringed and thus the relevant provision was deemed to breach the child offender's *right* to best interests under section 28(2) of the Constitution.

This case demonstrates the scope of the best interests principle under South African law. It can be used as a stand-alone right to challenge law and policy, and the assertion of a breach of this right leads the courts to consider other rights of relevance to the situation. This approach would certainly seem to be in keeping with that endorsed by the Committee.

Bonthuys, however, has argued that the best interests principle is treated differently to other constitutional rights by the South African courts. She notes:

> Instead of analysing and interpreting the contents of the best interests as they would have done with other fundamental rights, the courts simply assert that a particular rule or practice infringes the best interests of the child. Given the notorious uncertainty of the concept and the fact that people disagree strongly about what is good for children in general, this is noteworthy.[147]

[141] Above, para. 35.
[142] Above, para. 36.
[143] Above.
[144] Above, paras. 38–40.
[145] Above, para. 40.
[146] Above, para. 44.
[147] Bonthuys, above n. 133, 27.

Bonthuys further notes that 'once the conclusion is reached that the best interests of the child have been infringed, the [Constitutional Court] has not, with the exception of the *Sonderup* case, embarked on a full limitations enquiry'.[148] Bonthuys opines that the fact that the Constitutional Court has not dealt with the best interests principle in the same way that it treats other constitutional rights 'creates the impression that, contrary to their rhetoric, the best interests is not really a fundamental right, or at least not a right like all the others in the Bill of Rights'.[149]

Bonthuys' argument is countered by an analysis of *J* v. *National Director of Public Prosecutions and Another*, referred to above. In that case, the Constitutional Court provided a detailed analysis of the content of the best interests principle and its implications in the context of child offenders. It is, therefore, inaccurate to assert that the courts never analyse and interpret the contents of the best interests principle. Such analysis takes place on a case-by-case basis so as to respect the fact that the principle should be flexible and adaptable to suit the needs of individual children. As the Constitutional Court noted in *Minister of Welfare and Population Development* v. *Fitzpatrick and Others*, the best interests principle has 'never been given exhaustive content' in South African law because '[i]t is necessary that the standard should be flexible as individual circumstances will determine which factors secure the best interests of a particular child'.[150] Similarly, in *S* v. *M (Centre for Child law as Amicus Curiae)*, Sachs J was satisfied that, following the dicta of *Fitzpatrick*, 'indeterminacy of outcome is not a weakness. A truly principled child-centred approach requires a close and individualised examination of the precise real-life situation of the particular child involved.'[151] As such, the learned judge opined that applying a predetermined formula to determine the child's best interests would run contrary to the best interests principle. This flexible approach is also in keeping with the recommendations of the Committee on the Rights of the Child.[152]

Section 36 of the South African Constitution provides for the limitation of rights. This section applies to all rights, including the best interests principle. The South African courts have consistently held that the best

[148] Bonthuys, above n. 133, 27. See: *Sonderup* v. *Tondelli* 2001 (1) SA 1171 (CC).

[149] Bonthuys, above n. 133, 27.

[150] *Minister of Welfare and Population Development* v. *Fitzpatrick and Others* 2000 (3) SA 422 (CC), para. 18.

[151] *S* v. *M (Centre for Child law as Amicus Curiae)* 2008 (3) SA 232, para. 24.

[152] Committee on the Rights of the Child, above n. 3, para. 32.

interests principle is not absolute and is subject to limitation. In *De Reuck v. Director of Public Prosecutions*,[153] for example, the Constitutional Court emphasised that section 28(2) of the South African Constitution does not 'trump' other provisions. According to the Court, to allow the best interests principle to override the rights of others in all cases 'would be alien to the approach adopted by this Court that constitutional rights are mutually interrelated and interdependent and form a single constitutional value system'.[154] The Court noted that section 28(2), like the other rights enshrined in the Bill of Rights, is subject to limitations that are reasonable and justifiable in a democratic society.[155]

Similarly, in *S* v. *M*, Sachs J noted that although the best interests principle is to be applied in every matter concerning the child, '[t]his cannot mean that the direct or indirect impact of a measure or action on children must in all cases oust or override all other considerations'.[156] Furthermore, the judge was satisfied that 'the fact that the best interests of the child are paramount does not mean that they are absolute. Like all rights in the Bill of Rights their operation has to take account of their relationship to other rights, which might require that their ambit be limited.'[157] Therefore, it is evident that the South African courts do consider the interests of others when determining the question of best interests and that the best interests of the child are subject to the same limitations as other constitutional rights.

The above, however, raises another concern: if the best interests of the child do not always prevail, what is meant by the term 'paramount importance'? Indeed, as Friedman and Pantazis have questioned, 'if a child's best interests are not always supreme, what is the point of section 28(2)?'[158] A literal reading of section 28(2) would suggest that the best interests of the child should dictate the outcome of every case concerning a child or children and that no other consideration should take priority. As Sachs J noted in *S* v. *M*, '[t]he word "paramount" is emphatic'.[159] That expression, coupled with the phrase 'in every matter concerning the

[153] *De Reuck* v. *Director of Public Prosecutions (Withwatersrand Local Division)* 2004 (1) SA 406 (CC).

[154] Above, para. 55.

[155] Above, para. 55.

[156] *S* v. *M (Centre for Child law as Amicus Curiae)* 2008 (3) SA 232, para. 25.

[157] Above, para. 26.

[158] Adrian Friedman and Angelo Pantazis 'Children's rights' in Stu Woolman and Michael Bishop (eds.), *Constitutional law of South Africa* 2 ed. (Lansdowne: Juta and Co, Ltd., 2006).

[159] *S* v. *M (Centre for Child law as Amicus Curiae)* 2008 (3) SA 232, para. 25.

child', if taken literally, 'would cover virtually all laws and all forms of public action, since very few measures would not have a direct or indirect impact on children, and thereby concern them'.[160] However, it is clear that section 28(2) is not always the superseding factor. As Sachs J emphasised, the section does not mean that 'the direct or indirect impact of a measure or action on children must in all cases oust or override all other considerations'.[161] According to the judge, '[i]f the paramountcy principle is spread too thin it risks being transformed from an effective instrument of child protection into an empty rhetorical phrase of weak application, thereby defeating rather than promoting the objective of section 28(2)'.[162]

Thus, under section 28(2), the best interests of the child will not automatically outweigh the interests of others. The child's interests are still given special consideration, or a 'leg up' vis-à-vis other rights and values,[163] but those interests will not necessarily be absolute. To use the dicta from *S* v. *M*, once more:

> The paramountcy principle, read with the right to family care, requires that the interests of children who stand to be affected receive due consideration. It does not necessitate overriding all other considerations. Rather, it calls for appropriate weight to be given in each case to a consideration to which the law attaches the highest value, namely the interests of children who may be concerned.[164]

In this context, it could be argued that the South African best interests principle has more in common with the English and Irish conceptions of the principle than might have been first expected. The South African principle is not the supreme and dominating factor in every case but simply a 'consideration' for the court, albeit one 'to which the law attaches the highest value'.[165] Although at first glance the phrase 'of paramount importance' appears to be much stronger than 'paramount consideration', the South African Courts have established that the principle stands at the latter level. However, this does not mean that the application of the best interests principle in South Africa is equivalent to the English and Irish variations of the principle. The South African principle is far more robust. In a number of cases, the best interests

[160] Above.
[161] Above.
[162] Above.
[163] Friedman and Pantazis, above n. 158.
[164] *S* v. *M (Centre for Child law as Amicus Curiae)* 2008 (3) SA 232, para. 42.
[165] Above.

principle has been applied to drastically alter the South African legal landscape. The principle has been invoked to find, inter alia, that foreign citizens should be allowed to adopt South African-born children;[166] same-sex couples should be permitted to jointly adopt;[167] and two women should be permitted to be jointly registered as the parents of a child born via donor insemination.[168] The principle has not been used to the same effect in England or Ireland.

Furthermore, the South African case law emphasises the individualised nature of the best interests assessment. In *M* v. *The State*, for example, it was held:

> A truly principled child-centred approach requires a close and individualised examination of the precise real-life situation of the particular child involved. To apply a pre-determined formula for the sake of certainty, irrespective of the circumstances, would in fact be contrary to the best interests of the child concerned.[169]

Similarly, in *AD and Another* v. *DW and Others*, the Constitutional Court was satisfied that '[d]etermining the best interests of the child cannot be circumscribed by mechanical legal formulae or through rigid hierarchical rankings of care options'.[170] Evidently, there is an awareness amongst the judiciary that the best interests assessment requires that a contextualised, case-by-case enquiry is conducted and that this takes into account all of the circumstances relevant to the child in reaching a decision as to their best interests. This individualised assessment also aligns with the framework for best interests advanced above and that recommended by the Committee on the Rights of the Child.[171]

It is clear therefore that the South African best interests principle provides an expedient and robust means through which to protect and safeguard children and further that the application of the best interests principle mirrors the framework put forward by the Committee on the Rights of the Child. As noted above, section 28(2) sits alongside a comprehensive, non-exhaustive list of children's rights provided in

[166] *Minister of Welfare and Population Development* v. *Fitzpatrick and Others* 2000 (3) SA 422 (CC).

[167] *Du Toit and De Vos* v. *Minister of Welfare and Others* (CCT 40/01) [2002] ZACC 20.

[168] *J and B* v. *Director-General, Department of Home Affairs* (2003) (5) BCLR 463.

[169] *M* v. *The State* [2007] ZACC 18, para. 24.

[170] *AD and Another* v. *DW and Others (Centre for Child Law as Amicus Curiae; Department of Social Development as Intervening Party)* 2008 (3) SA 183 (CC), para. 50.

[171] Committee on the Rights of the Child, above n. 3, para. 32.

section 28(1).[172] The existence of these rights has led some authors to question whether there is any need for a separate provision to promote the child's best interests.[173] It is submitted, however, that a purely rights-based approach would not adequately protect children. As has been seen, the best interests principle is not only a right but also an interpretive principle which strengthens other rights, and it is a rule of procedure. Abandoning the principle would remove the priority afforded to children's rights in the determination process as was discussed in previous sections. The South African approach demonstrates the value in recognising the best interests principle as a threefold concept in line with the Committee's recommendations.

1.7 Conclusion

This chapter has demonstrated that the best interests principle is a valuable decision-making tool. The principle acknowledges the vulnerability of children – that it is more difficult for them to assert their rights than it is for adults. The principle allows for the interests of children to be elevated, which ensures that they are protected. By contrast, a purely rights-based approach would not offer such priority. In addition, it has been argued that the criticisms raised against the principle are not all-consuming and can be overcome. The 'problem' of indeterminacy, for example, is arguably not a problem at all given that so much of the law is indeterminate. It is a strength of the principle that it is flexible and therefore malleable to the specific circumstances of individual children. Social science literature can, in any case, be applied so as to reduce subjectivity from the assessment.

The South African application of the best interests principle would appear to be most in keeping with that which is recommended by the Committee on the Rights of the Child. This demonstrates that the Committee's vision of the principle is attainable and that it represents a realistic application of the principle. The principle, as endorsed by the Committee, has the potential to vastly improve the protection of not only children's interests but also their rights. As such, the conceptual framework identified in this chapter, which is based on the recommendations

172 The Constitution of the Republic of South Africa, s 28(1).

173 Bonthuys, for example, contends that many South African cases could have been decided by reference to the specific rights afforded to children in section 28(1) of the South African Constitution and, as such, it was not necessary for the courts to apply the best interests principle as a right. Bonthuys, above n. 133, 27.

of the Committee, allows individual States Parties to realise the full potential of the principle.

In the context of same-sex parenting, the best interests principle is an appropriate central theme given that, traditionally, resistance has built up against affording legal recognition to same-sex couples as parents on the basis that this is not 'best' for the children concerned.[174] The best interests principle, coupled with sociological and psychological data, can be used to assess the validity of this claim. The use of sociological and psychological data helps to reduce the subjectivity of this assessment and can be used to determine what is actually 'best' for children in this context. The procedural guarantees of Article 3 UNCRC also demand that the reasons for the decision are fully set out,[175] and so the decision-maker would have to justify its use or dismissal of the sociological evidence presented. Finally, if the extension of joint parental responsibilities and rights to same-sex couples is found to be in the child's best interests, the principle could then be used, in its manifestation as a right, to demand that these parental responsibilities and rights are extended.

The next chapter examines relevant sociological and psychological research to shed light on the meaning of 'best interests' in the context of same-sex parenting. Thereafter, the conceptual framework identified in this chapter is applied alongside these data to consider how the best interests principle should apply in specific contexts. The result is a child-centred analysis of parenting that is guided by evidence so as to ensure that each pathway to parentage that is discussed is regulated in a way that prioritises the child's interests.

[174] See Chapter 2.
[175] Committee on the Rights of the Child, above n. 3, para. 6.

2

The Best Interests of the Child

Sociological and Psychological Research

> This evil must stop for the sake of potential children and society, which both have enough problems without the extension of this horrific practice.
>
> Rhodes Byson, MP, speaking about lesbian parenthood in 1978.[1]

> There is no evidence to suggest that lesbian women or gay men are unfit to be parents or that psychosocial development among children of lesbian women or gay men is compromised.
>
> American Psychological Association, 2005.[2]

2.1 Introduction

The best interests principle frequently appears in discussions about same-sex parenting. In this context, the principle is often applied in a negative manner by those who are opposed to the legal recognition of gay and lesbian parents. Opponents of same-sex parenting claim that it is not in the best interests of children to be raised by gay and lesbian parents and therefore the law should not recognise these couples as legal parents.[3] During the 2015 marriage equality referendum in Ireland, for example, posters appeared across the country linking surrogacy to marriage equality, asserting that 'two men cannot replace a mother's love' and that 'a mother's love is irreplaceable'.[4] The 'No Campaign' argued against

[1] Susan Golombok, *Modern Families: Parents and Children in New Family Forms* (Cambridge: Cambridge University Press, 2015), p. 32.

[2] American Psychological Association, *Lesbian and Gay Parenting* (Washington, DC: American Psychological Association, 2005), p. 15.

[3] Jennifer Rosato, 'Children of same-sex parents deserve the security blanket of the parentage presumption' (2006) 44 *Family Court Review* 74, p. 74. Carlos Ball, *Same-Sex Marriage and Children* (Oxford: Oxford University Press, 2014); Iona Institute, *Made for Children: Why the Institution of Marriage Has Special Status* (Dublin: Iona Institute, 2010).

[4] Juno McEnroe, 'Tánaiste: No posters "sad and demeaning."', Irish Examiner, 5 May 2015.

marriage equality on this basis. Surrogacy was extraneous to the issue of marriage equality,[5] but, nonetheless, claims as to surrogacy and its implications for family formation were continually raised during the debates.[6] The common thread appearing in the arguments of the 'No Campaign' was that the legal recognition of same-sex parenting should be opposed so as to safeguard the best interests of children.

The quote from Rhodes Byson, MP, demonstrates that concerns about the welfare of children have also arisen in England and Wales in the context of same-sex parenting. Byson was speaking in 1978, but similar views have been aired throughout the intervening decades. For example, the best interests principle was referenced in opposition to provisions of the Adoption and Children Act 2002 that allow for joint adoption by same-sex couples.[7] Like the debates in Ireland, the central argument used to oppose the legislation was the claim that 'every child has a right to a mother and father'.[8]

Claims as to the existence of 'a right to a mother and father' are prevalent, but it must be acknowledged that this supposed right does not appear in the United Nations Convention on the Rights of the Child (UNCRC)[9] or in any other international instrument. Article 7 UNCRC supports the right of the child, as far as possible, to know and be cared for by their parents. The term 'parents' is not defined in the UNCRC and 'there is nothing in the drafting history of the Convention to suggest that the term "parents" was ever to be defined or confined to a man and woman'.[10] Thus, the claims as to best interests made by those who are opposed to the legal recognition of same-sex parenting can be regarded as a moral conception of the best interests principle, rather than one that is based on an understanding of the principle as enshrined in the UNCRC.

[5] Conor O'Mahony, 'The Constitution, the Right to Procreate and the Marriage Referendum' Constitution Project @ UCC, 21 April 2015 www.constitutionproject.ie/?p=503

[6] RTÉ News, 'Lawyer group say Yes vote for same-sex marriage will affect assisted reproduction rights' RTÉ News, 15 May 2015; Ronán Mullen, 'Head to Head: Ronán Mullen argues against same-sex marriage', Irish Times, 22 May 2015.

[7] John Tobin and Ruth McNair, 'Public international law and the regulation of private spaces: Does the convention on the rights of the child impose an obligation on states to allow gay and lesbian couples to adopt?' (2009) 23 *International Journal of Law, Policy and the Family* 110.

[8] Above pp. 111–112.

[9] United Nations Convention on the Rights of the Child, New York, 20 November 1989, in force 2 September 1990, Art. 7.

[10] Tobin and McNair, above n. 7, 112.

The arguments raised as to the best interests of children in this context echo the concerns noted in Chapter 1 about the subjectivity of the best interests principle – the use of the principle will be dependent upon the decision-maker's own values and ideals. Hence, the Irish 'No Campaign' interpreted the best interests principle to mean that children should not be raised by same-sex couples and that marriage should not be extended to such persons. By contrast, a coalition of Irish children's rights organisations, which included the Irish Society for the Prevention of Cruelty to Children (ISPCC), Barnardos, Youth Work Ireland and the Children's Rights Alliance (under the leadership of BeLongTo), supported a Yes vote in the referendum on the basis that this *would* be best for children.[11] Arguably, the children's rights organisations were better placed to assess the best interests of children in this situation, but the divergent views expressed serve to demonstrate the indeterminate nature of the best interests principle. While for some, the mantra of best interests seemed to dictate that same-sex couples should not be afforded the opportunity to marry, for others the best interests of children demanded that marriage equality be introduced.

This chapter examines sociological and psychological research concerning gay and lesbian parenting in order to guide the application of the best interests principle. It is argued that this research can reduce the indeterminacy of the principle by providing broader understanding of the social issues at play. The most common argument raised against same-sex parenting is that children do best when raised by their married, biological parents and where they are raised by both a mother and a father.[12] In attempting to use social science research to determine what is 'best' for children who are raised by same-sex couples, it is therefore prudent to examine the validity of the claims made as to the benefits to children of being raised by married, biological parents. Thereafter, the outcomes for children raised by gay and lesbian parents are analysed to understand whether children are disadvantaged where they are not raised by a parent of each sex.[13]

[11] Anna Carey, 'Marriage equality: The young movement that swung the Yes vote', *Irish Times*, 16 November 2015.

[12] Popenoe has argued that '[f]ew propositions have more empirical support in the social sciences than this one: Compared to all other family forms, families headed by married, biological parents are best for children'. David Popenoe quoted in Center for Marriage and Families, *The Scholarly Consensus on Marriage. Fact Sheet No. 2* (New York: Institute for American Values, 2006), p. 1.

[13] The 'outcomes' discussed include a variety of measures against which researchers assess the well-being of children, such as psychological outcomes and behavioural outcomes.

Social science literature is increasingly prevalent in law and policy decision-making. Its use in this context is also increasingly criticised as there is a danger of advocacy bias, selective reliance and misunderstanding. Before considering the findings of social science research in the area of gay and lesbian parenting, it is therefore necessary to examine the issue of subjectivity and bias in social science research to ensure that the analysis in the latter part of this chapter does not fall into this common pitfall.

2.2 Applying Social Science Research in Child Law

Social science research provides an evidence base to guide the creation of law and policy and to assist judicial decision-making. It can provide a clear statement about what is 'best' for children in particular situations, providing broader understanding of social factors and likely outcomes of best interests decisions. While it is impossible to predict the exact consequences of a certain legal decision, judges and policy makers can know 'as a matter of statistical probability' how their decision will affect the children concerned by relying on scientific data.[14]

In order for social science data to have a legitimate role in guiding law and policy, it must be appropriately applied. Inaccurate interpretations and analysis of empirical research by the legal community can have negative effects on children, as legal and policy decisions do not then align with their lived reality and existing needs. The use of social science data in child law is often inconsistent. As will be seen later in this chapter, there is a prevalence of advocacy bias in discussions about gay and lesbian parenting as opponents and advocates of legal recognition 'pick and choose' studies that support their contentions. Just as there are debates among legal scholars about particular issues, so too are there debates among social scientists, meaning that there is rarely just one social science view about an issue.[15] Hence, in applying social science data in law, there can be difficulties with the initial selection of research studies, interpretation of findings and the application of research to different societal groups. These points open up the possibility that the social science research will be

[14] Judith Cashmore and Patrick Parkinson, 'The use and abuse of social science research evidence in children's cases' (2014) 20 *Psychology, Public Policy, and Law* 239–250, p. 239.

[15] Zoe Rathus, 'A call for clarity in the use of social science research in family law decision-making' (2012) 26 *Australian Journal of Family Law* 81–115, p. 83.

misunderstood, disregarded or, worse still, manipulated to support a particular cause.[16]

When discussing 'new' family forms, problems also arise due to the nascent nature of the research: there may be a lack of longitudinal research with large sample sizes relating to these families since they either did not exist or were not visible within society until relatively recently. In this instance, questions arise as to whether social science research can legitimately be relied on by policy makers[17] or if it is simply 'inconclusive'.[18]

To address inconsistencies in the use of social science research in law, various bodies have proposed guidelines for the legal community when relying on such research.[19] For example, the Association of Family and Conciliation Courts (AFCC) proposes a set of sixteen guidelines that are designed to promote 'effective, responsible, and ethical use of social science research in family law–related practices, programs, and policies'.[20] These guidelines are directed at family law practitioners working in the courtroom environment, and so some recommendations are not directly applicable to discussions in this chapter. Nonetheless, broad guidance relevant to the present discussion can be drawn from the AFCC guidelines, as follows:

- Use only high-quality sources that have been evaluated through a peer review process by experts in the area of research.
- Ensure that individuals who evaluate the research have a basic understanding of research design and methodology to evaluate the strengths and limitations of research.
- Ensure that research studies are accurately reported to verify transparency and identify any potential research bias.

[16] Conor O'Mahony and Lydia Bracken, 'The child's right to family life: Shifting sands and social science' (International Journal of Children's Rights UNCRC 30th Anniversary Conference, 21 June 2019).

[17] Above.

[18] In *Zappone and Gilligan* v. *Revenue Commissioners* [2008] 2 IR 417, the Irish High Court found that there was simply not enough evidence to discern whether the welfare of children could be met by same-sex couples.

[19] Bryan Rodgers, Liz Trinder and Teresa Williams, *Towards a Family Justice Observatory to Improve the Generation and Application of Research* (London: Nuffield, 2015); Cashmore and Parkinson, above n. 14; Task Force on the Guidelines for the Use of Social Science Research in Family Law, *Guidelines for the Use of Social Science Research in Family Law* (Madison: Association of Family and Conciliation Courts, 2018).

[20] Task Force on the Guidelines for the Use of Social Science Research in Family Law, above.

- Consider the full range of research available on an issue, rather than selectively drawing on studies or research reviews that support a particular argument.
- Engage in up-to-date and comprehensive reviews of literature on a given topic.
- Verify the extent to which research claims can be generalised as conclusions from research conducted on specific groups of people might not apply to everyone.
- Understand and acknowledge the limitations of research design and methodology that may impact a study's findings.
- Consider and acknowledge alternative explanations of research claims.
- Identify areas of broad consensus and disagreement about the state of the research on an issue.
- Identify and disclose potential conflicts of interest that may influence or bias research.[21]

These points provide useful guidance for the application of social science literature in legal and policy decision-making. The guidance mirrors the recommendations of other social scientists and therefore reflects agreed general best practice in this area.[22] As the following sections demonstrate, advocates and opponents of same-sex parenting do not usually take such transparent steps in discerning the validity of research claims. The following sections evaluate the existing research in this area through the lens proposed by the AFCC to ensure a valid and comprehensive analysis of the research studies. However, the final point noted above must first be addressed: I must disclose that I am strongly in favour of the legal recognition of same-sex parenting and therefore am open to bias in evaluating the research. Nonetheless, a transparent approach will be adopted to ensure an objective analysis of competing claims based on social science data, starting with the claim that being raised by married, opposite-sex parents is best for children.

2.3 Are Married Opposite-Sex Parents the 'Ideal'?

The notion of family optimality is inescapable in debates about same-sex parenting. In many ways, it is an unsuitable standard in this context since

[21] Above.

[22] Cashmore and Parkinson argue that social science research should be based on 'rigorous peer review, the "pooling of evidence" (via replication and synthesis), and the extent to which the findings reflect general scientific consensus in the field'. Cashmore and Parkinson, above n. 14, 245.

we do not concern ourselves with 'optimality' when it comes to any other form of reproduction. If we did, most parenting arrangements would be subject to negative scrutiny. As Ball notes:

> [N]o one argues that only those with high incomes or college degrees be permitted to adopt children. Such social engineering . . . would clearly be misguided, because it would be inconsistent with the intuitive point, supported by the social science evidence, that there are many factors that account for child outcomes.[23]

Opponents of same-sex parenting (and marriage equality) often rely on the claim that children do 'best' when raised by their married biological parents. For example, during the Irish marriage equality debates, the Iona Institute (a Catholic campaign group that is opposed to marriage equality) claimed that marriage should be confined to opposite-sex couples because sociological studies demonstrate that children tend to fare best when raised by their genetic parents in a low-conflict marriage.[24] Similar arguments are made by opponents of same-sex parenting across the globe.[25]

An extensive body of research demonstrates the benefits to children of being raised by two biological parents in a low-conflict marriage.[26] For example, a study by Anderson Moore and others concludes that 'family structure matters for children, and the family structure that helps children the most is a family headed by two biological parents in a low-conflict marriage'.[27] In this study, the researchers conducted a review of existing literature, finding that the existing research is 'very consistent' as to the benefits to children of being raised by married parents.[28] However, these findings only apply to low-conflict marriage. Children who grow up

[23] Ball, above n. 3, 70.

[24] Iona Institute, above n. 3.

[25] Ball, above n. 3; Nick Evershed, 'Think of the kids: why marriage equality opponents are wrong on parenting', *The Guardian*, 17 August 2017.

[26] For example, Sara McLanahan and Gary Sandefur, *Growing Up with a Single Parent: What Hurts, What Helps* (Harvard: Harvard University Press, 1994); Neil Stewart, 'Marriage facts' (2008) 31 *Harvard Journal of Law and Public Policy* 313; David Ribar, 'Why marriage matters for child wellbeing' (2015) 25 *The Future of Children* 11–27; Maggie Gallagher and Joshua Baker, *Do Mothers and Fathers Matter?: The Social Science Evidence on Marriage and Child Well-Being* (Washington, DC: Institute for Marriage and Public Policy, 2004).

[27] Kristin Anderson Moore, Susan Jekielek, and Carol Emig, *Marriage from a Child's Perspective: How Does Family Structure Affect Children, and What Can We Do about It?* (Washington, DC: Child Trends, 2002), p. 6.

[28] Above, 1.

in an intact but high-conflict marriage have impaired emotional well-being and children whose parents divorce are at greater risk of depression, antisocial behaviour, impulsive/hyperactive behaviour and school behaviour problems.[29] It should also be noted that this study specifies that the research did not include an analysis of the available research on gay and lesbian families. Therefore, the authors note that 'no conclusions' can be drawn from the study about the well-being of children raised by gay and lesbian parents.[30]

Research by Gallagher and Baker has found that studies to date demonstrate 'powerful advantages of intact marriages of a mother and a father for children'.[31] However, the researchers also note that there is scholarly disagreement as to the 'size of the marital advantage'.[32] In particular, the researchers note that research on gay and lesbian parenting provides a competing body of evidence on the most advantageous family structure. The researchers cite the work of Stacey,[33] the American Psychological Association[34] and the American Academy of Pediatrics (AAP)[35] in this regard. Studies by these authors have found that children raised by lesbian and gay parents have positive outcomes and are not disadvantaged by their family structure. In response, Gallagher and Baker argue that there are methodological flaws in the research on same-sex parenting, which diminish its validity. Limitations include the lack of a nationally representative sample, limited outcome measures, reliance on maternal reports and the lack of long-term studies.[36] In addition, many studies on same-sex parenting at the time compared single lesbian mothers to single heterosexual mothers.[37] According to Gallagher and

[29] James Peterson and Nicholas Zill, 'Marital disruption, parent-child relationships, and behavior problems in children' (1986) 48 *Journal of Marriage and the Family* 295–307; Paul Amato, 'The consequences of divorce for adults and children' (2000) 62 *Journal of Marriage and the Family* 1269–1287.

[30] Anderson Moore et al., n. 27 above, 1.

[31] Gallagher and Baker, above n. 26, 171.

[32] Gallagher and Baker, above n. 26, 174.

[33] Judith Stacey, 'What Is Needed to Defend the Bipartisan Defense of Marriage Act of 1996?' Hearing Before the Subcomm. on the Constitution, Civil Rights and Property Rights of the Senate Comm. on the Judiciary, 108th Cong., 4 September 2003.

[34] American Psychological Association, *Lesbian and Gay Parenting* (Washington, DC: American Psychological Association, 1995).

[35] American Academy of Pediatrics, 'Coparent or second-parent adoption by same-sex parents' (2002) 109 *Pediatrics* 339–340.

[36] Gallagher and Baker, above n. 26, 3.

[37] Gallagher and Baker, above n. 26, 3.

Baker, this meant that the studies were not designed to shed light on family structure and hence

> cannot credibly be used to contradict the current weight of social science: family structure matters, and the family structure that is most protective a [*sic*] child well-being is the intact, married biological family.[38]

Assessing Gallagher and Baker's study against the criteria established by the AFCC, it is clearly a comprehensive and pragmatic review of existing literature. However, one practical difficulty with Gallagher and Baker's conclusion is that, if it is to be accepted that the studies relating to gay and lesbian families are 'not designed to shed light on family structure' or if they are not sufficiently longitudinal to provide conclusive findings, then, arguably, the inference should be that no conclusions can be drawn as to the *most* beneficial family structure. In the absence of conclusive evidence as to the impact of same-sex parenting, the claim that being raised by married opposite-sex parents is 'best' for children seems rather premature.

Moreover, in line with the AFCC guidelines, conflicting findings must also be assessed to understand whether there is consensus or disagreement in relation to the research literature on a particular topic. It is necessary, therefore, to explore the emerging contemporary literature in this area to understand the outcomes for children raised by same-sex parents and to assess the 'optimality' argument. A review of contemporary literature in this field demonstrates that disagreement among social scientists prevails.

In 2010, Biblarz and Stacey examined the results of eighty-one different studies on family formation only to conclude that '[c]ontrary to popular belief, studies have not shown that "compared to all other family forms, families headed by married, biological parents are best for children"'.[39] Biblarz and Stacey are critical of much of the existing research that emphasises the benefits of being raised by married opposite-sex parents. They note that many of those studies compared children who were raised by their married birth parents with those raised in single-parent families. In most of the studies, there was no comparison between marital children and those with two female or two male parents. As the authors note, '[b]ecause access to legal same-sex marriage is so new and rare, we do not yet have research that compares the children of

[38] Gallagher and Baker, above n. 26, 3.

[39] Timothy Biblarz and Judith Stacey, 'How does the gender of parents matter?' (2010) 72 *Journal of Marriage and Family* 3, p. 16.

married same-sex and different-sex couples'.[40] At the same time, the authors emphasise that there is a general consensus among researchers that children raised by unmarried lesbian parents develop at least as well as their counterparts with married heterosexual parents.[41] The AAP also highlights this consensus. Indeed, the AAP further notes that 'the fact that most data suggest that children grow up successfully in families created by gay and lesbian parents despite the almost-universal family disruption and social stigma they have experienced attests to the resilience of these families'.[42]

It is undeniable from the research that children raised by married, opposite-sex parents do very well, sometimes better than children raised in single-parent households (primarily explained by differences in socio-economic status).[43] As the AAP notes:

> Marriage supports permanence and security (the basic ingredients for the healthy development of children). Marriage is also the official societal mechanism for conferring rights, benefits, and protections that support couples as spouses and parents and their children financially and legally.[44]

Yet, marriage does not guarantee positive outcomes for children. Many children raised by married parents experience difficulties, just as many children raised by unmarried parents do.[45] From its review, the AAP concludes that stable, well-functioning families that consist of two parents (of any gender) provide the best environment in which children may be raised.[46] Hence, the AAP suggests that, although marriage may benefit children, the most important factor that influences their development is the presence of two stable and caring adults.

Contrary to the approach adopted by the opponents of same-sex parenting, the AAP has concluded that since marriage is beneficial to

40 Above 4.

41 For example: American Academy of Pediatrics, above n. 35; Stacey and Biblarz, above; Fiona Tasker, 'Lesbian mothers, gay fathers, and their children: A review' (2005) 26 *Developmental and Behavioral Pediatrics* 224 in Biblarz and Stacey above, p. 4.

42 Ellen Perrin, Benjamin Siegel and the Committee on Psychosocial Aspects of Child and Family Health, 'Promoting the well-being of children whose parents are gay or lesbian' (2013) 131 *Pediatrics* 1374–1383, p. 1380.

43 Michael Rosenfeld, 'Nontraditional families and childhood progress through school' (2010) 47 *Demography* 755.

44 Perrin, Siegel and the Committee on Psychosocial Aspects of Child and Family Health, above n. 42, 1381.

45 American Academy of Pediatrics, 'Task force on the family: Family pediatrics' (2003) 111 *Pediatrics* 1541, p. 1375.

46 Above 1375.

children, their best interests may demand that marriage is made available to their gay and lesbian parents. The security of marriage is known to be beneficial, and so 'it is in the best interests of children that they be able to partake in the security of permanent nurturing and care that comes with the civil marriage of their parents, without regard to their parents' gender or sexual orientation'.[47] In this light, it may be a somewhat self-defeating argument for those who are opposed to same-sex parenting and marriage equality, to hold marriage out as the ideal environment in which to raise children. In doing so, they indirectly advocate for certain children to be excluded from this 'ideal' unit, which arguably serves to hinder the best interests of those children.

In any case, holding marriage out as the ideal ignores the fact that many children are already being raised by unmarried same-sex couples. Denying rights to these families does not prevent same-sex couples from becoming parents. It simply deprives the child of the security of having a legal relationship with both of their parents. Thus, it is argued that claims as to the optimality of marriage do not justify limiting the legal recognition of same-sex parenting. The review of the literature above demonstrates that children raised by unmarried same-sex couples have broadly the same outcomes as those raised by married opposite-sex parents. Much of this research was undertaken before same-sex marriage was widely recognised, which is a testament to the resilience of gay and lesbian families. Although nascent, research on gay and lesbian families demonstrates that children raised in such families have positive outcomes, which provides further weight to arguments in favour of legally recognising such arrangements. This research is considered in the next section to provide a fuller picture of the literature in this area in line with the guidance provided by the AFCC. Research findings as well as research design and its limitations are considered to allow for an accurate and holistic analysis of the literature.

2.4 Outcomes for Children Raised by Gay and Lesbian Parents

There is a growing body of sociological and psychological literature on same-sex parenting. This can act as a guide to the application of the best interests principle by providing broader understanding of what is best for children in the context of parenting. Much of the existing literature shows that children raised by gay and lesbian parents have positive

[47] Above 1381.

psychological and social outcomes. However, a major limitation of this research relates to research design and methodology, which can reduce the authority and validity of research findings. It is therefore necessary to first address the limitations and parameters of the literature in order to assess the weight of research findings.

As outlined above, Gallagher and Baker identify four typical limitations in the research on gay and lesbian families: the lack of a nationally representative sample, limited outcome measures, reliance on maternal reports and the lack of any long-term studies.[48] Gallagher and Baker contend that these methodological issues mean that the research on gay and lesbian families lacks authority and cannot be used to challenge the research showing benefits to children of being raised by their married, biological parents.[49]

The Witherspoon Institute also highlights limitations in the research on gay and lesbian families, asserting that '[t]he current research on children reared by [same-sex couples] is inconclusive and underdeveloped – we do not yet have any large, long-term, longitudinal studies that can tell us much about how children are affected by being raised in a same-sex household'.[50] Stewart presents the same argument, namely that, in the absence of any long-term studies, '[t]he assertion that same-sex couples have equal child-rearing success lacks support from studies meeting usual standards for scientific validity'.[51]

The first empirical studies on lesbian mother families began in the 1970s[52] as those families became more visible in society and research was deemed necessary to understand questions raised in child custody disputes between lesbian mothers and their former male partners.[53] Research on gay fathers began later as more and more gay men were openly parenting children together. Numerous studies have now been conducted on gay and lesbian parenting, but it must be acknowledged that the sample sizes are often small, reflecting the fact that gay and lesbian parents are a minority when compared to opposite-sex parents. As large sample sizes simply do not exist, we must consider whether

48 Gallagher and Baker, above n. 26, 3.
49 Gallagher and Baker, above n. 26, 3.
50 Witherspoon Institute, *Marriage and the Public Good: Ten Principles* (Princeton: Witherspoon Institute, 2008), p. 18.
51 Stewart, above n. 26, 353.
52 Golombok, above n. 1, 37.
53 Golombok, above n. 1, 37.

social science literature can validly assess and compare the outcomes for children raised in these families.

Golombok opines that meta-analysis can be used to compensate for the small sample sizes involved in research on gay and lesbian families.[54] Meta-analysis is described as 'a statistical procedure that combines the findings of comparable investigations on a specific topic to increase statistical power and thus enable the identification of significant effects, should they exist'.[55] In a meta-analysis conducted by Crowl, Ahn and Baker,[56] no differences were found between children raised in gay and lesbian families and those raised in heterosexual families, although the quality of the parents' relationships with their children was found to be *better* in the gay and lesbian families. Golombok concludes that '[f]rom these meta-analyses, it appears that the failure to find greater psychological problems among the children of lesbian mothers in individual studies has not simply resulted from a lack of statistical power'.[57]

Other criticisms of the literature on same-sex parenting include maternal reporting and perceived sample bias. While the studies may validly be criticised for these reasons, there is now over thirty years of research in this field showing positive outcomes for children. The AAP argues that when this research is taken together, it provides 'robust, reliable, and valid assurance about the well-being of children raised by parents of the same gender'.[58] The AAP notes that more than 100 scientific publications conducted over 30 years demonstrate that children's well-being is affected much more by the quality of parenting and the presence of social and economic support for the family than by the gender or the sexual orientation of their parents.[59] The AAP contends that the weight of this evidence counteracts the argument that 'no conclusions' can be drawn from the research on gay and lesbian families.

No study to date has found any evidence that being raised by a same-sex couple is detrimental to children. As the AAP has noted, 'it is likely

[54] Golombok, above n. 1, 64.

[55] Golombok, above n. 1, 64.

[56] Alicia Crowl, Soyeon Ahn and Jean Baker, 'A meta-analysis of developmental outcomes for children of same-sex and heterosexual parents' (2008) 4 *Journal of GLBT Family Studies* 385–407.

[57] Golombok, above n. 1, 65.

[58] Perrin, Siegel and the Committee on Psychosocial Aspects of Child and Family Health, above n. 42, 1377–1378.

[59] Perrin, Siegel and the Committee on Psychosocial Aspects of Child and Family Health, above n. 42, 1378.

that the extensive research efforts that have been carried out would have documented serious and significant damages if they existed'.[60] No such negative results have been recorded. Indeed, it is notable that the findings of the world's largest 'anti-gay marriage study' have recently been discredited and have been shown to be scientifically inaccurate. This 2012 study by Regenerus had found that adults who grew up in a household with a gay or lesbian parent or parents were more likely to have been sexually abused, more likely to have attempted suicide and more likely to have had a sexually transmitted disease when compared to those who were raised by two biological parents.[61] In 2015, this study was replicated and reassessed by Cheng and Powell, who found that methodological defects in the original study had led to inaccurate results and that, in fact, the differences between children who are raised by gay or lesbian and heterosexual parents are minimal.[62]

In 2014, Crouch and others published the results of one of the largest studies to date on the outcomes for children raised by same-sex parents.[63] This parent-reported survey was completed by 315 parents representing 500 children. The study found no outcome differences between children raised by same-sex couples and those raised by opposite-sex couples. In fact, in certain areas, the children of same-sex parents had higher scores on measures of general behaviour, general health and family cohesion than their peers.[64]

Crouch and others' conclusions mirror those of earlier studies. For example, in 2010, Biblarz and Stacey concluded that children raised by same-sex parents have essentially the same outcomes in terms of development as children who are raised by opposite-sex parents.[65] In the course of their investigation, Biblarz and Stacey found more similarities than differences among children with lesbian and heterosexual parents, and the rare differences that were identified were deemed to favour the

60 Perrin, Siegel and the Committee on Psychosocial Aspects of Child and Family Health, above n. 42, 1380.

61 Mark Regenerus, 'How different are the adult children of parents who have same-sex relationships? Findings from the new family structures study' (2012) 41 *Social Science Research* 752.

62 Simon Cheng and Brian Powell, 'Measurement, methods, and divergent patterns: Reassessing the effects of same-sex parents' (2015) 52 *Social Science Research* 615.

63 Simon Crouch, Elizabeth Waters, Ruth McNair, Jennifer Power and Elise Davis, 'Parent reported measures of child health and wellbeing in same-sex parent families: a cross-sectional study' (2014) 14 *BMC Public Health* 635.

64 Above 644.

65 Biblarz and Stacey, above n. 39.

children raised by lesbian mothers.[66] For example, one study found that children with two mothers viewed their parents as more available and dependable[67] and another found that the lesbian mothers were more likely to discuss emotional issues with their children.[68] The latter study also reported that this family structure constrained aggressive behaviour in sons as well as daughters.[69] These findings led the researchers to conclude that '[i]f future research replicates these findings, it will pose substantial challenges to the view that children need both a female and male primary parent for optimal development'.[70]

The only negative result identified by Biblarz and Stacey related to a finding by MacCallum and Golombok from 2004,[71] which showed that six-year-old children raised in mother-only families (whether lesbian or heterosexual) described themselves as less competent physically and cognitively than their peers. However, when the children were interviewed again six years later, this difference did not appear. Furthermore, as Biblarz and Stacey note, '[b]ecause this study did not control for the number of parents in mother-only families, it could not help us determine whether the absence of a male parent or just of a second parent contributed to the lower self-esteem the younger children expressed'.[72]

MacCallum and Golombok's 2004 study also found that twelve-year-old boys raised in mother-only families (lesbian or heterosexual) did not differ from sons raised by a mother and father in terms of their masculinity but scored over a standard deviation higher on femininity scales.[73] According to Biblarz and Stacey, these results imply that 'growing up without a father did not impede masculine development but enabled boys to achieve greater gender flexibility'.[74] Gender flexibility is regarded as a positive trait as '[r]esearch implies that adults with androgynous

[66] Biblarz and Stacey, above n. 39, 13.

[67] Fiona MacCallum and Susan Golombok, 'Children raised in fatherless families from infancy: A follow-up of children of lesbian and single heterosexual mothers at early adolescence' (2004) 45 *Journal of Psychology and Psychiatry* 1407.

[68] Katrien Vanfraussen, Ingrid Ponjaert-Kristoffersen and Anne Brewaeys, 'Family functioning in lesbian families created by donor insemination' (2003) 73 *American Journal of Orthopsychiatry* 78.

[69] Above.

[70] Biblarz and Stacey, above n. 39, 13.

[71] MacCallum and Golombok, above n. 67.

[72] Biblarz and Stacey, above n. 39, 13.

[73] MacCallum and Golombok, above n. 67.

[74] Biblarz and Stacey, above n. 39, 14.

gender traits may enjoy social psychological advantages over more gender traditional peers'.[75] There were no reported comparable effects of fatherlessness on daughters: girls who were raised in mother-only families did not differ in terms of femininity or masculinity when compared to girls raised by a mother and a father.[76]

In light of the above findings, it would seem that the gender of parents has very little impact on child development. The findings cast doubt on the contention that children need both a mother and a father in order to thrive. Biblarz and Stacey note that the strengths typically associated with married mother–father families 'appear to the same extent in families with 2 mothers and potentially in those with 2 fathers'.[77] The researchers go so far as to conclude that it is arguable, based on the published findings, that two women actually parent better than a man and a woman. As they note, '[l]esbian co-parents seem to outperform married heterosexual parents on several measures, even while being denied the substantial privileges of marriage'.[78]

Some research suggests that same-sex relationships are less durable and are subject to a higher rate of relationship breakdown than opposite-sex unions.[79] Lau concludes that this increased rate of relationship breakdown is attributable to the fact that '[t]he lack of legal same-sex marriage in most jurisdictions means that same sex couples rarely face legal hurdles when they seek to dissolve their relationship'.[80] There are 'fewer investments to bind them together' and 'fewer barriers to exiting the union'.[81] Biblarz and Stacey opine that the durability of same-sex relationships, in particular lesbian relationships, may also be influenced by 'unequal biological and legal bases to parental status' which they believe 'can create distinctive fissures among lesbian comothers'.[82] The effects of unequal biological status on lesbian co-mothers were studied by Pelka in 2009.[83] Although that study did not examine the significance of

[75] Biblarz and Stacey, above n. 39, 14.

[76] MacCallum and Golombok, above n. 67.

[77] Biblarz and Stacey, above n. 39, 3.

[78] Biblarz and Stacey, above n. 39, 17.

[79] MacCallum and Golombok, above n. 67; Charles Lau, 'The stability of same-sex cohabitation, different-sex cohabitation, and marriage' (2012) 74 *Journal of Marriage and Family* 973.

[80] Lau, above 974.

[81] Lau, above 975.

[82] Biblarz and Stacey, above n. 39, 12.

[83] Suzanne Pelka, 'Sharing motherhood: Maternal jealousy among lesbian co-mothers' (2009) 56 *Journal of Homosexuality* 195.

this unequal status as regards relationship breakdown, it did note that 'feelings of exclusion coupled with the expectation of occupying equally nurturing "maternal" roles may cause emotional distress or conflict among co-mothers'.[84]

Where same-sex couples are able to have their relationships legally recognised, for example through civil partnership or marriage, the rate of relationship breakdown decreases. In a study conducted in relation to civil partnerships in England and Wales, for example, it was found that in the years 2005 to 2010, a higher number of opposite-sex marriages broke down than same-sex civil partnerships formed in the same year.[85] Furthermore, a study conducted by Rosenfeld in 2014 found that '[o]nce marriage and marriage-like unions are controlled for, same-sex couples and heterosexual couples have statistically indistinguishable rates of breakup'.[86] As such, in countries where same-sex couples have access to marriage or marriage-like institutions, the available research suggests that the rate of relationship breakdown among such couples decreases.

Most of the studies referenced thus far have focused on lesbian mothers. Less is known about gay male parents than lesbian parents due to the fact that there are simply fewer gay men parenting together than there are lesbian couples. Studies have, however, indicated that when two men co-parent, they do so in ways that seem closer, but not identical, to that of two lesbian women rather than to a heterosexual woman and man.[87] For example, a 2014 study of gay father families conducted by Golombok and others found that there was positive family functioning within these units with respect to quality of parenting and children's psychological well-being.[88] This research compared the functioning of 41 two-parent gay father families, 40 two-parent lesbian

[84] Above 198–199.

[85] Helen Ross, Karen Gask and Ann Berrington, 'Civil partnership five years on' (2011) 145 *Population Trends* 172 at p. 186.

[86] Michael Rosenfeld, 'Couple longevity in the era of same-sex marriage in the United States' (2014) 76 *Journal of Marriage and Family* 905.

[87] Charles Brinamen, 'On becoming fathers: Issues facing gay men choosing to parent' (2000) 61 *Dissertation Abstracts International* 2794; Gerald Mallon, *Gay men choosing parenthood* (Columbia: Columbia University Press, 2004); Judith Stacey, 'Gay male parenthood and the decline of paternity as we knew it' (2006) 9 *Sexualities* 27 in Biblarz and Stacey, above n. 39, 12.

[88] Susan Golombok, Laura Mellish, Sarah Jennings, Polly Casey, Fiona Tasker and Michael Lamb, 'Adoptive gay father families: Parent–child relationships and children's psychological adjustment' (2014) 85 *Child Development* 456.

mother families, and 49 two-parent heterosexual parent families with an adopted child aged 3 to 9 years.[89] The results found that gay fathers showed lower levels of both depression and parenting stress in comparison to heterosexual mothers and fathers.[90] Gay fathers were found to display more warmth towards their children, and they interacted with their children more than heterosexual parents.[91] Gay fathers also displayed greater levels of parent responsiveness and lower levels of disciplinary aggression.[92] Thus, the researchers note that '[w]here differences were identified between the gay father adoptive families and the heterosexual parent adoptive families, these reflected more positive functioning in the gay father families'.[93]

From the research, Golombok and others conclude that '[t]he findings of this study suggest that men can be just as competent at parenting as women, and that the absence of a female parent does not necessarily have adverse consequences for child adjustment'.[94] In this light, it is difficult to argue that same-sex couples should be denied parenting rights on the basis that it is 'better' for children to be raised by married opposite-sex parents. Neither the gender nor the marital status of parents seems to negatively affect children – it is the quality of parenting that is most important.

Despite the nascent nature of the research on gay and lesbian families, the review of the literature above demonstrates that there is no evidence to suggest that being raised by a gay or lesbian parent or parents is detrimental to children. By considering the full range of contemporary research in this area, it has been shown that there is broad consensus among researchers that children raised by same-sex couples develop just as well as those raised by opposite-sex parents. Although there are some limitations in the research on gay and lesbian families, there is no suggestion in any of the available research that same-sex parenting is harmful to children. The contention that same-sex couples are unsuitable to act as parents is therefore based on an unproven assumption that children *might* be harmed by being raised by same-sex parents. It is argued that a fear of abstract harm, that is not supported by any existing research, should not justify denying rights to gay and lesbian families.

89 Above 458.
90 Above 462.
91 Above.
92 Above.
93 Above 463.
94 Above 465.

2.5 Conclusion

The research discussed in this chapter challenges the traditional assumption that opposite-sex, married parents provide the optimum environment in which to raise children. It is clear from the research that same-sex couples can and do act as suitable parents. In fact, some of the research suggests that gay and lesbian parents may even surpass heterosexual couples in their parenting abilities. In this light, it is argued that the best interests of the child cannot legitimately be used to argue against the legal recognition of same-sex parenting. Plainly, the best interests of children can be secured by gay and lesbian parents, and it is notable that no study has found any adverse impact on the welfare of children who are raised by such parents. Therefore, any fears that may arise as to the welfare of children are essentially based on an unproven assumption. As Tobin and McNair conclude, examination of the available research reveals that arguments made to oppose the legal recognition of same-sex parenting arrangements 'based on the purported best interests of a child represent a misappropriation of this principle'.[95]

Perhaps the strongest argument against denying rights to gay and lesbian parents on the basis of an unconfirmed theory as to the best interests of children is the fact that children are currently being raised by same-sex couples. They are a generational reality with existing needs that must be met by lawmakers. It is submitted that an unproven risk of harm cannot justify denying rights to these children, and so legal recognition and protections must be put in place to ensure that children can obtain the security of having a legal relationship with both of their parents, whatever the gender or sexual orientation of those parents may be. Fear of abstract harm does not justify ignoring actual needs.

This chapter provides an evidence base to guide the application of the best interests principle. This evidence indicates that the most important determinant of favourable outcomes for children is the quality of parenting. Therefore, it is suggested that 'best interests' in the context of parenting means love, support and quality of interactions. The evidence shows that the best interests principle should not be used to argue against the recognition of same-sex parenting. The principle, guided by the existing sociological and psychological research, indicates that children's best interests can be met by gay and lesbian parents. This reality must be acknowledged and the best interests principle must be guided by this

[95] Tobin and McNair, above n. 7, 126.

existing research rather than by unproven assumptions and political agendas.

Having assessed the arguments pertaining to the best interests of children who are raised by gay and lesbian parents, these conclusions can now be applied to the various pathways to parentage available to same-sex couples, namely parental responsibility, adoption, donor conception and surrogacy. The objective of the following chapters is to identify a means of regulating each of these pathways in a manner that adheres to the best interests principle. In each of the chapters, reference is made to the relevant psychological and sociological research discussed in this chapter as well as additional research specific to the circumstances under consideration. In order to assess the implications of the best interests principle in these specific scenarios, reference will also be made to the relevant provisions of the UNCRC so as to guide the application of the principle in line with the framework for best interests that was identified in Chapter 1.

3

Parental Responsibility

3.1 Introduction

Parental responsibility is a concept that is separate to legal parentage or parenthood. Not all legal parents enjoy parental responsibility, and, in most jurisdictions, persons who are not legal parents have the possibility of acquiring it. The precise meaning of 'parental responsibility' differs from jurisdiction to jurisdiction, but it is generally understood as comprising the responsibilities and rights associated with raising a child. Different terminology is also adopted to describe this adult–child relationship. In England and Wales, the term 'parental responsibility' is used, in Ireland the concept is referred to as 'guardianship', while in South Africa, the phrase 'parental responsibilities and rights' is adopted. Each of these concepts is discussed in detail in this chapter. When discussing the concept generally, the term 'parental responsibility' is used in the chapter as this phrase is seen to best describe a child-centred understanding of the adult's role.[1]

Parental responsibility is an important mechanism through which to confer responsibilities and rights upon social parents. Social parents are persons who are not genetically or legally connected to the child but who undertake a parenting role. Some gay and lesbian parents have children from previous heterosexual relationships whom they now care for with a new partner.[2] In this situation, parental responsibility provides a mechanism whereby the new partner or spouse of the parent can acquire responsibilities and rights towards the child in a manner that does not affect the rights of the birth parents. Hence, the extension of

[1] Terminology is discussed further at 3.2.1.

[2] Jane Pillinger and Paula Fagan, *LGBT Parents in Ireland. Report from a study into the experiences of Lesbian, Gay, Bisexual and Transgender People in Ireland who are parents or who are planning parenthood* (Dublin: LGBT Diversity, 2013), p. 34; Carlos Ball, *Same-Sex Marriage and Children* (Oxford: Oxford University Press, 2014), p. 83.

parental responsibility to the social parent can be regarded as an important aspect of the best interests principle as it gives the social parent the legal tools that are necessary to properly care for the child. Article 7 of the United Nations Convention on the Rights of the Child (UNCRC) provides that the child has 'the right to know *and be cared for* by his or her parents'. The term 'parents' is not defined in the Convention and so can be taken to mean a genetic parent, a legal parent, a step-parent or anyone else acting in *loco parentis*.[3] Although it is acknowledged that the UNCRC only requires that the child's right to be cared for by their parents is protected 'as far as possible', the existence of this right provides weight to the argument that a social parent should be able to exercise parental responsibility so that they can fulfil the caring parental role.[4]

This chapter examines the operation of parental responsibility in England and Wales, Ireland and South Africa and assesses the suitability of the domestic laws from the perspective of the best interests of the child. The chapter draws on the conclusions of Chapters 1 and 2 to assess the demands of the principle in this context. The suitability of extending parental responsibility to social parents is considered, and it is argued that such a mechanism is vital to secure the best interests of the child. As part of this analysis, common arguments for and against the extension of parental responsibility are assessed. The chapter also considers the ways in which parental responsibility could be extended to social parents, and it is argued that a system that provides oversight of the extension better promotes the best interests of the child than a system whereby parental responsibility can be extended by way of a private agreement.

3.2 What Is Parental Responsibility?

3.2.1 Language and Terminology

Language and terminology are important in all legal contexts. Detailed rules on statutory and constitutional interpretation exist to enable

[3] John Tobin and Ruth McNair, 'Public international law and the regulation of private spaces: Does the convention on the rights of the child impose an obligation on states to allow gay and lesbian couples to adopt?' (2009) 23 *International Journal of Law, Policy and the Family* 110, p. 112.

[4] It should be recalled that the Committee on the Rights of the Child has indicated that the best interests principle is to be guided by the other rights contained in the UNCRC. Committee on the Rights of the Child, *General comment No. 14 (2013) on the right of the child to have his or her best interests taken as a primary consideration (art. 3, para. 1)* CRC/C/GC/14, para. 32.

lawyers and laypeople to understand legal provisions. Certain words, grammar and syntax have a profound effect on the meaning of laws and must, therefore, be chosen with care. Legal terminology can also have an effect on public attitudes as the language chosen by the legislature reflects the values within society and reinforces normative concepts.

As noted above, countries adopt different terminology to refer to the responsibilities that certain adults owe to children. It is often argued that use of the term 'parental responsibility' is preferable to that of 'guardianship' as a label for the adults' role.[5] This is because the former term is seen to emphasise the *responsibilities* of the adult(s) towards the child, whereas the latter is more concerned with the *rights* of the adult over the child.[6] As far back as 1984, the Committee of Ministers of the Council of Europe adopted a recommendation on parental responsibilities,[7] having agreed that that term

> described better the modern concept according to which parents are . . . given the task of educating, legally representing, maintaining etc their children. In order to do so they exercise powers to carry out duties in the interests of the child and not because of an authority which is conferred on them in their own interests.[8]

In 1988, the English Law Commission concluded that the language of 'parental responsibility' should be introduced in that jurisdiction in order to 'reflect the everyday reality of being a parent and emphasise the responsibilities of all who are in that position'.[9] More recently, in 2010, the Irish Law Reform Commission recommended that the existing Irish term of 'guardianship' should be replaced with 'parental responsibility' so as to better convey that parents and guardians have both rights and responsibilities towards their children. The term 'parental responsibility' is advantageous as it realigns the adult–child relationship so that the focus is on responsibilities, rather than parental power and control. As Judge Paul von Dadelszen, retired judge of the New Zealand District Court, has noted, 'if it became possible to speak in terms of parental

[5] See, for example, Law Reform Commission, *Consultation Paper on Legal Aspects of Family Relationships, LRC CP55-2009* (Dublin: Law Reform Commission, 2009), p. 28; Law Commission, *Family Law, Review of Child Law, Guardianship and Custody*, Law Com No. 172 of 1988 (London: Law Commission, 1988), p. 6.

[6] Law Reform Commission, above, 28; Andrew Bainham, *Children: The Modern Law*, 3 ed. (London: Family Law, 2005), p. 61.

[7] Recommendation No R(84)4.

[8] Nigel Lowe, 'The meaning and allocation of parental responsibility – a common lawyer's perspective' (1997) *11 International Journal of Law, Policy and the Family* 192, p. 193.

[9] Law Commission, above n. 5, 6.

responsibility . . . then perhaps parents might move away from thinking, even unconsciously, in such terms as owning, lending and borrowing'.[10]

Thus, the choice of terminology in child law can have an important symbolic or educational value and can influence societal attitudes.[11] Whereas the term 'guardianship' has proprietorial connotations of ownership and control, the phrase 'parental responsibility' seems to better reflect a modern version of the adult–child relationship that emphasises that adults owe responsibilities as well as duties to their children. As such, incorporating the latter term on a legislative footing could have a significant effect on reminding adults with parental responsibility (and wider society) of what that role entails.

In the context of gay and lesbian families, symbolic and educational values are particularly important. For many years, the law has failed to embrace the ways in which gay and lesbian couples become parents. Preservation of the term 'guardianship', with its adult-centred undertones of control, is arguably itself an example of a failure of the law to accommodate these parenting arrangements. It is very unlikely that the gay or lesbian partner of a parent would seek to acquire responsibilities and rights in respect of the child so as to 'control' or 'own' the child. Nor indeed, does it seem likely that society would be amenable to such an idea. Rather, it is submitted that the social parent should be encouraged to seek such responsibilities and rights so as to give legal effect to the parenting tasks already being undertaken and to fulfil the caring role referred to in Article 7 UNCRC. In this light, use of the term 'parental responsibility' is particularly important because it helps both society and the social parent to understand that it is 'responsibility' rather than 'ownership' that is being conferred.

Notwithstanding the above, it could equally be said that the choice of terminology, while useful in certain respects, is neither the panacea nor the ruin of family law. Arguably, the substance of the relationships is of far greater significance than the conceptual labels used to describe them.[12] Although it is argued that 'parental responsibility' looks better

[10] Paul von Dadelszen, 'Rights or obligations? – Review of the Guardianship Act 1968', Triennial New Zealand Law Society Conference and 4th New Zealand Family Law Conference, Christchurch, 6 October 2001.

[11] Andrew Bainham, 'Changing families and changing concepts – reforming the language of family law' (1998) 10 *Child and Family Law Quarterly* 1.

[12] Bainham, above n. 6, 101.

on paper than 'guardianship' as a label for the adult's role for the reasons set out above, the benefits of employing the former term would be negated if the State was to subsequently define that term in an inappropriate manner. In this regard, it is argued that the *most important* aspect of establishing the adult's role lies not in the title given to those who care for children but in the definition of what that role entails. It is necessary to define the role so that the adults and others are aware of their responsibilities and rights; to 'make explicit what is already implicit in the law'.[13] That said, it is submitted that any definition of parental responsibility should not be exhaustive because it would be impossible to include all of the relevant aspects in a single definition. Moreover, a strict definition would arguably run contrary to the best interests principle, which dictates that the law must remain flexible and adaptable to suit the needs of individual children. Instead, the argument here is that the definition of parental responsibility must provide meaningful guidance to the adults and others on what the role entails.[14]

The following sections examine the definitions of the concepts of parental responsibility, guardianship and parental responsibilities and rights that apply in England and Wales, Ireland and South Africa respectively. In each jurisdiction, the definition and practical application of the concepts are evaluated against the best interests principle to consider whether the legal regulation of the adult–child relationship adheres to the demands of the principle by providing appropriate guidance on the meaning of the concepts in question.

3.2.2 Parental Responsibility in England and Wales

In England and Wales, the term 'parental responsibility' is applied as a label for the responsibilities and rights that an adult may have in respect of a child.[15] Section 3(1) of the Children Act 1989 explains that 'parental

[13] Scottish Law Commission, *Parental Responsibilities and Rights, Guardianship and the Administration of Children's Property*, Discussion Paper No. 88 of 1990 (Edinburgh: Scottish Law Commission, 1990), p. 5.

[14] Lowe, above n. 8, 196.

[15] The term 'guardianship' is also used in England and Wales in the context of 'special guardianship'. This procedure allows for one or more persons to be appointed as a guardian of the child in circumstances where the child cannot be looked after by the birth parents but who is in need of a legally secure family placement. The special guardian(s) will exercise parental responsibility for the child to the exclusion of any other person (including the parent) with parental responsibility. See: Children Act 1989, ss 14A–14G, as inserted by Adoption and Children Act 2002, s 115.

responsibility' means 'all the rights, duties, powers, responsibilities and authority which by law a parent of a child has in relation to the child and his property'.[16] This is an expansive definition, yet it says very little about the content of the adult–child relationship. Instead, it relies on an implicit understanding of the legal rights and authority of parents without attempting to illuminate these concepts or minimise the potential for misconceptions. Moreover, the definition cannot be said to seriously emphasise the 'responsibilities' of being a parent, given that these are placed fourth on the list of elements. As Lowe has noted, the definition 'immediately throws one back to the rights and duties concept which "responsibility" was supposed to replace'.[17]

The English courts have provided an element of clarity in relation to the meaning of parental responsibility. In *Re H (Parental Responsibility)*, Butler Sloss LJ noted that parental responsibility gives a person 'the right to be consulted on schooling, serious medical problems, and other important occurrences in a child's life'.[18] The judge did not, however, clarify what constitutes an 'important' occurrence in the child's life.

Fortin opines that the English definition of parental responsibility reinforces the 'privatization of family life' and reflects 'an assumption that responsible parents will automatically protect their children's interests without legislative encouragement'.[19] While most parents do act in their children's best interests, Fortin believes that the legislative approach 'suggests a misplaced complacency over the existing state of family values'.[20] As discussed above, terminology and definitions are important. If the law was to provide a more detailed list of the incidents of parental responsibility, this would have a significant modelling effect on parental behaviour by emphasising the responsibilities owed to children. It is not suggested that the legislative definition should attempt to define every element of parental responsibility, but some guidance would be helpful. As such, it is unfortunate that the English legislation does not provide greater detail on the meaning of parental responsibility.

16 Children Act 1989, s 3(1).

17 Lowe, above n. 8, p. 195.

18 *Re H (Parental Responsibility)* [1998] 1 FLR 855, p. 859.

19 Jane Fortin, *Children's Rights and the Developing Law*, 3 ed. (Cambridge: Cambridge University Press, 2009), p. 324.

20 Above.

3.2.3 *Guardianship in Ireland*

In Ireland, there is no statutory definition of 'guardianship' per se. However, section 10(2)(a) of the Guardianship of Infants Act 1964 provides a definition of the guardian's role as follows:

> [A]s guardian of the person, [the guardian] shall, as against every person not being, jointly with him, a guardian of the person, be entitled to the custody of the infant and shall be entitled to take proceedings for the restoration of his custody of the infant against any person who wrongfully takes away or detains the infant and for the recovery, for the benefit of the infant, of damages for any injury to or trespass against the person of the infant.

This conception of guardianship is very much focused on the rights of the adult over the child. It fails to acknowledge that parents and other adults not only have rights in respect of their children but also have responsibilities to protect them.

The definition above is supplemented by the Children and Family Relationships Act 2015, which provides a more explicit, but non-exhaustive, list of the 'rights and responsibilities of a guardian' as follows:

(a) to decide on the child's place of residence;
(b) to make decisions regarding the child's religious, spiritual, cultural and linguistic upbringing;
(c) to decide with whom the child is to live;
(d) to consent to medical, dental and other health related treatment for the child, in respect of which a guardian's consent is required;
(e) to exercise the rights and responsibilities of a guardian as are set out in other enactments;[21]
(f) to place the child for adoption, and consent to the adoption of the child, under the Adoption Act 2010.[22]

It is encouraging that the Irish legislation refers to both the 'rights and responsibilities' of the guardian, but the list provided emphasises parental control in the different areas. The guardian is given the power 'to decide', 'to make decisions', 'to consent' and so on. There is no mention

[21] Specifically: Firearms Act 1925, s 2A(2); Protection of Young Persons (Employment) Act 1996, s 5; International Criminal Court Act 2006, ss 50 and 50A; Criminal Justice (Mutual Assistance) Act 2008, ss 79, 79A and 79B; Passports Act 2008, s 14; and under the Criminal Justice (Forensic Evidence and DNA Database System) Act 2014.

[22] Guardianship of Infants Act 1964, s 6C(11), as inserted by Children and Family Relationships Act 2015, s 49.

of any obligation to care for or to nurture the child or to help the child to make their own decisions.[23] This is notable since Article 5 UNCRC requires States to respect the responsibilities, rights and duties of parents, legal guardians and persons responsible for the child 'to provide, in a manner consistent with the evolving capacities of the child, appropriate direction and guidance in the exercise by the child of the rights recognized in the present Convention'. Thus, the UNCRC requires that States respect the adults' ability to provide direction and guidance to the child to help them make their own decisions. It is notable, therefore, that the Irish definition of guardianship does not refer to any such requirement.

3.2.4 Parental Responsibilities and Rights in South Africa

In South Africa, the term 'parental responsibilities and rights' is used. The focus in that jurisdiction is clearly on the responsibilities element of the concept as evidenced by the use of the phrase 'responsibilities and rights' rather than 'rights and responsibilities'. As Skelton has noted, this formulation 'is designed to stress the importance of responsibilities towards children first, whilst recognising the validity of parental rights'.[24] The concept of parental responsibilities and rights is comprised of four elements, namely the responsibility and the right

(a) to care for the child,
(b) to maintain contact with the child,
(c) to act as a guardian to the child, and
(d) to contribute to the maintenance of the child.[25]

Thus, 'parental responsibilities and rights' is an umbrella concept that encompasses four aspects of parenting. The concept is divisible such that the four elements embraced by the heading may be separated out to give a person 'full' or 'specific' parental responsibilities and rights in relation to the child.[26] The acquisition of 'full' responsibilities and rights means that the person obtains all of the responsibilities and rights set out above, while 'specific' responsibilities and rights entail

[23] Such responsibilities are bestowed upon guardians in New Zealand, for example. See: Care of Children Act 2004, s 16.

[24] Ann Skelton, 'Parental responsibilities and rights' in Trynie Boezaart (ed.), *Child Law in South Africa* (Cape Town: Juta and Co. Ltd., 2009), p. 63.

[25] Children's Act 38 of 2005, s 18(2).

[26] Children's Act 38 of 2005, s 18(1).

just one or some of these elements. As such, although a person may be awarded care of a child, this does not necessarily mean that they will also acquire guardianship. Such acquisition will be dependent on the specific reliefs sought by the person and on the court's determination of the demands of the best interests of the child at the centre of the application.[27]

'Guardianship' under the Children's Act 2005 is primarily concerned with administrative and contractual matters.[28] Each guardian is also entitled to give or refuse any consent required by law in respect of the child, for example in relation to the removal of the child from the jurisdiction or in respect of the adoption of the child.[29] By contrast, the South African concept of 'care' is, as the title suggests, concerned with the day-to-day caring, nurture and development of the child.[30] 'Care' is broadly defined so as to include

(a) within available means, providing the child with –
  (i) a suitable place to live;
  (ii) living conditions that are conducive to the child's health, well-being and development; and
  (iii) the necessary financial support;
(b) safeguarding and promoting the well-being of the child;
(c) protecting the child from maltreatment, abuse, neglect, degradation, discrimination, exploitation and any other physical, emotional or moral harm or hazards;
(d) respecting, protecting, promoting and securing the fulfilment of, and guarding against any infringement of, the child's rights set out in the Bill of Rights and the principles set out in Chapter 2 of this Act;
(e) guiding, directing and securing the child's education and upbringing, including religious and cultural education and upbringing, in a manner appropriate to the child's age, maturity and stage of development;
(f) guiding, advising and assisting the child in decisions to be taken by the child in a manner appropriate to the child's age, maturity and stage of development;

[27] See for example: *CM* v. *NG* 2012 (4) SA 452 (WCC).
[28] Children's Act 38 of 2005, s 18(3).
[29] Children's Act 38 of 2005, s 18(3)(c).
[30] Children's Act 38 of 2005, s 1.

(g) guiding the behaviour of the child in a humane manner;
(h) maintaining a sound relationship with the child;
(i) accommodating any special needs that the child may have; and
(j) generally, ensuring that the best interests of the child is the paramount concern in all matters affecting the child.[31]

'Care' not only confers upon the holder day-to-day decision-making powers and obligations to protect the child from various harms, it also includes an obligation to promote and protect the child's rights and to maintain a good relationship with the child. Furthermore, in contrast to the Irish legislation, which as discussed above is largely focused on the guardian's rights and powers, the South African legislation is framed more in terms of obligations to guide and assist the child in making their own decisions. The expansive definition of 'care' also stands in stark contrast to the rather concise definition of parental responsibility that is provided in the English Children Act 1989. As such, the South African approach is more in keeping with the best interests principle as it emphasises the responsibility elements of parenting rather than the entitlements of same, and it does so in a comprehensive manner.

3.2.5 Reflections on Terminology and Definitions

In light of the discussion above, it is submitted that the terminology that is used in family law is important, but the most significant aspect is how those terms are defined. In England and Wales and Ireland, the definitions of parental responsibility and guardianship fall short of the requirements of the best interests principle as they do not emphasise the responsibilities which should be central to the holder's role. In Chapter 2, it was concluded that the most important aspect of parenting is the quality of the parental role and the love and support provided by this person. Arguably, therefore, in failing to highlight the caring nature of the guardian's role, the English and Irish definitions fail to meet the requirements of the best interests principle. It is argued that the laws of each jurisdiction should expressly highlight the responsibility aspect of parental responsibility to ensure that it is understood as a child-centred concept and not merely as an extension of parental power.

[31] Children's Act 38 of 2005, s 1.

3.3 The Exercise of Parental Responsibility

Before considering why the exercise of parental responsibility is important, it is necessary to understand who can exercise it. The following subsections describe the laws pertaining to the allocation of parental responsibility in England and Wales, Ireland and South Africa. Having outlined the process for allocation, later sections will critically examine the motivations for various stakeholders seeking parental responsibility and will consider when it is appropriate, or not appropriate, to extend this status to known fathers and social parents.

3.3.1 England and Wales

In England and Wales, where the mother and father of a child are married to each other at the time of the child's birth, each has parental responsibility for the child.[32] An unmarried mother automatically acquires parental responsibility upon the birth of the child,[33] and, since 1 December 2003, an unmarried father acquires parental responsibility once he is registered on the child's birth certificate.[34] Where a second female parent is in a civil partnership with, or married to, the birth mother of the child at the time of the child's conception via assisted human reproduction (AHR), she automatically acquires parental responsibility once the child is born unless it is shown that she did not consent to the procedure at the relevant time.[35] If the second female parent does not obtain parental responsibility in this manner, she can acquire it by

- re-registering the birth to include the second female parent on the birth certificate;[36]
- entering into a parental responsibility agreement with the mother;[37]
- applying to the court for parental responsibility;[38]

[32] Children Act 1989, s 2(1).
[33] Children Act 1989, s 2(2)(a).
[34] Children Act 1989, s 4, amended by Adoption and Children Act 2002, s 111.
[35] Children Act 1989, s 2(1A), as inserted by Human Fertilisation and Embryology Act 2008, Sch 6 para. 26(2).
[36] Children Act 1989, ss 4(1)(a) and 4ZA(1)(a), as inserted by Human Fertilisation and Embryology Act 2008, Sch 6 para. 27.
[37] Children Act 1989, ss 4(1)(b) and 4ZA(1)(b), as inserted by Human Fertilisation and Embryology Act 2008, Sch 6 para. 27.
[38] Children Act 1989, ss 4(1)(c) and 4ZA(1)(c), as inserted by Human Fertilisation and Embryology Act 2008, Sch 6 para. 27.

- marrying or entering into a civil partnership with the mother;[39]
- being named in a child arrangements order.[40]

Thus, even where the female partner is not recognised as a legal parent, she has a number of opportunities to acquire parental responsibility. In each situation, section 2(6) of the Children Act 1989 clarifies that '[a] person who has parental responsibility for a child at any time shall not cease to have that responsibility solely because some other person subsequently acquires parental responsibility for the child'.[41] Furthermore, there is no limit on the number of persons who can exercise parental responsibility in respect of the same child.

The provisions above allow a social parent to acquire parental responsibility in respect of their partner's child. Once parental responsibility is extended to the social parent, they acquire the right to be consulted on important occurrences in a child's life and obtain the legal tools necessary to fully care for the child. The exercise of parental responsibility by any person (including a legal parent) can, however, be restricted by court order. The court may issue 'a prohibited steps order', which is 'an order that no step which could be taken by a parent in meeting his parental responsibility for a child, and which is of a kind specified in the order, shall be taken by any person without the consent of the court'.[42] Alternatively, the court may grant 'a specific issue order', which is 'an order giving directions for the purpose of determining a specific question which has arisen, or which may arise, in connection with any aspect of parental responsibility for a child'.[43]

In addition, specific limitations are imposed on the responsibilities of a person who acquires parental responsibility as a result of a child arrangements order. The person will not have the right

[39] A person who is married to, or is in a civil partnership with, a person who has parental responsibility for the child can obtain parental responsibility for that child by agreement with the parents or by court order. Children Act 1989, s 4A, as inserted by Adoption and Children Act 2002, s 112, and as amended by Civil Partnership Act 2004, s 75.

[40] The child arrangements order may specify that the child is to live with a specific person who is not a parent. In this situation, the named person shall have parental responsibility for the child while the order remains in force. Children Act 1989, s 12(2), as amended by Children and Families Act 2014, Sch 2 para. 21.

[41] Children Act 1989, s 2(6).

[42] Children Act 1989, s 8(1).

[43] Children Act 1989, s 8(1).

- to agree, or refuse to agree, to the making of an adoption order, or an order under section 84 of the Adoption and Children Act 2002, with respect to the child; or
- to appoint a guardian for the child.[44]

It should also be noted that the parental responsibility of certain persons can be terminated by court order. This includes the parental responsibility of a second female parent who has acquired it under section 4ZA of the Children Act 1989 and the parental responsibility of a step-parent who has acquired it under section 4A.[45] This demonstrates that parental responsibility is a temporary status that can, in some cases, be removed by the courts and will always come to an end once the child reaches the age of majority.

3.3.2 *Ireland*

In Ireland, where the parents of a child are married to each other at the time of the child's birth, both parents are automatically made joint guardians of the child.[46] Where the child is born outside of marriage, the mother is deemed to be the sole automatic guardian.[47] A non-marital father can obtain guardianship rights in relation to his child by subsequently marrying the mother, through cohabitation with the mother where certain conditions are met,[48] by agreement with her,[49] or by court order.[50] Once Parts 2 and 3 of the Children and Family Relationships Act 2015 are commenced, where the child is born through donor-assisted human reproduction (DAHR), the birth mother and the spouse or civil partner of the birth mother who has consented to being recognised as the child's second parent under section 5 of the 2015 Act will be recognised as guardians upon the birth of the child.[51] If the parents are unmarried and are not parties to a civil partnership, the woman who gives birth will be

[44] Children Act 1989, s 12(3).
[45] Children Act 1989, ss 4(2A),4ZA(5), 4A(3).
[46] Guardianship of Infants Act 1964, s 6(1).
[47] Guardianship of Infants Act 1964, s 6(4).
[48] Guardianship of Infants Act 1964, s 2(4A), as inserted by Children and Family Relationships Act 2015, s 43.
[49] Guardianship of Infants Act 1964, s 2(4), as inserted by Children Act 1997, s 4.
[50] Guardianship of Infants Act 1964, s 6A(1), as inserted by Status of Children Act 1987, s 12.
[51] Guardianship of Infants Act 1964, s 6B(1) and s 6B(2)(a), inserted by Children and Family Relationships Act 2015, s 49 and amended by Marriage Act 2015, s 16(b).

automatically regarded as a legal guardian of the child and her partner (male or female), who has consented to being recognised as the child's second legal parent under section 5 of the 2015 Act and who has cohabited with the mother for twelve consecutive months (including a period of three months after the birth of the child), will be recognised as a guardian.[52] If the second parent does not meet these cohabitation requirements, they will be able to acquire guardianship by way of statutory declaration[53] or court order,[54] in the same manner as the unmarried father described above.

In Ireland, before 2015, a person who was not a legal parent could only become a guardian in very limited circumstances provided for in sections 7 and 8 of the Guardianship of Infants Act 1964. Under section 7 of the 1964 Act, a guardian can appoint any person to act as a testamentary guardian in the event of their death, while section 8 allows for a court to appoint a person as a guardian where the child has no existing guardian. Thus, before 2015, there was no facility whereby the parent's spouse or partner could be made a *joint* guardian while that parent was alive.

The Children and Family Relationships Act 2015 has now extended the categories of persons who may apply for guardianship, thereby recognising the changing nature of Irish family relationships. The 2015 Act allows for a person who is not the child's parent to apply for guardianship where certain conditions are met:

1. He or she is married to or is in a civil partnership with, or has been for over 3 years a cohabitant of, a parent of the child, and has shared with that parent responsibility for the child's day-to-day care for a period of more than 2 years,[55] or
2. He or she has provided for the child's day-to-day care for a continuous period of more than 12 months, and the child has no parent or guardian who is willing or able to exercise the rights and responsibilities of guardianship in respect of the child.[56]

[52] Guardianship of Infants Act 1964, s 6B(2)(b), inserted by Children and Family Relationships Act 2015, s 49.

[53] Guardianship of Infants Act 1964, s 6B(4), amended by Marriage Act 2015, s 16(b).

[54] Guardianship of Infants Act 1964, s 6A(1), substituted by Children and Family Relationships Act 2015, s 48.

[55] Guardianship of Infants Act 1964, s 6C(2)(a), as inserted by Children and Family Relationships Act 2015, s 49.

[56] Guardianship of Infants Act 1964, s 6C(2)(b), as inserted by Children and Family Relationships Act 2015, s 49.

The first provision allows for a person acting in the capacity of a step-parent to be recognised as a guardian, while the second provision may be used where a person is caring for the child as a formal or informal foster carer. In each case, time limits apply before the application can be made. In applying for the appointment of an additional guardian, the consent of each guardian of the child will be required as will that of the proposed guardian.[57] The court may, however, dispense with the consent of one of the existing guardians where 'it is satisfied that the consent is unreasonably withheld and that it is in the best interests of the child to make such an order'.[58]

Where an additional guardian is appointed by court order, this 'shall not, unless the court otherwise orders, affect the prior appointment ... of any other person as guardian of the child'.[59] Thus, where a social parent is appointed as a guardian, they will act alongside the parent guardians and the appointment will not affect the parents' rights. There is no statutory limit on the number of guardians who can be appointed, but the court will consider the number of existing guardians and the degree to which those persons are involved in the upbringing of the child when deciding whether to appoint another.[60]

An additional guardian who is appointed by court order does not automatically acquire all of the same responsibilities and rights as other guardians. As noted above, the 2015 Act provides a list of the responsibilities and rights of a guardian, as follows:

(a) to decide on the child's place of residence;
(b) to make decisions regarding the child's religious, spiritual, cultural and linguistic upbringing;
(c) to decide with whom the child is to live;
(d) to consent to medical, dental and other health-related treatment for the child, in respect of which a guardian's consent is required;

[57] Guardianship of Infants Act 1964, s 6C(6), as inserted by Children and Family Relationships Act 2015, s 49.
[58] Guardianship of Infants Act 1964, s 6C(7), as inserted by Children and Family Relationships Act 2015, s 49.
[59] Guardianship of Infants Act 1964, s 6C(5), as inserted by Children and Family Relationships Act 2015, s 49.
[60] Guardianship of Infants Act 1964, s 6C(8)(b), as inserted by Children and Family Relationships Act 2015, s 49.

(e) to exercise the responsibilities and rights of a guardian set out in other enactments;[61]
(f) to place the child for adoption, and consent to the adoption of the child, under the Adoption Act 2010.[62]

Where one or both of the parents of the child are still living, the court-appointed non-parent guardian will only exercise such rights and responsibilities 'where the court expressly so orders' and 'to the extent specified in the order and in the case of the rights and responsibilities specified in any of paragraphs (a) to (e) of that subsection, subject to such limitations as are specified in the order'.[63] Therefore, the extent of the court-appointed guardian's rights and obligations will be at the discretion of the court. In deciding whether or not to limit the rights and responsibilities of the non-parent guardian, the court will have regard to the relationship between them and the child and to the best interests of the child.[64]

Although the restrictions on the role of the guardian noted above are similar to those that may be imposed on holders of parental responsibility in England and Wales, it is concerning that the Irish legislation almost creates a presumption in favour of restricting the rights and responsibilities of the court-appointed guardian. The restriction is the default position to apply unless the court *expressly* orders that this guardian can exercise the rights and responsibilities above. It is to be hoped that the best interests of the child will be used by the Irish courts to dictate that the non-parent guardian is given all of the relevant rights and responsibilities necessary to properly care for the child. Such legal tools are required to enable that guardian to fully protect the child. For example, one can easily envisage a situation whereby the child is in the care of the non-parent guardian and an accident occurs, such that medical or dental treatment becomes necessary. If the parent guardians are otherwise engaged or out of the country, the non-parent guardian must have the power to consent

[61] Specifically: Firearms Act 1925, s 2A(2); Protection of Young Persons (Employment) Act 1996, s 5; International Criminal Court Act 2006, ss 50 and 50A; Criminal Justice (Mutual Assistance) Act 2008, ss 79, 79A and 79B; Passports Act 2008, s 14; and under the Criminal Justice (Forensic Evidence and DNA Database System) Act 2014.

[62] Guardianship of Infants Act 1964, s 6C(11), as inserted by Children and Family Relationships Act 2015, s 49.

[63] Guardianship of Infants Act 1964, s 6C(9), as inserted by Children and Family Relationships Act 2015, s 49.

[64] Guardianship of Infants Act 1964, s 6C(10), as inserted by Children and Family Relationships Act 2015, s 49.

to the child's medical or dental treatment. Otherwise, a situation might arise whereby the child would remain untreated (provided that it is not an emergency procedure) until such time as the parents become available. In this context, imposing restrictions on the non-parent guardian's responsibilities and rights could be seen as running contrary to the child's best interests. Indeed, given that the very reason for appointing the non-parent as a guardian in the first instance will be to allow them to fully care for and protect the child on a day-to-day basis, it seems to be counter-productive not to give the non-parent all of the legal tools that are required to fulfil this role.

A court-appointed guardian also lacks the power to appoint a testamentary guardian unless they have custody of the child to the exclusion of any living parent.[65] Similarly, unless the non-parent guardian has sole custody of the child, they will not be able to appoint a temporary guardian to exercise rights and responsibilities on their behalf in the event that they become incapable through serious illness or injury of exercising the rights and responsibilities of guardianship.[66] By contrast, parental guardians may appoint such persons.

Where the appointment of the non-parent guardian is no longer of benefit to the child, that guardian may be removed by court order. The court will consider whether the removal is in the best interests of the child and the appointed guardian must either

(i) consent to their removal,
(ii) be unable or unwilling to exercise the powers, responsibilities and entitlements of guardianship in respect of the child, or
(iii) have failed in their duty towards the child to such extent that the safety or welfare of the child is likely to be prejudicially affected if the guardian is not removed from office.[67]

This provision ensures that only those actually caring for the child and acting in their best interests enjoy the status of guardian.

[65] Guardianship of Infants Act 1964, s 7(2), as inserted by Children and Family Relationships Act 2015, s 50.

[66] Only 'qualifying guardians' as defined in the Guardianship of Infants Act 1964, s 2, as amended by Children and Family Relationships Act 2015 s 43, may appoint temporary guardians: Guardianship of Infants Act 1964, s 6E, as inserted by Children and Family Relationships Act 2015, s 49.

[67] Guardianship of Infants Act 1964, s 8(7)(d), as inserted by Children and Family Relationships Act 2015, s 51.

3.3.3 *South Africa*

In South Africa, the birth mother of the child always has full parental responsibilities and rights, unless she herself is an 'unmarried child'.[68] As discussed in Chapter 5, where a married couple, of the same or opposite sex, have a child together through assisted fertilisation,[69] they are both recognised as legal parents and automatically have full parental responsibilities and rights in respect of the child.[70] If the partners are unmarried in this situation, only the birth mother is regarded as a legal parent and only she acquires parental responsibilities and rights upon the birth of the child.[71]

A person who is not recognised as a legal parent of the child may acquire parental responsibilities and rights through agreement with one of the parents.[72] This agreement will only take effect where it is registered with a family advocate or where it is made an order of court.[73] This registration will only occur where the family advocate or court is satisfied that the agreement is in the best interests of the child.[74] Furthermore, it should be noted that a parent may only confer such parental responsibilities and rights on another person by agreement as they already have in respect of the child.[75] Thus, the extent of the assignment by agreement of responsibilities and rights to a social parent is dependent on the existing responsibilities and rights of the parents. However, responsibilities and rights may also be assigned by court order: under the Children's Act 2005, 'any person having an interest in the care, well-being or development of a child' may apply to court for contact, care[76] or guardianship[77] in respect of a child.

As was discussed earlier in this chapter, the umbrella concept of parental responsibilities and rights is divisible in South African law such that the four elements embraced by the heading may be separated out to give a person 'full' or 'specific' parental responsibilities and rights. By allowing for either full or specific responsibilities and rights to be conferred upon a person, it is arguable that the South African legislature has adopted a more child-centred approach than the other jurisdictions as the

68 Children's Act 38 of 2005, s 19. Where the mother is an 'unmarried child', she will not have guardianship in respect of the child.

69 'Assisted fertilisation' is the phrase used in the Children's Act 38 of 2005.

70 Children's Act 38 of 2005, s 40(1)(a).

71 Children's Act 38 of 2005, s 40(2).

72 Children's Act 38 of 2005, s 22.

73 Children's Act 38 of 2005, s 22(4).

74 Children's Act 38 of 2005, s 22(5).

75 Children's Act 38 of 2005, s 22(2).

76 Children's Act 38 of 2005, s 23.

77 Children's Act 38 of 2005, s 24.

allocation of responsibilities and rights can be tailored to suit the needs of the individual child. There may be circumstances where it is not necessary to confer the full bundle of responsibilities and rights upon a person so as to protect the child. For example, where a social parent is acting in a parental capacity towards the child, it may be prudent to confer the rights and duties of 'care' upon them, but their position as a social parent may not necessarily require that they also manage the child's property interests. The social parent should only be awarded such responsibilities and rights as are required in the specific circumstances of the case. Under this approach, the best interests of the child dictate the extent of the responsibilities and rights which are conferred upon the social parent.

It is acknowledged that earlier comments made in this chapter in respect of the Irish system suggest that a social parent with parental responsibility should acquire all of the same rights and responsibilities as other guardians. However, in the Irish system, the rights and responsibilities of the court-appointed guardian that may be restricted relate to the caring aspects of the guardian's role. It is argued that the non-parent guardian's administrative abilities should rightly be curtailed in certain circumstances, but that guardian should not be deprived of the responsibilities and rights that are necessary to fulfil the caring and protective role. In the context of the South African system, it is suggested that it may not always be necessary to confer the full bundle of responsibilities and rights upon a person so as to protect the child. However, where the person is awarded 'care', they should be able to fully exercise all incidents of that caring role.

The Children's Act 2005 also places certain responsibilities on persons who do not have parental responsibilities and rights but who care for children 'either indefinitely, temporarily or partially'.[78] In this situation, the person must, while the child is in their care,

(a) safeguard the child's health, well-being and development; and
(b) protect the child from maltreatment, abuse, neglect, degradation, discrimination, exploitation and any other physical, emotional or mental harm or hazards.[79]

This person may also exercise any parental responsibilities and rights that are reasonably necessary to comply with the obligations above. This may include providing consent to the child's medical treatment where consent

[78] Children's Act 38 of 2005, s 32(1).
[79] Children's Act 38 of 2005, s 32(1).

cannot reasonably be obtained from a parent or guardian. The responsibilities and rights of this person may, however, be restricted by court order.[80] These provisions ensure that a person caring for a child, but who has not been awarded parental responsibilities and rights, can legally fulfil the caring role and ensure that the child is protected.

The sections above demonstrate that, in each of the comparator jurisdictions, a person who is not a legal parent has the opportunity to acquire parental responsibility. Thus, in the context of gay and lesbian families, the partner of a legal parent may acquire a legal relationship with the child in this way. This recognises the reality of the child's life and the existing caring role undertaken by the social parent. There is sometimes a concern that the child's relationship with their non-resident birth parent may be undermined where parental responsibility is extended to the social parent.[81] It is important, therefore, that any decision as to whether to extend parental responsibility to a social parent must be based on the best interests of the child and must be assessed on a case-by-case basis according to the specific circumstances of the child.

3.4 Extending Parental Responsibility for Status and Security

Parental responsibility confers responsibilities and rights on adults in relation to the upbringing of children. The extension of parental responsibility to social parents who care for children offers legal recognition of that caring role. Importantly, it also gives the social parent legal responsibilities and rights that are necessary to care for and protect the child. Parental responsibility typically includes matters such as consent to medical treatment, application for a passport for the child and decisions concerning the child's religious or educational upbringing. Without parental responsibility, the social parent has no legal connection, and hence no legal powers or duties, towards the child notwithstanding the reality of the social relationship. This leaves the child in a vulnerable position as the person caring for them on a daily basis may lack the legal tools required to do so. The social parent without parental responsibility may also be excluded from other aspects of the child's life, such as attendance at parent–teacher meetings or providing consent for a class trip. While these latter difficulties may appear to be mundane matters, for

80 Children's Act 38 of 2005, s 32(3).
81 Bainham, above n. 6, 236.

the children directly affected by these issues, they represent very relevant concerns. These issues have the potential to frustrate routine family life and to reinforce the stigma experienced by gay and lesbian families, therefore directly impacting on the best interests of children raised within such families.

Parental responsibility is different to the status of legal parentage and many significant legal consequences attach to parentage that do not arise in respect of parental responsibility. For example, in contrast to legal parentage, parental responsibility does not create a line of lineage, and so the child does not acquire any automatic inheritance rights in respect of the social parent.[82] Parental responsibility does not create any legal relationship between the child and the social parent's extended family, nor does it have implications in terms of citizenship. Furthermore, parental responsibility comes to an end once the child reaches the age of majority or earlier by court order. As such, once the child becomes an adult, the social parent will no longer exercise parental responsibility and will not have any lasting legal relationship with the child beyond this point. By contrast, although a legal parent also loses their decision-making capacity vis-à-vis the child when the child reaches the age of majority, they remain a legal parent for life.[83] These points should be borne in mind when considering whether to extend parental responsibility to the social parent or whether some other legal mechanism should be used to create a legal relationship between the social parent and the child.

The extension of parental responsibility is not just a concern for social parents. As noted above, not all legal parents automatically exercise parental responsibility. In many countries, unmarried fathers do not automatically hold this status and may seek to acquire it through the available mechanisms under domestic law. Depending on the applicable domestic law, a sperm donor may also have the opportunity to apply to acquire parental responsibility. For example, pending commencement of Parts 2 and 3 of the Children and Family Relationships Act 2015 in Ireland, a sperm donor is regarded as the child's legal father where the child is conceived by way of DAHR, and the Irish Supreme Court has confirmed that this man has the same opportunity as any other unmarried father to apply for guardianship (parental responsibility) in respect of the child.[84]

[82] The social parent is, of course, at liberty to voluntarily provide for the child in their will.

[83] Legal parentage can be terminated where the child is subject to an adoption order or a parental order.

[84] *JMcD* v. *PL and BM* [2010] 2 IR 199.

3.4.1 *Known Fathers and Parental Responsibility*

The extension of parental responsibility to a sperm donor in cases where the child is intended to be raised by two women gives rise to complex legal and social issues. On the one hand, it could be argued that the child's right to identity and right to be cared for by their parents, as protected by Articles 7 and 8 UNCRC, would be best protected by legally recognising the child's relationship with the genetic father by extending parental responsibility to him. After all, Article 18 UNCRC requires that States Parties recognise that 'parents have *common responsibilities* for the upbringing and development of the child'. On the other hand, the extension of parental responsibility to the genetic father may undermine the status of the child's nuclear family that is comprised of the two female parents. Indeed, status and visibility are common themes in disputes about parental responsibility. For example, in the English case of *Re D (Contact and Parental Responsibility: Lesbian Mothers and Known Father)*,[85] discussed further below, a father applied for parental responsibility and, in order to ease concerns relating to this application, agreed that he would not exercise any rights or responsibilities in relation to the child's medical or educational upbringing. Thus, as Black J noted, the granting of parental responsibility in these circumstances amounted to 'a grant of a status, stripped of practical effect'.[86] The extension of parental responsibility to the father recognised a role for him in the child's life without giving him many practical legal responsibilities and rights, suggesting that status and recognition were more important to the father in this instance than a functional parenting role.

The child's best interests must be paramount in deciding whether parental responsibility should be extended. Those best interests must be determined on a case-by-case basis according to the child's specific circumstances, situation and needs.[87] As discussed in Chapters 1 and 2, this determination should be guided by reference to the child's rights, and sociological and psychological evidence can help to reduce subjectivity in determining what is best for the child in light of their particular situation.

In a number of cases, the English courts have considered requests from known fathers for parental responsibility. In *Re D (Contact and Parental*

[85] *Re D (Contact and parental responsibility: lesbian mothers and known father)* [2006] EWHC 2 (Fam), [2006] 1 FCR 556.

[86] Above, para. 21.

[87] Committee on the Rights of the Child, above n. 4, para. 32.

Responsibility: Lesbian Mothers and Known Father),[88] referenced above, the applicant agreed to father a child who was subsequently raised by the birth mother and her female partner after they advertised for a man who would be interested in fathering a child. The child was conceived through sexual intercourse between the father and the birth mother. From the outset, the father wished to play an active role in the child's upbringing whereas the female couple intended that the man would be acknowledged as the child's father but would exercise a minor role in the child's life.[89] The applicant sought parental responsibility in relation to the child. This application was opposed by the female parents as they felt that the father would use his parental responsibility to interfere in their upbringing of the child. At the time of the hearing, both female parents exercised parental responsibility in respect of the child.

In order to ease concerns relating to his application, the applicant gave assurances that he would not exercise his parental responsibility, if granted, in a way that would interfere with the decision-making capacity of the female parents, in particular in the areas of medical treatment and schooling. Dr Sturge, a consultant child and adolescent psychiatrist, presented the view that extending or refusing parental responsibility to the father in this case would have little impact on the child's development or identity formation. Rather, she found that contact and knowledge of her father and his family would have the greatest impact on the child in these areas.[90] The psychiatrist also found that extending parental responsibility to the father may have the effect of undermining the child's security within her nuclear family that was comprised of the two women.[91] As such, she concluded that the best solution 'would be if the father could receive official recognition in some way but not be allowed to involve himself in the nitty gritty of [the child's] life'.[92] Ultimately, the judge decided in favour of granting the father parental responsibility subject to the conditions that he had proposed, including that he would not visit or contact the child's school for any purpose or contact any health professional involved in her care, without the prior written consent of the female parents.

88 *Re D (Contact and Parental Responsibility: Lesbian Mothers and Known Father)*, above n. 85.

89 Above, para. 5.

90 Above, para. 73.

91 Above, paras. 81–82.

92 Above, para. 83.

Re D (Contact and Parental Responsibility: Lesbian Mothers and Known Father) emphasised the centrality of the nuclear family, which in this case was comprised of the two female parents and the child. The nuclear family is not defined in the judgment but appears to be based loosely on the sexual family model that is comprised of two parents who are in a committed relationship with one another.[93] While the acceptance and recognition of same-sex parenting in this case is to be welcomed (the decision dates back to 2006), it is argued that the focus on the nuclear family fails to acknowledge that children often have broader networks of family relationships outside of the traditional two-parent model. Moreover, the emphasis on the nuclear family obscures the assessment of the child's best interests. As McCandless notes, 'family form became the integral consideration of [the child's] best interests in the case, rather than substantive parenting'.[94]

The conclusions of the psychiatrist in this case are also notable, in particular the finding that '[p]arental responsibility to a third, outside the family individual, in any situation, potentially undermines the completeness of the nuclear family unit. It is a signal of anomaly'.[95] This statement has negative implications for families that do not come within the definition of 'nuclear family'. In particular, the reference to 'any situation' and use of the term 'anomaly' to describe a third parent is hardly encouraging. What does this say about situations where the 'nuclear' family is split across two households or where the legal parents are not in a sexual relationship? Would the extension of parental responsibility to a step-parent also be regarded as an 'anomaly'?[96]

In situations where there are two households, presumably neither household would be designated as the 'nuclear' family and so, based on the psychiatrist's statement, the extension of parental responsibility would not be deemed to be anomalous. Therefore, a generous interpretation of the meaning of 'nuclear family' as discussed in *Re D* is that it is

93 Martha Fineman described the sexual family as 'the traditional or nuclear family, a unit with a heterosexual, formally celebrated union at its core'. Martha Fineman, *The Neutered Mother, the Sexual Family and Other Twentieth Century Tragedies* (London: Routledge, 1995), p. 143. In *Re D*, the discussion is based on the same-sex union, but the reconceptualised sexual family continues to emphasise a sexual affiliation between two adult partners.

94 Julie McCandless, 'Status and anomaly: Re D (contact and parental responsibility: Lesbian mothers and known father) [2006] EWHC 2 (Fam), [2006] 1 FCR 556' (2008) 30 *Journal of Social Welfare and Family Law* 63, p. 68.

95 *Re D*, above n. 85, para. 61.

96 See further McCandless, above n. 94.

simply used as a shorthand method to describe the situation where the child is primarily raised by two parents in the one household. In this sense, the phrase is simply a reflection of the reality of the child's upbringing; that certain adults are primary carers and other adults play a secondary role. It is a rather clumsy phrase as it seems to confine primary care to two adults who are in a committed relationship with each other, but it does not necessarily exclude other family types. It is necessary, however, to reassess the language that is used according to the specific circumstances of the case. The absence of appropriate terminology to refer to different parenting roles and family forms is unfortunate but, as long as the best interests of the child remain the paramount consideration in deciding who should exercise parental responsibility, it is not calamitous to the present discussion.

In later cases concerning lesbian parents and known fathers, the English courts have continued to focus on protecting the nuclear family and, in some cases, have declined to grant parental responsibility to the genetic father on the basis that doing so would interfere with the stability of the nuclear family and thereby negatively affect the child. For example, in cases such as *Re B (Role of Biological Father)*[97] and *R v E and F (Female Parents: Known Father)*,[98] the courts declined to award parental responsibility to genetic fathers on the basis that this would interfere with the autonomy of the nuclear family. In each decision, the best interests of the child were the paramount consideration for the court, and the judgments demonstrate that the courts will also take into account the reality of the child's upbringing in considering the practical effect of granting or refusing the extension of parental responsibility.

The Irish courts have also had the opportunity to consider whether a man who donated sperm to a female couple should be permitted to obtain guardianship in respect of the child. In the case of *JMcD* v. *PL and BM*,[99] the applicant (referred to as 'McD'), donated sperm to a lesbian couple so that they could conceive a child. Prior to this, the parties had entered into an agreement that the respondents would be the child's parents, that McD would not have any responsibility for the child's upbringing and that his role would be similar to that of a 'favourite uncle'. Over time, relations between the parties deteriorated and the respondents sought to travel to Australia with the child for a period of

[97] *Re B (Role of Biological Father)* [2007] EWHC 1952 (Fam), [2008] 1 FLR 855 (CA).
[98] *R* v. *E and F (Female Parents: Known Father)* [2010] EWHC 417 (Fam), [2010] FLR 383.
[99] *JMcD* v. *PL* [2010] 2 IR 199.

one year. McD applied to be appointed as a guardian of the child in an attempt to block the trip to Australia.

In the Irish High Court, Hedigan J concluded that the lesbian couple and their child constituted a de facto family for the purpose of Article 8 of the European Convention on Human Rights, and this finding had a strong influence on his conclusion that neither guardianship nor access should be granted to the applicant. Upon appeal, the Supreme Court was unanimous in dismissing the applicant's claim as to guardianship.[100] Notably, the Supreme Court clarified that the de facto family does not exist as a rights-bearing institution under Irish law. As such, the mother's partner, as a non-genetic parent, had no rights in respect of the child at the centre of the case. Despite this finding, the Court noted that the partner's relationship with the child was still a factor that had to be considered in determining the best interests of the child. As Murray CJ stated:

> That is not to say that the de facto position of the [social parent] could or should be totally ignored in considering the issues in this case since so much turns on the ultimate interests of the child. The [social parent's] relationship with the [mother] and their relationship with the child are among the factors to be taken into account in that context.[101]

Denham J was of a similar view, remarking:

> On the issue of a *de facto* family, the learned High Court judge fell into error. However, that has little significant effect on the analysis in the circumstances of this case of what is in the best interests of the child. The respondents are a loving couple, taking care of the child, in a settled environment. These are key factors in considering the welfare of the child.[102]

Thus, similar to the English case law, the child's best interests and the reality of the parenting arrangements were paramount in considering this application for guardianship. In the Irish case, however, there was no discussion of the 'nuclear' family, because, at the time, the family comprised of the two female parents was not recognised as a family under Irish law. Nonetheless, the child's actual relationships within this family were considered when determining the best interests of the child.

There have been significant changes to the Irish law regulating guardianship and family recognition since the *JMcD* decision was handed

[100] Following a further hearing, the High Court (Hedigan J) granted access by the applicant to the child, subject to certain conditions.

[101] *JMcD* v. *PL* [2010] 2 IR 199, pp. 255–256.

[102] Above 270.

down. Once fully commenced, the Children and Family Relationships Act 2015 will regulate the area of donor-assisted human reproduction (DAHR) and will provide that, where all relevant statutory conditions are met, a sperm donor will not be a legal parent and hence will not automatically be eligible to apply for guardianship where a child is conceived via DAHR.[103] However, where a child is conceived through DAHR performed outside of the clinical setting (for example, through home insemination), the conception will fall outside of the ambit of the 2015 Act and the donor may be recognised as a legal parent. As such, the Irish courts may still encounter applications for guardianship from known donors in the years to come and will need to assess each application in light of all of the circumstances of the case and the best interests of the child.

3.4.2 *Social Parents and Parental Responsibility*

There are many potential benefits for the child in extending parental responsibility to the social parent who is already undertaking a parenting role. Yet, it might equally be argued that the proliferation of parental responsibility could have negative effects where a number of persons are required to share decision-making for the child. This section critiques the use of parental responsibility as a legal tool to recognise the relationship between children and social parents. The focus is on the extension of parental responsibility to a social parent in circumstances where that social parent is part of the child's nuclear family unit and actively cares for the child with one of the legal parents on a regular basis. The child may also have an ongoing relationship with the 'other' legal parent, and so the discussion centres on the extension of parental responsibility to 'multiple' (i.e. more than two) persons.

3.4.2.1 Arguments in Favour of Extending Parental Responsibility to Multiple Persons

The main argument in favour of allowing three or more people to exercise parental responsibility in respect of the same child is that, in many cases, the child will already have three or more persons acting in a parental capacity and so the law should reflect this. This point was made by the Irish Law Reform Commission in its Report on Legal Aspects of Family Relationships. In this Report, the Commission emphasised that the statutory framework for guardianship in that country needed to 'reflect the reality that in some circumstances a child may have more

[103] Children and Family Relationships Act 2015, s 5.

than two adults fulfilling parental roles'.[104] As such, it recommended that legislation should be enacted to facilitate the extension of parental responsibility to civil partners and step-parents in a manner that would not remove parental responsibility from the legal parents of the child.[105]

As was previously noted, Article 7 UNCRC provides that the child has the right, as far as possible, to be cared for by their parents. As such, using this Article to inform the application of the best interests principle, it is argued that it is in the child's best interests for the social parent to be able to acquire the legal responsibilities necessary to fulfil their parental role. This argument is strengthened by reference to the Committee on the Rights of the Child's suggestion that, when determining the child's best interests, the decision-maker should have regard to preserving the family environment, maintaining relations and to the care, protection and safety of the child.[106] Parental responsibility allows the adult to acquire a legal relationship with the child and gives them at least some of the legal tools necessary to protect the child. Legal recognition of all of the child's existing parental relationships is therefore deemed to be in keeping with the best interests principle and should not be arbitrarily restricted.

Allowing more than two persons to exercise parental responsibility in respect of the same child recognises the role that each of them plays in the child's life, and it provides an alternative to step-parent adoption. Step-parent or second-parent adoption is an increasingly common mechanism to recognise and regularise existing family relationships. However, the effect of the adoption order is to extinguish all legal ties with the 'other' birth parent and extended family. For this reason, step-parent adoption is often regarded as an inappropriate method to create a legal relationship between the social parent and the child.[107] By contrast, the extension of parental responsibility not only allows all of the adults to maintain a legal relationship with the child but also allows for the reality of the child's life to be legally recognised.

[104] Law Reform Commission, *Report on Legal Aspects of Family Relationships*, LRC 101–2010 (Dublin: Law Reform Commission, 2010), p. 39.

[105] Above. As discussed earlier in the chapter, multiple persons can now acquire guardianship in Ireland under reforms introduced by the Children and Family Relationships Act 2015.

[106] Committee on the Rights of the Child, above n. 4, paras. 58–74.

[107] See Chapter 4.

3.4.2.2 Arguments against Extending Parental Responsibility to Multiple Persons

Where multiple persons share parental responsibility, they have an equal say in matters concerning the most important aspects of the child's life. This has the potential to create a difficult emotional environment for the adults, and by implication the children, involved. Parenting becomes more onerous as the adults must consult with a third or fourth person on matters concerning the child where previously they simply had to consult with one another. This is particularly difficult where there is an acrimonious relationship between the parties. As Bainham has commented, '[w]hile a triangular sharing of parental responsibility may work well where all parties have an interest in the child and wish to enter into a co-operative arrangement, it could be a recipe for conflict where this is not the case'.[108]

The potential difficulties regarding co-operation are particularly pertinent in jurisdictions where persons with parental responsibility are required by law to consult with one another. In England and Wales, section 2(7) of the Children Act 1989 provides that persons with parental responsibility are permitted to act independently of one another in most circumstances, but there are situations where they are required to consult with others.[109] As Eekelaar notes, the English courts generally take the view that a parent with parental responsibility has the right to be consulted on 'important matters regarding the child's upbringing' even if consultation on these matters is not expressly required by legislation.[110] For example, section 13(1) of the Children Act 1989 provides that where a child arrangements order (previously referred to as a residence order) is in force with respect to a child, no person can change the child's surname without either the written consent of every person who has parental responsibility for the child or leave of court.[111] Nonetheless, in *Re PC (Change of Surname)*,[112] the Court 'effectively ignored s 2(7) in deciding that a parent with parental responsibility should have the right to be consulted over a change of surname, even though no residence order had

108 Bainham, above n. 6, 236–237.

109 Children Act 1989, s 2(7). Some situations require the consent of all persons with parental responsibility. For example, the consent of each parent of the child is required before an adoption order can be made.

110 John Eekelaar, 'Rethinking parental responsibility' (2001) 31 *Family Law* 426, pp. 428–429.

111 Children Act 1989, s 13(1).

112 *Re PC (Change of Surname)* [1997] 2 FLR 730.

been made'.[113] A right to be consulted has also been found to arise in the rather vague category of decisions concerning 'important occurrences in the child's life' such as schooling and serious medical problems.[114] Thus, persons holding parental responsibility in England and Wales may act independently except where the decision concerns an 'important matter'.

In South Africa, co-holders of parental responsibilities and rights may act independently and without the consent of the other co-holder or co-holders.[115] There are certain areas, however, where the consent of all co-holders of guardianship will be required, such as consent to the child's adoption or marriage.[116] A limited duty to consult is also imposed upon the co-holders of parental responsibilities and rights. Under section 31(2) of the Children's Act 2005, where a decision is 'likely to change significantly, or to have a significant adverse effect on, the co-holder's exercise of parental responsibilities and rights in respect of the child', the person taking the decision must give due consideration to any views and wishes expressed by any co-holder of parental responsibilities.[117]

In Ireland, there is no specific requirement placed upon the guardians to consult with each other, but the consent of all guardians is required for certain matters, such as where the child is placed for adoption.[118]

One would hope that where parental responsibility is exercised by a number of people, all of the parties would work in harmony with one another to promote the best interests of the child. Indeed, it is notable that Article 18 UNCRC specifically states that the best interests of the child should be the 'basic concern' of parents and legal guardians. There may be a case where parental responsibility is extended to a social parent against the wishes of the non-resident parent. In this situation, the extension of parental responsibility may increase, or indeed cause, acrimony between the parties, making it more difficult to act collaboratively. However, it must be remembered that parental responsibility exists for the benefit of the child. As such, if the extension of parental responsibility to the social parent is deemed to be in the child's best interests, this should be a more relevant factor than consideration of any potential

[113] Eekelaar, above n. 110, 428. A similar result was reached in *Re T (Change of Surname)* [1998] 2 FLR 620.

[114] *Re H (Parental Responsibility)* [1998] 1 FLR 855.

[115] Children's Act 38 of 2005, s 30(2).

[116] Children's Act 38 of 2005, s 18(3).

[117] Children's Act 38 of 2005, s 31(2). The views and wishes of the child must also be considered in respect of certain decisions. Children's Act 38 of 2005, s 31(1).

[118] Guardianship of Infants Act 1964, s 6C(11), as inserted by Children and Family Relationships Act 2015, s 49.

inconvenience that the adults may experience. On the other hand, if the conflict between the parents is such that it impedes decision-making in respect of the child, this would clearly not operate in that child's best interests. An aggrieved parent could frustrate the whole process.

A non-resident parent (who does not live with the child on a fulltime basis) may be concerned that giving the social parent an enhanced status would interfere with, or even diminish, the non-resident parent's role in the child's life. Bainham suggests that this has occurred in some cases in England and Wales,[119] and so it is a valid concern. Bainham opines that 'to share decision-making for a child between three rather than two adults is clearly a weakening of the position of the parent who is not in the household'.[120] While this issue will not arise in every case, the fact that the non-resident parent is not physically present in the family home may, in some cases, lessen their role to a certain extent. However, this is not so much a problem with the extension of parental responsibility to a social parent but is one that stems simply from the fact that the parents are living apart.[121] The extension of parental responsibility to a social parent does not reduce the parental responsibility of the legal parents. The non-resident parent will therefore have the same legal authority and responsibility in respect of the child notwithstanding the extension of parental responsibility. Although the parent with custody will naturally have more control over the day-to-day care of the child, the non-resident parent with parental responsibility has an equal input in relation to the most important aspects of the child's life, and this will not be diluted where a social parent also acquires parental responsibility.

The seemingly unlimited nature of the extension of parental responsibility and the fact that a number of persons may exercise it during the child's lifetime also give pause for thought. Bainham, for example, questions 'whether the proliferation of parental responsibility which could occur where children are caught up in serial marriages would be in their best interests, or workable at all, on a practical level'.[122] In many jurisdictions, the parental responsibility of a social parent can be terminated by court order or otherwise where the termination is in the best interests of

[119] Bainham, above n. 6, 236.

[120] Above.

[121] Arguably, this situation is no different to the conventional scenario whereby the resident parent has primary or sole custody.

[122] Bainham, above n. 6, 237.

the child.[123] This is a sensible approach. It would not be appropriate for parental responsibility to terminate simply by virtue of divorce or dissolution of a civil partnership. After all, the very reason for the initial extension of responsibility is the fact that the social parent was acting as a parent towards the child and the extension was deemed to be in the child's best interests. Therefore, it does not follow that the child should lose their legal relationship with the social parent just because the adults have ended their relationship. Furthermore, allowing for parental responsibility to be removed by court order is appropriate because it ensures that only those actually caring for the child and acting in the best interests of the child exercise responsibilities.

In this light, it is submitted that the potential for multiple persons to exercise parental responsibility should not be viewed in a negative manner. As long as each adult continues to act in the child's best interests, there is no reason to bemoan the potential for the proliferation of parental responsibility. The child's best interests must be paramount in deciding who should exercise parental responsibility. As such, all of the persons who have a parental relationship with the child should be eligible to exercise responsibilities and rights. That is not to say that every social parent should automatically acquire parental responsibility; instead, the extension of parental responsibility will be considered against the best interests standard. If the best interests of the child demand that the social parent should exercise parental responsibility, then it should not be curtailed.

3.4.2.3 Extension Mechanisms

As was seen above, England and Wales, Ireland and South Africa adopt different procedures for allocating parental responsibility to social parents. In England and Wales[124] and South Africa,[125] parental responsibilities may be extended to social parents either by way of agreement with the parents or by application to court. By contrast, in Ireland, guardianship can only be extended to the social parent by way of court order.[126]

[123] See, for example, Children Act 1989, s 4A(3); Guardianship of Infants Act 1964, s 8(7), as inserted by Children and Family Relationships Act 2015, s 51; Children's Act 38 of 2005, s 28.

[124] Children Act 1989, s 4A, as inserted by Adoption and Children Act 2002, s 112 and as amended by Civil Partnership Act 2004, s 75.

[125] Children's Act 38 of 2005, ss 22–24.

[126] Guardianship of Infants Act 1964, s 6C, as inserted by Children and Family Relationships Act 2015, s 49.

This section considers the suitability of the mechanisms for extending parental responsibility to social parents from the perspective of the best interests of the child. It is questioned whether the extension of parental responsibility should be a private matter for the parties to agree themselves or whether an element of oversight is required in order to ensure that the child's best interests are secured.

One advantage of allowing for parental responsibility to be extended to a social parent by way of agreement is that this mechanism provides a straightforward and efficient means to extend responsibilities. The court process can be expensive and time-consuming, and so both cost and delay can be minimised through the use of a private agreement. The private agreement also has the potential to enhance co-operation between the parties as they will all be actively involved in the appointment decision, leading to a more collaborative process.

The main difficulty that arises in allowing for parental responsibility to be extended by private agreement to a person who is not a parent is that there would typically be no oversight of this type of appointment. The person would not be subject to any independent vetting or screening as would be required in the case of an adoption or fostering arrangement. As such, the best interests of the child could be overlooked in a system that prioritises the adult's decisions in this regard without any supervision of their choices.

In Scotland, parental responsibility can only be allocated to non-parents by way of a court order.[127] Extending parental responsibility by agreement was rejected in that jurisdiction on the basis that it would be difficult to ensure that any such agreement was in the best interests of the child. It was felt that the wishes and welfare of the child were more likely to be given due consideration where the decision lay solely with the court.[128]

Use of the court process to extend parental responsibility to a social parent ensures that the person is subject to independent approval. In many countries, the courts are required to refer to the domestic 'best interests checklist'[129] when considering whether the person should exercise parental responsibility. Although the use of such checklists was criticised in Chapter 1, they at least ensure that various factors relevant

[127] Children (Scotland) Act 1995, s 11.

[128] Law Reform Commission, above n. 5, 96; Ian Dey and Fran Wassoff, 'Mixed Messages: Parental Responsibilities, Public Opinion and the Reforms of Family Law' (2006) 20 *International Journal of Law, Policy and the Family* 225, p. 236.

[129] See Chapter 1.

to the child are considered in the decision-making process. By contrast, there might not be an obligation on the parties to consider the best interests of the child in this manner where there is a private agreement. For example, the current legislation in England and Wales[130] and Ireland[131] only requires that the *court* has regard to the best interests of the child in reaching a decision as to parental responsibility. By contrast, in South Africa, the best interests principle applies '[i]n all matters concerning the care, protection and wellbeing of the child' and does not restrict this duty to the courts.[132]

Claims in favour of judicial oversight may be particularly relevant where the parents are involved in a number of re-marriages or subsequent partnerships. In most jurisdictions, there is no stated limit on the number of persons who can exercise parental responsibility, and so it is perhaps appropriate that there should be independent assessment of such appointments so as to ensure that the best interests of the child remain the paramount focus.

In Ireland, a waiting period applies before a step-parent (that is, the spouse, civil partner or cohabitant of a legal parent) can be appointed as an additional guardian: the person must have shared responsibility for caring for the child with the child's parent for at least two years before they can be appointed.[133] This waiting period ensures that the prospective additional guardian has shown an intention and an ability to act as a parent before the appointment can take place. Nonetheless, it is submitted that some mechanism should still exist to analyse whether the intended guardian has, in fact, proved their worth and has genuinely acted as a parent during this waiting period.

In South Africa, where a parent enters into a parental responsibilities and rights agreement with another person, the agreement will only take effect if it is registered with a family advocate or if it is made an order of court.[134] This registration will only occur where the family advocate or court is satisfied that the agreement is in the best interests of the child.[135] This approach seems to strike a balance between the issues outlined above. It allows the parties to enter into a co-operative agreement as to

130 Children Act 1989, ss 1(1) and 1(3).

131 Guardianship of Infants Act 1964, s 3, as amended by Children and Family Relationships Act 2015, s 45; Guardianship of Infants Act 1964, s 31(2), as inserted by Children and Family Relationships Act 2015, s 63.

132 Children's Act 38 of 2005, ss 7 and 9.

133 Guardianship of Infants Act 1964, s.6C(2)(a), as inserted by Children and Family Relationships Act 2015, s 49.

134 Children's Act 38 of 2005, s 22(4).

135 Children's Act 38 of 2005, s 22(5).

parental responsibilities but at the same time it provides independent oversight of the appointment. This ensures that the best interests of the child will be paramount in deciding whether or not the social parent should exercise parental responsibility. As such, it is submitted that the South African approach represents the most favourable method for regulating parental responsibilities agreements. This approach not only offers the expediency of a private agreement but also offers a mechanism to ensure that the child's best interests are secured.

In light of the above, it is submitted that some element of oversight of the extension of parental responsibility to a person who is not a legal parent is preferable to ensure that this action is in the best interests of the child. Parental responsibility concerns the most important aspects of the child's upbringing and so there should be oversight of its proliferation. This need for oversight does not necessarily demand that parental responsibilities agreements should be excluded, as the South African example reveals. Parental responsibilities agreements promote co-operation and obviate the need for recourse to the adversarial court process. Consequently, it is submitted that it would be preferable to allow for the allocation of parental responsibility *either* by way of court order or through agreement in circumstances where this agreement is subject to independent approval.

3.5 Conclusion

Gay and lesbian families are formed in many different ways, and so it is important that the law has different mechanisms in place to recognise diverse family relationships. Parental responsibility provides a mechanism whereby the social parent can acquire a legal relationship with the child but is not recognised as a legal parent, which is important in situations where the child has an ongoing relationship with both birth parents.

This chapter has examined the concept of parental responsibility and explored how this concept should operate in accordance with the best interests of the child. In order for the concept to complement the best interests of children, it was argued that the *responsibilities* of adults must be emphasised and further that the reality of the child's life should be central in considering whether parental responsibility should be allocated to a particular adult. In each of the comparator jurisdictions, parental responsibility can be extended to social parents, recognising the important role that these persons play in the child's life. In many cases, the extension of parental responsibility to a social parent is more appropriate than step-parent or second-parent adoption. However, as is continually emphasised in this book, the best interests of children are not uniform or static. As such, the widest range of legal options must be in place to ensure that the best interests of each individual child can be met. With this in mind, the following chapter focuses on adoption as a mechanism to establish legal family relationships and considers in particular the suitability of second-parent adoption as an option to formalise existing social ties between adults and children.

4

Adoption

4.1 Introduction

Adoption is a mechanism that creates a new legal family for a child. The process terminates the parental responsibilities and rights of the birth parents and transfers these to the adoptive parents. Once the adoption order is made, the child becomes a full, permanent member of the new legal family. Pursuant to Article 21 of the United Nations Convention on the Rights of the Child (UNCRC), State Parties that recognise and/or permit a system of adoption 'shall ensure that the best interests of the child shall be the paramount consideration'.[1] Adoption must, therefore, be a child-centred process and the child's interests must be the paramount focus in any decision concerning the adoption of a child.

This chapter argues that, from a children's rights perspective, there is no logical basis for refusing to allow same-sex couples to access joint adoption and further that the best interests principle demands that such access is made available. Unlike other chapters in this book which seek to identify a way to regulate different pathways to parentage in accordance with the conceptual framework for the best interests principle endorsed in Chapter 1, this chapter focuses more on the transformative potential of the best interests principle as an advocacy tool to advance the rights of children. Case law from selected jurisdictions, namely England and Wales, Northern Ireland and South Africa, is analysed to support this premise. Judicial dicta from these jurisdictions demonstrate an awareness amongst the judiciary of the benefits for the child of having a secure legal relationship with both of the adults who care for the child on a daily basis. The cases also emphasise the need for individual solutions to suit the needs of individual children.

[1] United Nations Convention on the Rights of the Child, New York, 20 November 1989, in force 2 September 1990, Art. 21.

Discrete aspects of adoption law that are of particular relevance to same-sex parenting are also assessed in this chapter, namely the need for specific regulation in respect of second-parent adoption and issues arising in the context of intercountry adoption by same-sex adopters. The discussion begins with an examination of the appropriateness of adoption as a means of securing existing family relationships. It is argued that, although adoption is not always appropriate in this context, where a child is already being cared for by a same-sex couple, there is a strong argument that the child should be able to benefit from a legal adoptive relationship with the partner or spouse of the parent.[2] Thereafter, the provisions regulating adoptions by same-sex couples in England and Wales, Ireland and South Africa are assessed and are benchmarked against the best interests of the child standard.

The approach of the European Court of Human Rights (ECtHR) to the question of adoption by same-sex couples is also assessed. It is argued that although the ECtHR has not yet found that same-sex couples enjoy a general right to jointly apply to adopt under Article 8 of the European Convention on Human Rights (ECHR), the Court has failed to appropriately examine the rights of the child in such cases. It is submitted that these cases could have been decided differently through analysis of the rights and best interests of the children at the centre of the proceedings.

4.2 Adoption as a Means of Securing Existing Family Relationships

Traditionally, adoption was understood as a process that allowed orphaned or abandoned children to benefit from a new legal family. Increasingly, the process is used as a way to legally fasten existing family relationships.[3] This may be achieved through 'step-parent' or 'second-parent' adoption. This form of adoption allows a parent's new spouse or partner to adopt the parent's biological or adoptive child in a manner that does not affect the parental rights and responsibilities of that parent. By contrast, in traditional joint adoption, the rights and responsibilities of

[2] See: American Academy of Pediatrics, 'Coparent or second-parent adoption by same-sex parents' (2002) 109 *Pediatrics* 339.

[3] Figures in Ireland show that the majority of domestic adoption orders made in the years 2002–2016 were in favour of a step-parent adopting jointly with a birth parent. For example, in 2016, 65 of the 95 domestic adoption orders granted were step-parent adoptions. See: Adoption Authority of Ireland, *Annual Report 2016* (Dublin: Adoption Authority of Ireland, 2016), p. 25.

both of the existing parents are extinguished upon the making of the adoption order.

4.2.1 The Appropriateness of Second-Parent Adoption

Second-parent adoption allows a person who is acting in the capacity of a step-parent to acquire full parental responsibilities and rights in respect of their partner's child. The process is somewhat controversial given that the effect of the adoption order is to extinguish the child's legal relationship with the 'other' birth parent (i.e. that parent who is not in a relationship with the step-parent) and extended family.[4] As such, in cases where the child has an ongoing relationship with that other parent, this legal procedure may be regarded as an inappropriate means through which to regularise familial ties in the reconstituted step-family. In England and Wales, there has been a policy of discouraging step-parent adoptions since the 1970s for this reason.[5] On the other hand, there may be situations where step-parent adoption is appropriate, for example where the other parent is absent or unknown. As Lowe and Douglas have commented:

> Although it is tempting to say that step-parent adoptions should be prohibited, it is submitted that it would not be right to do so for there are occasions where adoption is appropriate, though in case of the death of one of the birth parents, one wonders whether guardianship would be more appropriate.[6]

At present in England and Wales, the courts, in deciding upon an adoption application, are directed to consider the alternative orders available (such as parental responsibility or residence orders) and to decide which order would best promote the child's welfare.[7] As such, there is an acknowledgement in that jurisdiction that second-parent adoption may, in some cases, prove to be the most effective option, but other avenues must first be explored.

[4] Second-parent adoption should be distinguished from 'simple' adoption. Simple adoption is only available in a handful of jurisdictions and operates to create a new parent–child relationship between the adopter and the child without severing the family ties between the child and their biological family.

[5] Andrew Bainham and Stephen Gilmore, *Children: The Modern Law*, 4 ed. (London: Family Law, 2013), p. 652.

[6] Nigel Lowe and Gillian Douglas, *Bromley's Family Law*, 10 ed. (Oxford: Oxford University Press, 2007), p. 848.

[7] Adoption and Children Act 2002, s 1(6).

As has been discussed in Chapter 3, the extension of parental responsibility to a social parent may often be regarded as a more appropriate means through which to confer rights and responsibilities upon that person. However, as noted in that chapter, legal parentage gives rise to many important legal consequences that do not attach to parental responsibility. Legal parentage has implications for the child's inheritance rights and in determining citizenship. Parentage also creates a legal relationship with members of the parent's extended family. Parental responsibility does not have any legal impact on these areas. Moreover, legal parentage is a lifelong status. By contrast, parental responsibility comes to an end once the child reaches the age of majority, or earlier by court order.

Adoption creates secure and lasting family relationships, and it allows the child to be fully integrated into their family. It may also give rise to social and psychological benefits for the child as it indicates to the child that the social parent is committed to them. Hence, while the extension of parental responsibility to a social parent may improve the position of the family in many respects, it is not a panacea, nor will it be the most appropriate solution for every child. As the best interests of the child must be assessed on a case-by-case basis, it is submitted that the widest range of options should be available so that the best individual solution can be found for each individual child. This means that both second-parent adoption and the extension of parental responsibility should be available as options to enable a social parent to acquire a legal relationship with the child.

In the context of extending parenting rights to same-sex couples, second-parent adoption seems to be a less divisive option than allowing for the joint adoption of 'stranger' children by such couples.[8] This is perhaps explained by the fact that where a child is already being raised by a same-sex couple and being cared for by them on a daily basis, the child's need for security within this unit is apparent.[9] By contrast, in joint adoption, where the child does not yet have a relationship with the prospective adopters, it may be more difficult for society to view the

[8] Maarit Jänterä-Jareborg, 'Parenthood for same-sex couples – Scandinavian developments' in Katharina Boele-Woelki and Angelika Fuchs (eds.), *Legal Recognition of Same-Sex Relationships in Europe: National, Cross-Border and European Perspectives*, 2 ed. (Cambridge: Intersentia, 2012).

[9] For a discussion of the arguments in favour of second-parent adoption, see: American Academy of Pediatrics, above n. 2.

possibility of such an adoption through the lens of the best interests principle.[10]

In many countries, the introduction of second-parent adoption for same-sex couples was accepted by society without vocal public resistance.[11] In these cases, society seemed

> to share or at least accept the legislator's view that stepchild adoption is a way of strengthening the legal position of children living in families with two same-sex adults … the step-parent's sex or sexual orientation is regarded as irrelevant from the perspective of the child's best interests.[12]

By contrast, the introduction of joint adoption rights for same-sex couples has often proved to be much more controversial.[13] As noted above, second-parent adoption allows existing relationships to be legally recognised, whereas joint adoption is 'more about conferring the right to build a family' and so the policy considerations, and public understanding, are different.[14] As a result, some countries allow second-parent adoption for same-sex couples but do not permit them to apply for joint adoption.[15]

It is suggested that the rationale for resisting joint adoption in this context is rather short-sighted. In countries where second-parent adoption is already available to same-sex couples, it is seemingly futile to preclude same-sex couples from jointly adopting 'stranger' children. Firstly, where second-parent adoption is permitted, this negates any argument that gay and lesbian couples are unfit to act as joint adoptive parents. In such circumstances, the State has accepted that such persons can act as suitable adoptive parents. Secondly, if the prohibition on joint adoption by same-sex couples was to be maintained in circumstances where second-parent adoption is available, that prohibition could easily be circumvented by a couple seeking to jointly adopt as one member of the couple could adopt as a single applicant and thereafter the partner

[10] Arguably, the joint adoption of children by same-sex couples should also be seen to operate in the best interests of those children because, by widening the pool of prospective adopters, it is more likely that their specific needs will be met through the process. Mia Dambach, 'The international legal context governing intercountry adoptions by gay men and lesbians' (2011) 35 *Adoption and Fostering* 65.

[11] Jänterä-Jareborg, above n. 8, 102–103.

[12] Jänterä-Jareborg, above n. 8, 102–103.

[13] Jänterä-Jareborg, above n. 8, 104.

[14] Tim Amos and Joe Rainer, 'Parenthood for same-sex couples in the EU' in Katharina Boele-Woelki and Angelika Fuchs (eds.), *Same-Sex Relationships and Beyond*, 3 ed. (Cambridge: Intersentia, 2017), p. 85.

[15] Above.

could apply for second-parent adoption.[16] Thus, it would be a meaningless prohibition in practice.

However, while it may be legitimate to allow same-sex couples to evade the rules governing joint adoption in the domestic context, different considerations may arise in respect of the use of second-parent adoption following an intercountry adoption. This is because the regulation of intercountry adoption is premised on co-operation between States where the sending country makes the placement decision. This ethos of co-operation is potentially undermined where the receiving country subsequently approves a change to the child's legal parental status. As intercountry adoptions are becoming more prevalent, it is necessary to consider the appropriateness of the second-parent adoption process in this specific context.

4.2.2 The Appropriateness of Second-Parent Adoption in the Context of Intercountry Adoptions

Intercountry adoption occurs where the resident of one country seeks to adopt a child who is resident in a different country. In the context of such adoptions, concern might be raised that the second-parent adoption mechanism would be used to circumvent the eligibility and suitability laws of the 'sending' country in an intercountry application. Some 'sending' countries are unwilling to recognise same-sex couples as eligible adopters.[17] As such, it is quite possible that one member of the couple would proceed with an intercountry adoption as a single applicant and, thereafter, the couple would seek a domestic second-parent adoption in order to confer rights upon the partner.[18] Alternatively, a single person may adopt a child from a foreign jurisdiction and then, some years later,

[16] In Germany, for example, prior to the introduction of joint adoption for same-sex couples in 2017, second-parent adoption was possible and could be used to circumvent the prohibition on joint adoption. See further: BVerfG, Judgment of the First Senate of 19 February 2013 – 1 BvL 1/11.

[17] Dambach, above n. 10.

[18] Gonzalez-Beilfuss notes that in Spain, because many sending countries refuse to assign children to same-sex couples, it is 'not uncommon for same-sex couples to resort to individual adoption abroad, and then to regularize the situation in Spain through step-parent adoption'. Christina Gonzalez-Beilfuss, 'All or nothing: The dilemma of southern jurisdictions' in Boele-Woelki and Fuchs, above n. 8, 49. See also Roberta Messina & Salvatore D'Amore, 'Adoption by lesbians and gay men in Europe: Challenges and barriers on the journey to adoption' (2018) 21 *Adoption Quarterly* 59.

enter into a new relationship and seek to acquire parental rights for this new partner.

A question arises in these circumstances as to whether it is appropriate that provision be made available for a domestic second-parent adoption to take place after the child has been adopted from the foreign jurisdiction by a single applicant. On the one hand, the child's immediate needs may dictate that the partner, as a person caring for the child on a day-to-day basis, should be permitted to adopt their partner's child. After all, the child has the right to be cared for by their parents pursuant to Article 7 UNCRC. On the other hand, a second-parent adoption by the gay or lesbian partner may run contrary to the adoption regulations of the child's country of origin and may, therefore, be seen as circumventing the rules of the sending country, thereby tainting the ethos of co-operation that is central to the intercountry adoption process.[19]

In Denmark,[20] Iceland[21] and Norway,[22] second-parent adoptions by a parent's gay or lesbian partner are not permitted in respect of children who were initially adopted from a foreign jurisdiction by a single applicant.[23] Jänterä-Jareborg explains that the objective behind these restrictions is

> to prevent the creation of a *limping second adoption* which is not valid in the child's country of origin. It is assumed that the countries of origin of adopted children will normally not recognise registered partnerships as being equal to marriage or regard same-sex couples as suitable adoptive parents.[24]

According to Jänterä-Jareborg, this restrictive approach is in keeping with the underlying ideology of any intercountry adoption 'as a joint venture between the child's country of origin and the receiving state, where both parties respect each other's laws and the country of origin takes the placement decisions'.[25] Similarly, Dambach notes that the spirit of respect for the eligibility rules of the sending country

[19] Hague Convention on Protection of Children and Co-operation in Respect of Intercountry Adoption, 29 May 1993, in force 1 May 1995, Art. 1.

[20] Danish Act on Registered Partnerships, s 4, as amended by Act No. 360/1999.

[21] Icelandic Act on Registered Partnerships, s 6, as amended by Act No. 52/2000.

[22] Norwegian Act on Registered Partnerships, as amended by Act 36/2001 and 612/2001. It should be noted that if the child's country of origin permits the second-parent adoption, then this may be allowed in Norway.

[23] Jänterä-Jareborg, above n. 8, 103.

[24] Jänterä-Jareborg, above n. 8, 103 [emphasis in original].

[25] Jänterä-Jareborg, above n. 8, 104.

> is completely undermined when single people are permitted to adopt a child without revealing their sexual orientation but with an intention of undergoing a second parent adoption in the receiving country to get the same-sex couple recognised as parents.[26]

In addition, preservation of the child's cultural background is often regarded as an important element of the child's right to identity. Therefore, if the child was originally adopted from a jurisdiction that does not recognise same-sex couples as joint parents, it may run contrary to the child's cultural background to allow for the second-parent adoption to take place.[27]

On the other hand, at the time of the second-parent adoption, the child will have lived in the receiving country for a number of years. The supervision of the adoption will have passed to the courts of that country, and, at this stage, they will be best placed to determine the best interests of the child.[28] In this light, a more flexible approach is required because the second-parent adoption may be in the best interests of the child who is already being raised by the partner of the parent.

In this situation, it is submitted that the child's immediate interests should take precedence. The best interests of the child must be paramount in cases of adoption and the concept of best interests must be flexible and adaptable to accommodate the needs of the child.[29] As such, although at the time of the initial adoption, the sending country will have made its own determination as to the best interests of the child, this decision should not be viewed as absolute, and it should be capable of review by the domestic courts of the receiving country. If the second-parent adoption is subsequently deemed to be in the child's best interests, it is argued that the fact that the child was originally subject to an intercountry adoption order should not prevent those best interests from being realised. The application for second-parent adoption should be assessed on a case-by-case basis in line with the child's best interests.

4.3 Domestic Adoption

The domestic laws of England and Wales, Ireland and South Africa allow same-sex couples to apply to jointly adopt children. There is no such

[26] Dambach, above n. 10, 74.

[27] Dambach, above n. 10, 67.

[28] Jänterä-Jareborg, above n. 8, 104.

[29] Committee on the Rights of the Child, *General comment No. 14 (2013) on the right of the child to have his or her best interests taken as a primary consideration (art. 3, para. 1)* CRC/C/GC/14, para. 32.

thing as a 'right' to adopt. Instead, each application for adoption must be considered in light of the best interests of the child, and so the domestic laws confer rights on same-sex couples to apply for adoption and to have their applications considered against the best interests standard. This section examines the evolution of the domestic adoption laws of the three comparator jurisdictions and demonstrates the centrality of the best interests principle to the development of law and policy. Case law pertaining to Northern Ireland is also discussed to highlight the transformative role played by the best interests principle in the reform of adoption laws in that jurisdiction. The final part of the section examines jurisprudence from the ECtHR and, in doing so, argues that the full potential of the best interests principle as an advocacy tool in cases concerning same-sex adoption has not yet been realised before the European Court.

Before turning to consider the role of the best interests principle in the context of domestic adoption, it is important to highlight the practical reality that some adoptions are intercountry in nature,[30] though there has been an overall global decline in intercountry adoption.[31] It is important that the domestic law allows for same-sex couples to jointly submit an application for intercountry adoption (and to have this adoption subsequently recognised in the home jurisdiction), but the ability of same-sex couples to engage in this type of adoption may be limited by the number of 'sending' countries that are willing to accept them as parents. For example, Sweden changed its domestic laws to allow for same-sex adoption in 2003, but the first intercountry adoption by a same-sex couple did not take place until 2017.[32] The restrictive eligibility criteria applied by sending countries were blamed for the paucity of intercountry adoptions by same-sex couples during this fourteen-year period.[33] It is important to remain cognisant of this international context when considering the domestic laws below.

4.3.1 England and Wales

In England and Wales, joint adoption is available to both married and unmarried same-sex couples. Section 50 of the Adoption and Children

[30] Messina and D'Amore, above n. 18.

[31] European Parliament, *Adoption of children in the European Union* (Briefing, June 2016).

[32] The Local, 'First same-sex overseas adoption takes place in Sweden', The Local, 5 September 2017.

[33] Above.

Act 2002 provides that '[a]n adoption order may be made on the application of a couple where both of them have attained the age of 21 years'.[34] The term 'couple' is subsequently defined in the 2002 Act to mean two persons who are married to each other, two people (whether of different sexes or the same sex) living as partners in an enduring family relationship or two people who are civil partners of each other.[35] The question of whether the partners are in 'an enduring family relationship' is based on consideration of the circumstances of the relationship and no statutory period is specified as to the length of the relationship.[36]

Unlike some of the other examples in this chapter, the introduction of joint adoption rights for same-sex couples in England and Wales resulted from parliamentary initiative rather than from litigation from aggrieved couples. The parliamentary process was, however, marred by significant disagreement and debate on whether the link between marriage and adoption should be preserved or severed.[37] As a result of this divergence of opinions, the proposals extending joint adoption to unmarried couples (whether of the same or opposite sex) were only agreed 'at the eleventh hour'.[38] In particular, the proposals met with strong opposition in the House of Lords. Consideration of the welfare of the children who would subsequently be raised by unmarried couples seemed to be the main factor inducing hesitance among the Lords on this matter.[39] As Baroness Blatch commented during the House of Lords debates, children 'should have the greatest stability and love . . . the surest way of achieving that is to place a child in a family with a mother and a father'.[40]

Attitudes in England and Wales have now become more accepting of same-sex couples as adoptive parents. Figures show that, in that jurisdiction, 12 per cent (460) of adoptable children were adopted by same-sex couples during the year ending 31 March 2018,[41] compared to just 4 per cent in 2010.[42] Marriage rights were extended to same-sex couples

34 Adoption and Children Act 2002, s 50.

35 Adoption and Children Act 2002, s 144(4), as inserted by Civil Partnership Act 2004, s 79(12).

36 *Re T and M (Adoption)* [2010] EWHC 964 (Fam), [2011] 1 FLR 1487.

37 Andrew Bainham, *Children: The Modern Law*, 3 ed. (London: Family Law, 2005), p. 273.

38 Above.

39 For a summary of the parliamentary proceedings, see: A. Marshall, 'Comedy of Adoption – When Is a Parent Not a Parent?' [2003] *Family Law* 840.

40 Hansard, HL, vol. 640, col 601, 5 November 2002 in Marshall, above, 841.

41 CoramBAAF, 'Statistics: England' www.corambaaf.org.uk/fostering-adoption/looked-after-children-adoption-fostering-statistics/statistics-england.

42 Department of Education, 'Statistical First Release' SFR 27/2010 (September 2010).

in England and Wales in 2014, thereby removing the last hurdle to legal equality for gay and lesbian families.[43] The English judiciary has also become more accepting of same-sex couples as parents. For example, one magistrate was temporarily suspended in 2015 for objecting to the adoption of a child by a same-sex couple. He was reported to the Judicial Conduct Investigations Office after making various comments to other magistrates to the effect that it would be better for a child to be placed 'with a mother and father' than with a same-sex couple.[44]

In deciding the 2008 Northern Irish case of *Re P (Adoption: Unmarried Couple)*,[45] the House of Lords found that it was contrary to the best interests of the child to exclude unmarried opposite-sex couples from the joint adoption process. This reasoning was subsequently adopted by the Northern Irish courts and was extended to find that unmarried same-sex couples should also be able to access joint adoption.[46] As such, even in the traditionally conservative Northern Irish jurisdiction, there is judicial recognition that the rights and interests of children demand that joint adoption rights should be made available to same-sex couples.

In *Re P (Adoption: Unmarried Couple)*, the House of Lords was asked to consider whether a Northern Irish provision, Article 14 of the Adoption (Northern Ireland) Order 1987, which permitted only married couples and single persons to adopt, was contrary to the ECHR. The Lords concluded that the provision was inconsistent with Article 8 ECHR, read together with Article 14.

In this case, the House of Lords spoke at length about the implications that eligibility criteria in adoption have for securing a child's best interests. Lord Hoffmann emphasised the fact that eligibility to *apply* for an adoption order is but the 'first step on the road to adoption'.[47] After this, the applicants are thoroughly scrutinised to satisfy the court that adoption by them is in the interests of the child.[48] The difficulty for Lord Hoffmann was that the prohibition on adoption by unmarried couples meant that highly suitable prospective adopters who passed all of the relevant tests had to be refused their application on the sole ground that

[43] The Marriage (Same Sex Couples) Act 2013 came into force on 29 March 2014.

[44] 'Family court magistrate suspended after objecting to same-sex parents', *Pink News*, 18 January 2015.

[45] *Re P (Adoption: Unmarried Couple)* [2008] UKHL 38.

[46] *The Northern Ireland Human Rights Commission's Application* [2012] NIQB 77; *In the Matter of an Application by the Northern Ireland Human Rights Commission* [2013] NICA 37.

[47] *Re P (Adoption: Unmarried Couple)* [2008] UKHL 38, para. 11.

[48] Above.

they were unmarried. The judge held that this bright-line rule against unmarried couples could not be justified because the law requires the interests of each child to be examined on a case-by-case basis.[49]

Lord Hoffman acknowledged that it was a reasonable generalisation to prefer married couples over unmarried couples as potential adopters given the stability of the marital relationship. However, it was not reasonable to assume that all married couples are suitable adopters and all unmarried couples are not. The prevailing interest had to be the interest of the child, not the marital status of the prospective adopters.

Baroness Hale focused on the question of whether the discrimination against the unmarried couple in this case could be justified by objective and reasonable grounds so as to comply with Article 14 ECHR.[50] She noted that the protection of the traditional family based on marriage is 'in principle capable of being a legitimate aim'.[51] As she remarked,

> being married does at least indicate an initial intention to stay together for life. More important, it makes a great legal difference to their relationship. Marriage brings with it legal rights and obligations between the couple which unmarried couples do not have.[52]

Nonetheless, Baroness Hale acknowledged that '[t]he law cannot force any couple, married or unmarried, to stay together'.[53] Moreover, she noted that there were some couples who could not marry, many of whom were already caring for children and now wished their relationship to have the security of adoption.[54] Thus, the choice was not between placing a child with a married couple or an unmarried couple but between 'the child remaining in that home with one legal parent or remaining there with two'.[55] Furthermore, the fact that single persons could adopt under the Northern Irish law undermined the legitimacy of excluding the unmarried couple.[56] Ultimately, consideration of the best interests of the child led the judge to conclude that there was no longer an objective

49 Above, para. 16.
50 Above, para. 108.
51 Above.
52 Above.
53 Above.
54 Baroness Hale noted, for example, that '[s]trange though it may seem to some, there are people who have conscientious objections to divorce, but who do not have conscientious objections to living together outside marriage'. *Re P*, above, para. 110.
55 Above.
56 Above.

and reasonable justification for the 'blanket ban' on joint adoption by unmarried couples.[57]

In the subsequent case of *The Northern Ireland Human Rights Commission's Application*,[58] the Northern Irish High Court endorsed the reasoning of the Lords in *Re P* and confirmed that the ruling extended to same-sex couples. This case arose because, after *Re P*, the impugned laws remained in force in Northern Ireland. As such, the Northern Ireland Human Rights Commission brought a claim challenging the ongoing failure of the Government to amend the laws. In the High Court, Treacy J was satisfied that '[t]he justification for retaining the current eligibility criteria when considered from the point of view of a child's right to be adopted has been demolished by the judgment in Re. P'.[59] According to the judge:

> Excluding persons from the whole adoption process on the sole basis of their relationship status can only serve to narrow the pool of potential adopters which cannot be in the best interests of children for the reasons identified in Re P. The rigorous scrutiny and assessment of suitability will ensure that only persons capable of providing a loving, safe and secure adoptive home will ultimately be considered. Looked at in this light it is clear that the complete bar to applying to adopt that the current eligibility criteria create cannot bear a reasonable relationship of proportionality to that aim.[60]

The judge concluded that the Article 8 rights of unmarried couples, whether of the same or opposite sex, read together with Article 14 ECHR, had been breached by the continued denial to them of the opportunity to apply to adopt jointly. This case is also notable due to the fact that the respondent had attempted to argue that, because other mechanisms such as residence orders and parental responsibility orders were available to facilitate the extension of parental responsibility to social parents, this rendered 'the practical reality convention compliant'.[61] Treacy J was unconvinced by this argument, finding that 'the arguments in relation to the alternatives available under the relevant orders hold no weight. It cannot be in the best interests of a child to deny that child of the full benefits of having two fully legal adoptive parents.'[62]

[57] Above, para. 112.
[58] *The Northern Ireland Human Rights Commission's Application* [2012] NIQB 77.
[59] Above, para. 72.
[60] Above, para. 80.
[61] Above, para. 39.
[62] Above, para. 81.

This case was subsequently appealed to the Divisional Court, which dismissed the appeal and endorsed the findings of Treacy J.[63] This demonstrates that, according to the Northern Irish courts, the best interests of the child mandate that joint adoption is made available to their parents regardless of whether those parents are married or not. As has been seen, the best interests of the child are given priority in that jurisdiction and, for the Northern Irish judiciary, it is the benefit of a two-parent home, regardless of the gender or sexual orientation of the parents, that best adheres to that principle.

The judgments above align with the ethos of adoption as a child-centred concept that prioritises the best interests of the child. They recognise that children are the group most affected by the law's refusal to recognise their family relationships and emphasise the practical reality of non-recognition. Moreover, they acknowledge the individualised nature of best interests assessments, as endorsed by the Committee on the Rights of the Child,[64] and emphasise that individualised assessments are impeded where a blanket ban on adoptions by particular adults is in place.

The focus of the House of Lords in *Re P*, and the reasoning subsequently adopted by the Northern Irish courts in the above cases, has not yet found favour with the ECtHR. Although the ECtHR has increasingly recognised that gay and lesbian families fall within the ambit of Article 8 ECHR and that they enjoy 'family life' as understood under that Article, the Court has stopped short of finding that restrictions on such family life – such as the exclusion of same-sex couples from the joint adoption process – constitute a breach of their rights under that Article.

4.3.2 *Ireland*

Until recently in Ireland, same-sex couples could not jointly adopt a child together. Under the Adoption Act 2010, adoption was only available to married couples or single persons.[65] As marriage was not available to same-sex couples prior to 2015,[66] this meant that a single gay or lesbian

[63] *In the Matter of an Application by the Northern Ireland Human Rights Commission* [2013] NICA 37.

[64] Committee on the Rights of the Child, above n. 29, para. 32.

[65] Adoption Act 2010, ss 33–34.

[66] Same-sex couples may now enter into civil marriages in Ireland following the enactment of the Marriage Act 2015 which was introduced on foot of the Thirty-Fourth Amendment of the Constitution (Marriage Equality) Act 2015.

person could adopt a child, but a same-sex couple could not. Furthermore, section 33 of the Adoption Act 2010 precluded the recognition of adoptions effected outside of the State where the adopters were a same-sex couple.[67] Under this provision, the Adoption Authority could only recognise an adoption by more than two persons effected in a foreign jurisdiction where the applicants were a married couple.[68] Therefore, a foreign adoption by a same-sex couple (whether domestic or intercountry) could not be recognised in Ireland.

The Children and Family Relationships Act 2015 made significant changes to the eligibility criteria for adoption. Section 114 of the 2015 Act amended section 33 of the Adoption Act 2010 to provide that married couples, single persons, civil partners and cohabiting couples were eligible to adopt. These provisions were never commenced. Instead, the adoption provisions set out in the 2015 Act were transferred to the Adoption (Amendment) Act 2017. Following commencement of that Act, civil partners and cohabiting couples of the same or opposite sex are now eligible to apply to jointly adopt a child for the first time in Ireland.[69] Married couples and single persons also remain eligible to apply for adoption.[70]

Second-parent adoption is also addressed in the 2017 Act. The 2017 Act amends the Adoption Act 2010 to provide that where a child is adopted by a step-parent, the child is deemed to be the child of that step-parent and the step-parent's spouse, civil partner or cohabitant, as the case may be.[71] The step-parent is defined as the spouse, civil partner or cohabitant of a birth parent.[72] In order to be eligible to adopt, the child must have lived with the step-parent and the birth parent for a continuous period of not less than two years.[73]

The provisions relating to second-parent adoption represent long overdue reform of Irish adoption law. Prior to the enactment of the 2017 Act, there was no specific provision for second-parent adoption in Ireland. This meant that where a step-parent wished to adopt their partner's child, the effect of the adoption order was to terminate the legal parental rights and responsibilities of the birth parent and to

67 Adoption Act 2010, s 33(1).

68 Adoptions by single persons could also be recognised.

69 Adoption Act 2010, s 33, amended by Adoption (Amendment) Act 2017, s 16.

70 Adoption Act 2010, s 33, amended by Adoption (Amendment) Act 2017, s 16.

71 Adoption Act 2010, s 58A, inserted by Adoption (Amendment) Act 2017, s 26.

72 Adoption Act 2010, s 37(b), amended by Adoption (Amendment) Act 2017, s 18.

73 Adoption Act 2010, s 37(b) as amended by Adoption (Amendment) Act 2017, s 18.

transfer all parental rights to the step-parent. Consequently, in a situation where the step-parent wished to adopt the child, the birth parent (who already had full parental responsibilities and rights in respect of the child) was required to give up their existing parental rights and to jointly adopt the child alongside the step-parent. This was an overly burdensome requirement with negative consequences for all stakeholders. The process had implications for the child's right to identity and arguably ran contrary to the best interests principle. The child's right to identity was concerned because, in effecting this form of adoption, the biological child thereafter became the adoptive child of the birth parent. Although the adoption would not disrupt the child's day-to-day life, the child's legal status changed in respect of the biological parent. As Margaret Dromey, former chief executive of Treoir,[74] noted, the previous process meant that 'when a child produces a certificate, it is an adoption certificate and no longer a birth certificate, and that is an issue that can be difficult for people'.[75] Thus, the introduction of specific provisions to facilitate second-parent adoption is most welcome.

Overall, the new provisions concerning adoption in Ireland are positive as they allow for children who are being raised jointly by same-sex couples to benefit from the security of adoption by their social parent, if this is deemed appropriate in their particular circumstances. As was discussed in the previous section, adoption may not be appropriate in every case given that its effect is to extinguish all legal ties between the child and the birth parents. However, given that the best interests of the child are to be assessed on a case-by-case basis, the widest range of options should be available to ensure that the best interests of the individual child can be met. Second-parent adoption should not be encouraged or discouraged but instead be seen simply as another option available to ensure that the best interests of the individual child can be realised.

The Irish legislation imposes some restrictions on the use of second-parent adoption. It is only available where the second parent is the spouse, civil partner or cohabitant of one of the legal parents. In addition, the second parent must care for the child for at least two years before they are eligible to apply for adoption. As such, there is a two-year waiting period before second-parent adoption can be used. Where the child is less than two years of age, only joint adoption is possible whereby the birth

[74] Treoir is an organisation that represents unmarried parents in Ireland.

[75] Fiona Gartland, 'Change sought to anomaly in adoption law' *Irish Times*, 28 June 2014.

parent is required to give up their existing parental rights in order to jointly adopt with the second parent in the manner described above.

Irish law does not prevent the use of second-parent adoption in respect of a child who was already subject to an intercountry adoption order.[76] Given that intercountry adoption is now the most common form of adoption in Ireland,[77] it will be interesting to see how the Irish courts approach applications for second-parent adoption in these circumstances should any such case arise. It is unlikely that the legislation would be interpreted as imposing a prohibition on second-parent adoption in this context. Article 42A.3 of the Irish Constitution provides that '[p]rovision shall be made by law for the voluntary placement for adoption and the adoption of *any* child'.[78] Thus, any prohibition on the adoption of certain categories of children would arguably run contrary to the constitutional mandate. Moreover, as previously noted, the best interests of the child must be assessed on a case-by-case basis. A blanket ban on second-parent adoption following intercountry adoption would impede assessment of the best interests of the child. Any court considering an application for second-parent adoption in respect of a child who was previously subject to an intercountry adoption order will have to consider the child's best interests in light of the actual circumstances of the case. In deciding on any adoption application, the Irish courts must consider the best interests of the child and are directed to take account of

(a) the child's age and maturity,
(b) the physical, psychological and emotional needs of the child,
(c) the likely effect of adoption on the child,
(d) the child's views on their proposed adoption,
(e) the child's social, intellectual and educational needs,
(f) the child's upbringing and care,
(g) the child's relationship with their parent, guardian or relative, as the case may be, and
(h) any other particular circumstances pertaining to the child concerned.[79]

[76] As noted earlier in the chapter, some Scandinavian countries impose this type of restriction.

[77] In 2016, 214 intercountry adoptions were registered in the register of intercountry adoptions, while 95 domestic adoption orders were granted. Adoption Authority of Ireland, above n. 3, 29.

[78] Bunreacht na hÉireann, Art 42A.3 [emphasis added].

[79] Adoption Act 2010, s 19(2), as amended by Adoption (Amendment) Act 2017, s 9.

This individualised assessment would be meaningless if a prohibition or presumption against second-parent adoption was applied by the courts in respect of a child originally subject to an intercountry adoption order. In this situation, in line with the arguments advanced earlier in this chapter, the child's need for security within their current family should weigh heavily in the best interests assessment.

The Irish reforms represent a major overhaul of adoption law in that country. The best interests of the child are now central to the adoption process and will determine the outcome of any application. Other areas of adoption law, however, still require attention. For example, at present in Ireland, adopted persons have no specific right of access to their birth records, which impedes attempts at contact between adoptees and their birth parents. The Adoption (Information and Tracing) Bill 2016 proposes to provide for a scheme whereby adoption information, including the information required to obtain a birth certificate, may be provided to an adopted person in certain circumstances and subject to conditions. This Bill is currently under consideration by the Irish Parliament. If enacted, it will result in further changes to Irish law, but the suitability of the reforms will depend on the final agreed text.[80]

4.3.3 *South Africa*

In South Africa, the joint adoption of children by same-sex couples has been possible since the Constitutional Court judgment of *Du Toit and De Vos* v. *Minister of Welfare and Others*[81] was handed down in 2002. In this case, the Constitutional Court found that provisions which excluded same-sex couples from the joint adoption process were unconstitutional on the basis that they did not adhere to the paramountcy of the best interests principle as enshrined in section 28(2) of the South African Constitution[82] and further that the provisions infringed the principle of equality as set out in section 9(3).[83]

[80] Many adopted persons have expressed dissatisfaction with the provisions proposed in the Adoption (Information and Tracing) Bill 2016 as it stands at the time of writing. See: Lydia Bracken, *Child Law in Ireland* (Dublin: Clarus Press, 2018), pp. 138–141.

[81] *Du Toit and De Vos* v. *Minister of Welfare and Others* (CCT 40/01) [2002] ZACC 20.

[82] Section 28(2) of the Constitution of the Republic of South Africa provides that '[a] child's best interests are of paramount importance in every matter concerning the child'.

[83] Section 9(3) of the Constitution of the Republic of South Africa provides that '[t]he state may not unfairly discriminate directly or indirectly against anyone on one or more grounds, including race, gender, sex, pregnancy, marital status, ethnic or social origin,

The applicants in this case were partners in a long-standing lesbian relationship. Pursuant to sections 17(a), 17(c) and 20(1) of the Child Care Act 1983 and section 1(2) of the Guardianship Act 1993, the joint adoption and guardianship of children were confined exclusively to married couples. As the applicants were not permitted to marry under South African law at that time,[84] it was decided that the second applicant would alone become the adoptive parent of two children. Some years later, the couple instituted proceedings challenging the constitutionality of the above-mentioned provisions. They argued, inter alia, that the provisions violated the applicants' rights to equality and dignity and that they did not give paramountcy to the best interests of the child as required by section 28(2) of the South African Constitution. The High Court found that the contested provisions violated the Constitution and ordered the reading in of certain words into the impugned provisions so as to allow for joint adoption and guardianship of children by same-sex life partners.[85] The applicants subsequently sought confirmation of same from the Constitutional Court.[86]

The Constitutional Court noted that the impugned provisions affected persons who, but for the fact that they were unmarried same-sex partners, would otherwise meet the criteria for eligibility for adoption.[87] According to the Court, such exclusion

> surely defeats the very essence and social purpose of adoption which is to provide the stability, commitment, affection and support important to a child's development, which can be offered by suitably qualified persons ... Excluding partners in same sex life partnerships from adopting children jointly where they would otherwise be suitable to do so is in conflict with the principle [of the paramountcy of the best interests of the child].[88]

colour, sexual orientation, age, disability, religion, conscience, belief, culture, language and birth'.

84 South Africa extended marriage rights to same-sex couples in 2006. See: Civil Union Act 17 of 2006.

85 The High Court judgment is reported as *Du Toit and Another* v. *Minister of Welfare and Population Development and Others* 2001 (12) BCLR 1225.

86 Such confirmation is required under South African law. Section 172(2)(a) of the Constitution of the Republic of South Africa provides that '[t]he Supreme Court of Appeal, a High Court or a court of similar status may make an order concerning the constitutional validity of an Act of Parliament, a provincial Act or any conduct of the President, but an order of constitutional invalidity has no force unless it is confirmed by the Constitutional Court'.

87 *Du Toit and De Vos* v. *Minister of Welfare and Others* (CCT 40/01) [2002] ZACC 20, para. 21.

88 Above, paras. 21–22.

The Court found that the applicants were highly suitable to adopt and so preventing them from doing so served to 'deprive children of the possibility of a loving and stable family life'.[89] The Court held that the contested provisions failed to accord paramountcy to the best interests of the child as required by section 28(2) of the Constitution and therefore were in breach of that constitutional guarantee. Following this finding, the Court went on to read into the legislation wording to allow for joint adoption and guardianship by same-sex couples. In doing so, however, the Court was careful to emphasise that

> in each decision concerning adoption, prospective adoptive parents should be evaluated on a case-by-case basis as provided for in the Child Care Act. In so doing, care will be taken to ensure that only suitable couples will be entitled to adopt children jointly.[90]

Section 231 of the Children's Act 2005 now makes statutory provision for joint adoptions by same-sex couples. This section provides that a child may be adopted jointly by

(i) a husband and wife;
(ii) partners in a permanent domestic life-partnership; or
(iii) other persons sharing a common household and forming a permanent family unit.[91]

The terms 'husband and wife' must be read as including a reference to civil union partners.[92] As such, both married and unmarried same-sex couples are permitted to jointly adopt under South African law. In addition, the Children's Act 2005 specifically allows for the spouse or partner of a parent to adopt the child of that parent.[93] Until recently, however, there was some confusion among the South African courts as to whether this form of second-parent adoption was legally permissible. This confusion stemmed from the fact that section 230(3) of the Children's Act 2005 provides that a child shall be 'adoptable' where

(a) the child is an orphan and has no guardian or care-giver who is willing to adopt the child;
(b) the whereabouts of the child's parent or guardian cannot be established;

[89] Above, para. 22
[90] Above, para. 43.
[91] Children's Act 38 of 2005, s 231(1)(a).
[92] Civil Union Act 17 of 2006, s 13(2)(b).
[93] Children's Act 38 of 2005, s 231(1)(c).

(c) the child has been abandoned;
(d) the child's parent or guardian has abused or deliberately neglected the child, or has allowed the child to be abused or deliberately neglected; or
(e) the child is in need of a permanent alternative placement.[94]

The above provision made it unclear as to whether a step-child was an 'adoptable' child for the purposes of the statute. In particular, given that the step-child would already have at least one guardian, it was felt that they would not be adoptable under section 230(3).[95]

Furthermore, section 242 of the 2005 Act provides that the effect of an adoption order is to terminate 'all parental responsibilities and rights any person, including a parent, step-parent or partner in a domestic life partnership, had in respect of the child immediately before the adoption'.[96] As a result of this provision, the Children's Courts developed a policy of refusing applications for second-parent adoptions on the basis that it was understood that the biological parent would lose their parental rights in respect of the child if the adoption was allowed to take place.[97]

These issues were finally resolved by the Pretoria High Court in *Centre for Child Law* v. *Minister of Social Development*.[98] This case was instituted by the Centre for Child Law[99] following a number of approaches from parents, step-parents and practitioners who had been turned away from the Children's Court when seeking to apply for adoption by a step-parent. The Centre sought a number of orders from the court, including orders

(i) declaring that section 230(3) of the Children's Act 2005 did not preclude a child from being adoptable in cases where the child has a guardian and where the person seeking to adopt is the spouse or permanent life-partner of the guardian of the child; and
(ii) declaring that s 242 of the Act did not automatically terminate all of the parental responsibilities and rights of the guardian of a child whose spouse or permanent life-partner seeks to adopt the child.[100]

[94] Children's Act 38 of 2005, s 230(3).
[95] *Centre for Child Law* v. *Minister of Social Development* 2014 (1) SA 577 (GSJ), para. 7.
[96] Children's Act 38 of 2005, s 242(1).
[97] *Centre for Child Law* v. *Minister of Social Development*, 2014 (1) SA 577 (GSJ), paras 4–5.
[98] Above.
[99] The Centre for Child Law is a law clinic whose objective is to contribute, within its means, to establish and promote the best interests of the child and to use the law as an instrument to advance such interests.
[100] *Centre for Child Law* v. *Minister of Social Development* 2014 (1) SA 577 (GSJ), para. 1.

According to the High Court, where a non-custodian parent has consented to the adoption of their child, such parent had to be taken to have 'abandoned' the child as contemplated in section 230(3)(c).[101] The Court noted that the term 'abandoned' was defined in section 1 of the Children's Act 2005 to mean 'a child who has obviously been deserted by the parent, guardian or care-giver'.[102] According to the Court, this definition did not require that the child be abandoned by both parents. As such, the Court was satisfied that where a non-custodian parent consents to the adoption of their child by the spouse or partner of the custodian parent, it followed that the child would be 'adoptable' in those circumstances within the meaning of section 230(3)(c).[103]

The Court also found that a child could be deemed to have been 'abandoned' where the child has, for no apparent reason, had no contact with the parent, guardian or care-giver for a period of at least three months. Again, the Court opined that this definition did not require that the child must have had no contact with both parents for this period. Similarly, the Court held that a child could be deemed to be adoptable in terms of section 230(3)(b) of the Children's Act 2005 where the whereabouts of one of the guardians could not be established and further that this section did not require that the whereabouts of both parents or guardians must be unknown.[104]

In relation to section 242, the High Court noted that the Children's Court had overlooked the fact that this section states that the effect of an adoption order is to terminate the responsibilities and rights of the parents 'except when provided otherwise in the order'.[105] Consequently, the High Court found that the Children's Court has discretion to order that the responsibilities and rights of a child's parent or guardian will not terminate upon the granting of an adoption order to the step-parent. According to the High Court, '[i]t will, save in exceptional circumstances, clearly be in the best interests of the child that such

101 Above, para. 8.

102 Above.

103 Above. This finding presents an interesting contrast to the Irish judgment of *N* v. *Health Service Executive* [2006] 4 IR 374. In that case, the Supreme Court found that the natural parents of a child had not failed in their duties towards her (as previously set out in Art 42.5 of the Irish Constitution) by placing the child for adoption and, as such, the child was returned to the natural parents. Essentially, the Court was satisfied that placing the child for adoption did not constitute abandonment by the parents.

104 *Centre for Child Law* v. *Minister of Social Development* 2014 (1) SA 577 (GSJ), para. 9.

105 Children's Act 38 of 2005, s 242.

an order be made'.[106] As a result, the reliefs sought by the Centre for Child Law were granted by the Court. Therefore, second-parent adoption in South Africa permits a same-sex partner or spouse to adopt their partner's biological or adoptive child without terminating the first parent's legal status as a parent, and it has been acknowledged by the High Court that this situation will typically be in the best interests of the child.[107]

4.3.4 *Summary of Comparative Jurisdictions*

The discussion above shows that each comparator jurisdiction allows same-sex couples to apply to adopt children and offers flexibility in the regulation of adoption law that enables the best interests of the child to be assessed on a case-by-case basis. Case law from Northern Ireland and South Africa emphasises the need for individualised best interests assessments in adoption, which cannot be achieved where certain prospective adopters are precluded entirely from the process. It is argued that this case law supports the contention that the widest range of legal options should be available to recognise the lived reality and best interests of individual children. In this vein, it is further argued that the best interests principle can be used to demand that same-sex couples should have access to both second-parent adoption and joint adoption to ensure that the broad range of mechanisms necessary to secure the child's best interests are in place.

The ECtHR has taken a more restrictive approach to cases concerning same-sex adoption. Although it is noted that the ECtHR is constrained by its supervisory and subsidiary jurisdiction, it is argued that the approach of the Court in cases concerning same-sex parenting has failed to adequately consider the position and rights of children who are at the centre of such cases. It is thus instructive to contrast the ECtHR jurisprudence with that of the comparator jurisdictions addressed above.

4.4 Approach of the ECtHR

Article 8 of the ECHR protects the right to respect for private and family life. In a number of cases decided by the ECtHR, this article has operated to advance the rights of gay and lesbian parents and to ensure that they do

[106] *Centre for Child Law* v. *Minister of Social Development* 2014 (1) SA 577 (GSJ), para. 14.
[107] Above.

not experience discrimination as a result of their sexual orientation.[108] The Court has not yet extended this reasoning to joint adoption by same-sex couples. In *X and Others* v. *Austria*,[109] the ECtHR held that Article 14 ECHR, taken in conjunction with Article 8 ECHR, had been breached by provisions that excluded same-sex couples from the second-parent adoption process. In so holding, however, the Court emphasised that the ruling did not concern the wider question of parenting rights for same-sex couples but was confined to the particular circumstances of the case. For the most part, the ECtHR has emphasised that adoption falls within the margin of appreciation of each State, and so there is no general right to apply to adopt under the ECHR.[110]

This section examines recent case law from the ECtHR to understand the approach of the Court in cases concerning joint adoption by same-sex couples. It is submitted that, in these cases, the ECtHR failed to adequately consider the rights and interests of the child. It is argued that consideration of the best interests of the child may in fact demand that the opportunity to jointly adopt is extended to same-sex couples.

4.4.1 *Adoption and Marriage*

In many countries, the inability of same-sex couples to jointly adopt takes the form of an indirect prohibition: joint adoption is only available to married couples and marriage itself is confined to opposite-sex couples.[111] As a result, adoption becomes inextricably linked with marriage, and so same-sex couples' inability to access to marriage creates the indirect barrier to adoption.

In *Schalk & Kopf* v. *Austria*,[112] the ECtHR held that laws that prevented same-sex couples from entering into (same-sex) marriage were not a violation of their rights under Article 8 ECHR nor under Article 12 ECHR (the right to marry). The Court found that the right to marry that is enshrined in Article 12 is no longer limited to marriage between two persons of the opposite sex. However, the Court held that 'the question

[108] For example, *Salgueiro Da Silva Mouta* v. *Portugal*, app. no. 33290/96, 21 December 1999; *EB* v. *France*, app. no. 43546/02, 22 January 2008; See further Lydia Bracken, 'Strasbourg's response to gay and lesbian parenting: Progress, then plateau?' (2016) 24 *International Journal of Children's Rights* 358.

[109] *X and Others* v. *Austria*, app. no. 19010/07, 19 February 2013.

[110] *Gas and Dubois* v. *France*, app. no. 25951/07, 15 March 2012.

[111] This was the situation in Ireland prior to the introduction of the Marriage Act 2015.

[112] *Schalk & Kopf* v. *Austria*, app. no. 30141/04, 24 June 2010.

whether or not to allow same-sex marriage is left to regulation by the national law of the Contracting State'.[113] This conclusion was influenced by the fact that there was no European consensus on the question of same-sex marriage at the time of the judgment with just six of the forty-seven Contracting States allowing for same.[114] The ECtHR did, however, find, for the first time in this case, that 'family life' as understood under Article 8 existed between the members of the same-sex couple.

In the subsequent case of *Oliari and Others* v. *Italy*,[115] the ECtHR found that there is a positive obligation on States to allow for registered partnerships to take place between persons of the same sex. According to the Court, '[t]o find otherwise today, the Court would have to be unwilling to take note of the changing conditions in Italy and be reluctant to apply the Convention in a way which is practical and effective'.[116] The Court stopped short, however, of finding that this positive obligation should also extend to marriage. Although it was noted that the number of European countries that recognise same-sex marriage had increased since the judgment in *Schalk*, there was not yet a consensus on the matter. Consequently, the Court was satisfied that the question of whether to allow for same-sex marriage remained a matter that fell within the margin of appreciation of each Member State.[117]

Thus, the ECtHR has indicated that until there is a European consensus on the question of same-sex marriage, access to same will fall within the margin of appreciation of each State. The margin of appreciation is the means through which effect is given to the principle of subsidiarity. The Contracting States have primary responsibility for securing the rights and freedoms contained in the ECHR, while the European Court exercises a supervisory role. Various factors determine the breadth of the margin of appreciation in a particular situation. Often, the existence or non-existence of a European consensus will be influential: where there is no European consensus on a particular matter, the State is generally afforded a wide margin of appreciation to make decisions in that area; where there is a European consensus, the margin will be narrowed. In questions concerning marriage and the family, States are also typically afforded a large measure of regulatory discretion on the basis that the national authorities are 'better placed' than the ECtHR to

113 Above, para. 61.
114 Above, para. 58.
115 *Oliari and Others* v. *Italy*, app. nos. 18766/11 and 36030/11, 21 July 2015.
116 Above, para. 186.
117 Above, para. 192.

understand local conditions affecting these areas. As discussed below, this approach was adopted in *Gas and Dubois* v. *France*,[118] to find that there was no violation of the ECHR where a woman was prevented from adopting the child of her partner.

4.4.2 Gas and Dubois *v.* France

In *Gas and Dubois*, one partner in a same-sex couple sought to adopt a six-year-old child born to the other partner by artificial insemination. The child had lived all her life in the applicants' shared home. The application for simple adoption was refused by the domestic courts on the basis that Article 365 of the French Civil Code would have operated to terminate the birth mother's parental responsibility in respect of the child and to transfer it to her partner if the adoption order was made. An exception to this situation existed under Article 365 whereby the parental responsibility of the birth parent did not terminate upon the adoption of the child by the 'spouse' of the birth parent. The applicants in the instant case had entered into a *pacte civil de solidarité* (PACS) but were not regarded as 'spouses'. Consequently, the French tribunal reasoned that it was not in the best interests of the child for the adoption to take place due to the consequences this would have for the child's legal relationship with her birth mother. This refusal was upheld by the Versailles Court of Appeal.

The applicants subsequently brought a case to the ECtHR arguing that, as a same-sex couple, they had been subjected to an unjustified difference in treatment compared with opposite-sex couples, whether married or not, because they could not avail of the 'spousal exception' contained in Article 365 of the Civil Code. They argued that this difference in treatment was contrary to Articles 8 and 14 ECHR.

The ECtHR began its assessment by noting that, in order for an issue to arise under Article 14 ECHR, there must be a difference in the treatment of persons in relevantly similar situations and that the difference in treatment will only amount to discrimination where the action does not pursue a legitimate aim or where it violates the principle of proportionality. It was therefore necessary to first compare the applicants' legal situation with that of a married couple. Following the reasoning in *Schalk*, the Court noted that the ECHR does not impose an obligation on Member States to allow same-sex couples to marry and that where

[118] *Gas and Dubois* v. *France*, app. no. 25951/07, 15 March 2012.

Member States offer same-sex couples some form of legal recognition (such as civil partnership or PACS), they enjoy a wide margin of appreciation in determining the exact nature of the status conferred. In considering whether the applicants' position was sufficiently similar to that of a married couple, the Court emphasised that 'marriage confers a special status on those who enter into it'[119] and that it gives rise to social, personal and legal consequences. For the purpose of second-parent adoption, the applicants' legal situation was not comparable to that of a married couple.

By contrast, the ECtHR found that the applicant's position was comparable to that of an unmarried opposite-sex couple. However, given that unmarried opposite-sex partners were also excluded from the Article 365 spousal exception, the Court did not find any discrimination on the basis of sexual orientation.[120] The Court also rejected the applicants' argument based on indirect discrimination (the couple, in contrast to opposite-sex couples, could not get married in order to take advantage of Article 365). In considering this contention, the Court simply referred back to Article 12 ECHR and restated its findings in relation to access to marriage for same-sex couples.[121]

It is well established in the case law of the ECtHR that Article 14 ECHR allows States to impose differential treatment upon similarly placed individuals where such treatment pursues a legitimate aim.[122] Moreover, as was discussed earlier, States enjoy a wide margin of appreciation in matters pertaining to marriage and the family. Thus, the Court's finding in *Gas* that marriage confers a 'special status' on those who enter into it and that married couples can legitimately avail of an adoption regime that is denied to other couples, while at the same time restricting access to marriage, aligns with the prior jurisprudence of the court.

However, while differential treatment concerning adults may be permissible in these circumstances, it is argued that different considerations arise when the rights of the child are considered. The child in this case was clearly treated differently to the child of a married opposite-sex couple as she could not be adopted by her social parent, but the child of a married opposite-sex couple could be. This difference in treatment derived from the fact that her parents were part of a same-sex couple and

[119] Above, para. 68.
[120] Above, para. 69.
[121] Above, paras. 70–71.
[122] See, for example, *Saucedo Gomez* v. *Spain*, app. no. 37784/97, 26 January 1999.

was thus a difference in treatment based on sexual orientation. Yet, one struggles to find any analysis of the rights and interests of the child in the majority judgment. Only the dissenting judgment of Judge Villiger addressed the position of the child. Judge Villiger found that the child had been subject to differential treatment as she could not be adopted by the partner of her parent, whereas the child of a married opposite-sex couple could be. The judge concluded that this difference of treatment could not be justified from the perspective of the child's best interests.[123] According to the judge:

> In the best interests of a child born into a same-sex relationship, I believe that the child should be offered the best possible treatment afforded to other children born into a heterosexual relationship – which is joint parental custody.[124]

In line with Article 21 UNCRC, the best interests of the child are to be paramount in cases of adoption, and those best interests must be assessed on a case-by-case basis. The ECtHR is permitted to make reference to the UNCRC and has frequently applied the best interests principle as the 'paramount consideration' in cases concerning children.[125] Indeed, regardless of the breadth of the margin of appreciation in a particular case, the ECtHR has indicated that the best interests of the child must always be paramount in the decision-making process. As the Court stated in *Mennesson* v. *France* (a case concerning surrogacy):

> the solutions reached by the legislature – even within the limits of this margin – are not beyond the scrutiny of the Court. It falls to the Court to . . . determine whether a fair balance has been struck between the competing interests of the State and those directly affected by that solution . . . In doing so, it must have regard to the essential principle according to which, whenever the situation of a child is in issue, the best interests of that child are paramount.[126]

Therefore, although States enjoy a wide margin of appreciation in cases concerning family life, particularly where there is no European consensus on the matter, the best interests of the child must still be paramount. In *Gas*, the interests of the child were not even considered by the majority of the court and certainly were not 'paramount' in the decision. The Court

[123] Dissenting Opinion of Judge Villiger. *Gas and Dubois v France*, app. no. 25951/07, 15 March 2012, p. 24.

[124] Above, 25.

[125] See, for example, *Yousef* v. *Netherlands*, app. no. 33711/96, 5 November 2002.

[126] *Mennesson* v. *France*, app. no. 65192/11, 26 September 2014, para. 81.

approached the issues purely from the perspective of the adult applicants without considering the disadvantaged position of the child vis-à-vis other children.

It should also be noted that the margin of appreciation afforded to the State will normally be restricted where the case concerns a particularly important facet of an individual's existence or identity[127] or where it is based on sex or sexual orientation.[128] In these situations, there is a burden on the State to show that the difference in treatment is necessary to achieve the stated legitimate aim.[129] In *Gas*, the French Government argued that restricting the spousal exception to married couples was designed to safeguard children's interests because marriage offers greater stability to children.[130] However, as has been seen in Chapter 2, there is no evidence to suggest that children raised by unmarried same-sex couples are disadvantaged when compared to those raised by married couples. Moreover, it must be acknowledged that marriage is not a guarantee of stability. As Baroness Hale noted in *Re P*, '[t]he law cannot force any couple, married or unmarried, to stay together'.[131] All of these considerations create considerable doubt as to whether the restriction on second-parent adoption by same-sex couples was in fact proportionate when considered from the perspective of the child.[132]

The *Gas* case represents an adult-centred view of adoption, which is in complete contrast to the approach of the courts in the comparator jurisdictions. As has been seen in the case law of South Africa and Northern Ireland, the best interests principle provides a powerful basis from which to argue that joint adoption rights should be made available to same-sex couples. As such, it is submitted that the ECtHR's failure to consider the best interests of the child in *Gas* represents a significant oversight. The best interests principle is not only a right but also an interpretive principle, and so it is argued that the issues in cases of adoption must be considered from the perspective of the child's best interests in cases heard by the ECtHR.[133]

[127] *Evans* v. *United Kingdom*, app. no. 6339/05, 10 April 2004.

[128] *Karner* v. *Austria*, app. no. 40016/98, 24 July 2003.

[129] Above.

[130] *Gas and Dubois v France*, app. no. 25951/07, 15 March 2012, para. 49.

[131] *Re P (Adoption: Unmarried Couple)* [2008] UKHL 38, para. 108.

[132] See further: Bracken, above n. 108.

[133] For a children's rights revision of the *Gas* judgment see: Lydia Bracken, 'Gas and Dubois v France' in Helen Stalford, Kathryn Hollingsworth and Stephen Gilmore (eds.), *Rewriting Children's Rights Judgments From Academic Vision to New Practice* (Oxford: Hart Publishing, 2017).

4.4.3 X and Others *v.* Austria

In the later case of *X and Others* v. *Austria*,[134] the ECtHR held that provisions that excluded same-sex couples from the second-parent adoption process violated Article 14 ECHR, taken in conjunction with Article 8 ECHR. In this case, the impugned Austrian law permitted the unmarried opposite-sex partner of the parent to adopt the child of their partner in a manner that did not affect the status of that parent. By contrast, the adoption of a partner's child by an unmarried same-sex partner had the effect of severing the relationship between the parent and child. Due to these specific circumstances, the Court emphasised that the case did not concern 'the question of adoption by same-sex couples in general' but was 'a narrowly defined issue of alleged discrimination between unmarried different-sex couples and same-sex couples in respect of second-parent adoption'.[135] The principal consideration for the Court was whether the exclusion of unmarried same-sex couples from the second-parent adoption process served a legitimate aim and whether it was proportionate to that aim.

From the outset, the ECtHR found that there was 'no doubt' that the law created a distinction between unmarried opposite-sex and same-sex couples in respect of second-parent adoption.[136] The Court found that the unmarried female couple (the first and third applicants) were in a comparable position to an unmarried opposite-sex couple and noted that unmarried opposite-sex couples were permitted to avail of second-parent adoption under the Austrian law. The Court was satisfied that the difference in treatment was 'inseparably linked to the fact that the first and third applicants formed a same-sex couple, and was thus based on their sexual orientation'.[137] This point distinguished the instant case from the Court's previous ruling in *Gas and Dubois* because, in that case, the French law denied second-parent adoption to all unmarried couples regardless of their sexual orientation.[138]

The Austrian Government submitted that the contested provisions served a legitimate aim in that they were designed to protect the traditional family. This assertion was based on the argument that 'in accordance with biological reality, a minor child should have two persons of

[134] *X and Others* v. *Austria*, app. no. 19010/07, 19 February 2013.
[135] Above, para. 134.
[136] Above, para. 116.
[137] Above, para. 130.
[138] Above, para. 131.

opposite sex as parents'.[139] The ECtHR noted that the protection of the traditional family is 'in principle, a weighty and legitimate reason which might justify a difference in treatment'.[140] However, the Court noted that, in making such an argument, the burden of proof was on the Government to show that the protection of the traditional family and the protection of the child's interests required the exclusion of same-sex couples from second-parent adoption. The Austrian Government had not provided any evidence to this effect. On the contrary, the Government conceded that same-sex couples could be 'as suitable or unsuitable' as opposite-sex couples as potential adopters.[141] The ECtHR further noted that the Austrian law lacked consistency in that single gay and lesbian persons were permitted to adopt and where the single adopter had a registered same-sex partner, that partner's consent was required before the adoption could take place. The Court was satisfied that this situation demonstrated that '[t]he legislature therefore accepts that a child may grow up in a family based on a same-sex couple, thus accepting that this is not detrimental to the child'.[142] The Court concluded that that there had been a violation of Article 14 ECHR, taken in conjunction with Article 8 ECHR.

Although *X and Others* v. *Austria* may be regarded as advancing the rights of same-sex couples with children, the significance of the judgment is limited by the specific facts of the case. The ruling does not impose a general obligation on States to make second-parent adoption available to same-sex couples. The decision simply indicates that where second-parent adoption is made available to unmarried opposite-sex couples, it is not legitimate to exclude unmarried same-sex couples from the process. By extension, the ruling also implies that where second-parent adoption is made available to married opposite-sex couples, it must also be available to married same-sex couples.

The judgment is disappointing for the lack of attention paid to the position of the child. Notwithstanding that the child was a party to the proceedings, the central question for the Court concerned the potential discrimination against the adults – there was no discussion of potential discrimination against the child caused by his lack of legal relationship with his second parent. Once more, the best interests of the child were not discussed as a substantive matter, which is another blemish in the

[139] Above, para. 137.
[140] Above, para. 138.
[141] Above, para. 72.
[142] Above, para. 144.

ECtHR's recent case law. As discussed above, it is arguable that a child-centred approach could radically alter the ECtHR's approach to cases concerning second-parent adoption by same-sex couples and may even demand that this form of adoption is made available.

The case may, however, indirectly support future challenges concerning the inability of same-sex couples to jointly adopt due to the Court's finding that the contested provisions were not required to protect the traditional family or to protect the interests of children. Given that these are the most common arguments raised against the legal recognition of same-sex parenting,[143] it will be much harder to now claim legitimate reasons for discrimination against same-sex parents in future cases. This, coupled with a child-centred approach to the decision-making could likely result in a finding of a violation of the ECHR in a future case concerning the inability of same-sex couples to jointly adopt.

4.5 Conclusion

This chapter has demonstrated the value of the best interests principle as an advocacy tool to advance the rights of children who are raised by same-sex couples. In particular, it has been argued that resourceful application of the principle could be used to demand that same-sex couples be permitted to apply for adoption. This argument is stronger where the child is already being raised by gay and lesbian parents, but equally it could be said that providing the widest range of prospective adoptive parents allows greater opportunity for the needs of individual children to be met. Furthermore, where second-parent adoption is made available to same-sex couples, the State will have acknowledged that same-sex couples are competent to act as joint adoptive parents. This negates any argument that same-sex couples should not be allowed to apply for the joint adoption of 'stranger' children. It is encouraging that the laws of England and Wales, Northern Ireland, Ireland and South Africa allow for this possibility.

Laws allowing for the adoption of children by same-sex couples are necessary to offer the child security within the family unit. The introduction of adoption laws may also have symbolic importance in that they have the potential to 'normalise' the concept of same-sex parenting by making such families more visible. Research in Ireland conducted prior to the introduction of joint adoption rights, for example, found that,

[143] See Chapter 2.

despite the existence of laws allowing for adoption by single persons (and a European Court judgment signalling that discrimination in this area is not tolerable),[144] many gay and lesbian persons had negative experiences when trying to adopt in Ireland.[145] It is to be hoped, therefore, that the introduction of laws expressly allowing for joint adoption by same-sex couples will lead to a change in this regard. Overall, the emphasis should be on the needs of children, and it is submitted that this emphasis provides a commanding argument as to why access to adoption for same-sex couples should be available.

144 *EB* v. *France*, app. no. 43546/02, 22 January 2008.

145 Jane Pillinger and Paula Fagan, *LGBT Parents in Ireland: Report from a study into the experiences of Lesbian, Gay, Bisexual and Transgender People in Ireland who are parents or who are planning parenthood* (Dublin: LGBT Diversity, 2013), p. 57.

5

Donor Conception

5.1 Introduction

Assisted human reproduction (AHR) involves several types of medical treatment designed to result in pregnancy. Donor conception is an increasingly common form of AHR.[1] This process involves the use of donated gametes (sperm/ova) or embryos as part of the conception. For female couples, this may involve the injection of semen into the vaginal tract in time with one partner's ovulation in an attempt to conceive a child. Reciprocal IVF may also be used by female couples whereby the eggs of one partner are inseminated in vitro with donor sperm and the resultant embryo is carried by the other partner. Male couples require the assistance of a surrogate to have a child through donor conception. As such, this chapter focuses on planned lesbian families created through donor conception, while Chapter 6 examines the use of surrogacy by male couples. Of course, lesbian couples may also engage in surrogacy, but this route to parentage is more commonly used by opposite-sex couples and male couples.

In most countries, the laws that apply to determine the parentage of children conceived by sexual intercourse between a man and woman do not, in themselves, accommodate the use of donor procedures. This is unsurprising given that the laws applicable to conception following sexual intercourse were developed long before donor conception was commonplace. Traditional parentage laws typically determine legal maternity based on the act of giving birth and legal paternity based on the marital status of the father or his genetic connection to the child. In the context of donor conception

[1] Susan Golombok, 'Lesbian mother families' *in Modern Families: Parents and Children in New Family Forms* (Cambridge: Cambridge University Press, 2015).

by lesbian couples, these provisions are insufficient as they do not recognise the position of the non-gestational female partner. This leaves the child in a vulnerable position as this partner, who will jointly raise and care for the child from birth, has no legal rights or responsibilities towards them.[2]

This chapter argues that the best interests of the child demand that specific laws are introduced to determine legal parentage in the context of donor conception and to ensure that the child's intended parents are recognised as legal parents, with full responsibilities and rights to care for the child from birth. The chapter examines the domestic laws of England and Wales, Ireland[3] and South Africa in an attempt to identify a way to regulate donor conception that aligns with the best interests of the child. The chapter draws on the conclusions of Chapters 1 and 2 in order to identify best practice in this area.

In addition to discerning the implications of the best interests principle in the context of parentage, the chapter addresses related aspects of donor conception that are particularly relevant to planned lesbian families, including the child's right to identity, retrospective parentage, non-clinical procedures and access to services. The chapter assesses the demands of the best interests principle in each of these areas to identify a framework for the regulation of donor conception that best supports the rights and interests of the child.

In this chapter, the terms 'donor conception' and 'donor insemination' will primarily be used. However, when discussing the laws of the comparator jurisdictions, the domestic terminology is adopted. Hence, the term 'donor insemination' is used when discussing the laws of England and Wales; in Ireland, the term 'donor-assisted human reproduction' or 'DAHR' is adopted, while in South Africa, the discussion centres on 'artificial fertilisation'.

[2] Recent news reports highlight this issue: 'Lesbian mums can't register baby in Italy' BBC News, 19 April 2018; Lydia Bracken, 'The kids are not alright: Why some children are in a legal bind' RTÉ Brainstorm, 25 May 2018.

[3] In European jurisdictions, donor conception is further regulated by the European Tissues and Cells Directive (Directive 2004/23/EC). That directive is not subject to scrutiny in this chapter as its provisions have largely been incorporated into the domestic legislation of EU countries.

5.2 The Legal Framework for Donor Conception in England and Wales, Ireland and South Africa

5.2.1 England and Wales: Human Fertilisation and Embryology Acts 1990 and 2008

5.2.1.1 Allocation of Parentage

The Human Fertilisation and Embryology Act 1990 broke new ground when it was first enacted in England and Wales. The legislation was the first in the world to create a national system of regulation for AHR with a specific body, the Human Fertilisation and Embryology Authority, to oversee all aspects of the regulation. The legislation provided that where a woman availed of reproductive treatment as part of a joint enterprise with either her spouse[4] or non-marital male partner,[5] that man would be regarded as the child's legal father. The sperm donor did not acquire any parental status.[6]

Same-sex couples were largely excluded from the provisions of the 1990 Act. As Gamble and Ghevaert note, 'the 1990 Act framed assisted reproduction law for heterosexual couples, aiming to shore up traditional family values and the institution of marriage and to discourage same sex and single parents'.[7] The first difficulty for same-sex couples seeking access to fertility treatment was that the parentage provisions did not offer any opportunity for the female partner of the birth mother to be recognised as a legal parent. This difficulty would be alleviated in later years due to the introduction of joint adoption for same-sex couples,[8] but it remained the case that same-sex couples could not be automatically regarded as joint legal parents at the time of the child's birth. Secondly, under the 1990 Act, clinics had to consider a child's 'need for a father' before offering treatment.[9] This provision was designed to make it more difficult for single women and lesbian couples to access treatment and resulted in a reluctance among many clinicians to treat women

[4] Human Fertilisation and Embryology Act 1990, s 28(2).
[5] Human Fertilisation and Embryology Act 1990. s 28(3).
[6] Human Fertilisation and Embryology Act 1990, s 28(4).
[7] Natalie Gamble and Louisa Ghevaert, 'The human fertilisation and embryology act 2008: Revolution or evolution?' (2009) 39 *Family Law* 730, p. 730.
[8] The Adoption and Children Act 2002 was fully implemented on 31 December 2005. This legislation allows for joint adoption by same-sex couples. Joint adoption for same-sex couples in England and Wales is discussed in Chapter 4 of this book.
[9] Human Fertilisation and Embryology Act 1990, s 13(5).

without a male partner.[10] The 'need for a father' consideration is discussed in detail later in this chapter.

The Human Fertilisation and Embryology Act 2008 was introduced to modernise the law and to accommodate same-sex couples who sought access to reproductive treatment. This legislation brought about important changes to the parentage provisions and to the licensing conditions. The 2008 Act allows for the female spouse,[11] civil partner[12] or female partner (who is not a party to a civil partnership)[13] of the woman receiving treatment to be regarded as the child's second legal parent.[14] The allocation of legal parentage to the female spouse or civil partner is automatic unless she is shown not to have consented to the birth mother's treatment at the relevant time.[15] Where the women are not married or not in a civil partnership, the partner will only be regarded as a parent where both parties have expressly consented to same.[16] The sperm donor will not acquire any legal connection to the child in question.[17] The 2008 Act also removed the 'need for a father' consideration and replaced it with a requirement that clinics consider the child's need for 'supportive parenting'.[18]

When considering a child's need for 'supportive parenting', the HFEA Code of Practice directs clinics to consider the following definition:

> Supportive parenting is a commitment to the health, wellbeing and development of the child. It is presumed that all prospective parents will be supportive parents, in the absence of any reasonable cause for concern that any child who may be born, or any other child, may be at risk of significant harm or neglect. Where centres have concern as to whether

[10] Eric Blyth, Vivian Burr and Abigail Farrand, 'Welfare of the child assessments in assisted conception: A social constructionist perspective' (2008) 26 *Journal of Reproductive and Infant Psychology* 31.

[11] Human Fertilisation and Embryology Act 2008, s 42, as amended by Marriage (Same-Sex Couples) Act 2013, Sch 7, para. 40.

[12] Human Fertilisation and Embryology Act 2008, s 42.

[13] Human Fertilisation and Embryology Act 2008, s 43.

[14] It should be noted that while the male partner of the birth mother is deemed to be the child's legal 'father', a female partner is not regarded as second 'mother' but rather as a 'second parent'. See Lydia Bracken, 'Challenging normative constructions of parentage in Ireland' (2017) 39 *Journal of Social Welfare and Family Law* 316.

[15] Human Fertilisation and Embryology Act 2008, s 42(1), as amended by Marriage (Same-Sex Couples) Act 2013, Sch 7, para. 40.

[16] Human Fertilisation and Embryology Act 2008, s 44.

[17] Human Fertilisation and Embryology Act 2008, s 41.

[18] Human Fertilisation and Embryology Act 2008, s 14(2).

this commitment exists, they may wish to take account of wider family and social networks within which the child will be raised.[19]

This definition establishes that there is a presumption in favour of providing treatment and that the burden of proof is on the clinic to establish that treatment should not be provided in a particular case. This reform has resulted in greater access to fertility services for lesbian women. Indeed, a study by Lee and others found that English clinics often view lesbian couples as 'ideal patients'.[20] The authors note that the presumption to treat, endorsed by the Code of Practice, has led to 'a continued trajectory towards the disappearance of group exclusions by clinics in relation to perceptions of the desirable family form'.[21]

5.2.1.2 Non-clinical Procedures

Where a married couple (whether of the opposite sex[22] or same sex[23]) or civil partners[24] engage in fertility treatment, the spouse or civil partner of the birth mother is automatically regarded as the child's second legal parent unless the partner or spouse did not consent to the treatment at the time of the procedure. Thus, the second parent is legally recognised regardless of whether the procedure takes place in a clinical or non-clinical setting. By contrast, where the couple are not married or not in a civil partnership, the second parent is only recognised as a legal parent where the treatment takes place 'under a license':[25] that is where the treatment takes place in a licensed fertility clinic.[26] As such, in respect of these couples, where the donor insemination has been carried out in a non-clinical setting which is not subject to a license, the second intending parent is not regarded as a legal parent upon the birth of the child.

[19] Human Fertilisation and Embryology Authority, *Code of Practice*, 9 ed. (London: Human Fertilisation and Embryology Authority, 2019), para. 8.15.

[20] Ellie Lee, Jan Macvarish and Sally Sheldon, 'Assessing child welfare under the human fertilisation and embryology act 2008: A case study in medicalisation?' (2014) 36 *Sociology of Health and Illness* 500, p. 501.

[21] Above, 511.

[22] Human Fertilisation and Embryology Act 2008, s 35.

[23] Human Fertilisation and Embryology Act 2008, s 42 as amended by Marriage (Same-Sex Couples) Act 2013, Sch 7, para. 40.

[24] Human Fertilisation and Embryology Act 2008, s 42.

[25] Human Fertilisation and Embryology Act 2008, ss 36 and 44.

[26] Human Fertilisation and Embryology Act 1990, Sch 2, outlines the activities for which a license may be granted. Para. 4 of Sch 2 provides that the license can only authorise activities to be carried on the premises specified in the license and under the supervision of an individual specified in the license.

The English legislation therefore creates a statutory presumption of parentage in favour of married couples and civil partners in respect of donor insemination. The inclusion of married same-sex couples and civil partners in this presumption is significant since most jurisdictions have confined such presumptions to married opposite-sex couples.[27] In Ireland, for example, the presumption of parentage is only available to married opposite-sex couples.[28] It is notable, therefore, that such a presumption is extended to married same-sex couples and civil partners in England and Wales, even if it is confined to the specific area of donor insemination. Where a child is conceived by non-clinical donor insemination and the parents are not married or in a civil partnership, the second parent is not automatically regarded as a legal parent and the child will not have a legal relationship with that parent at birth. Instead, the sperm donor would be regarded as the child's legal father. This situation is common across the three comparator jurisdictions discussed in this chapter. The implications of excluding non-clinical procedures from the parentage provisions that apply to clinical procedures, and the effect this has on the best interests of the child, are examined later in the chapter to consider whether the best interests principle requires that such procedures are subject to legal regulation.

5.2.2 Ireland: Children and Family Relationships Act 2015

Before 2015, there was no specific legislation in place in Ireland governing the allocation of parentage in situations where donor-assisted human reproduction (DAHR) was used. This meant that where a couple conceived a child by way of a donor procedure (using donated sperm/ovum/embryo), the woman who gave birth was regarded as the legal mother; if she was married, her husband was presumed to be the legal father;[29] and if she was unmarried, the man listed on the child's birth certificate was presumed to be the legal father.[30] This approach failed to accommodate the second intended parent (male or female) who was not genetically or gestationally connected to the child. In particular, where same-sex

[27] Bracken, above n. 14.

[28] Status of Children Act 1987, s 46(1). This provision is not amended by the Marriage Act 2015, which was introduced to allow for same-sex marriages to take place.

[29] Status of Children Act 1987, s 46(1), amended by Children and Family Relationships Act 2015, s 88.

[30] Status of Children Act 1987, s 46(3), amended by Children and Family Relationships Act 2015, s 88.

couples engaged in this process, the partner of the birth mother had no opportunity to be recognised as a legal parent at the time of the child's birth.

The Children and Family Relationships Act 2015 provides for the regulation of DAHR for the first time in Ireland. For the purpose of the legislation, DAHR is defined as a procedure where one or both of the gametes from which the embryo has been or will be formed have been provided by a donor, or where the embryo has been provided by a donor.[31] The Act does not comprehensively regulate DAHR; only certain aspects of the DAHR process are addressed, such as provisions to determine the parentage of children born through DAHR and safeguards for the child's right to identity. The Act does not regulate other issues pertaining to DAHR.

Although the Irish legislation was enacted in 2015, the provisions relating to DAHR (Parts 2 and 3) have not been commenced at the time of writing. As such, parentage continues to be allocated in the manner described above such that female same-sex couples cannot be jointly registered as legal parents where a child is born through DAHR – at present, only the birth mother can be legally recognised as a mother when the child is born. The delay in commencing the relevant provisions was initially due to a typographical error in the wording of a sub-section of the 2015 Act. This error was corrected by amending legislation in 2018.[32] Further errors were subsequently identified in Part 9 of the 2015 Act, which required amendment before the DAHR provisions could be commenced. These errors were addressed by the Civil Registration Act 2019. At the time of writing, the final barriers to commencement of Parts 2 and 3 of the 2015 Act concern administrative and operational arrangements that must be put in place by the Department of Health. These include the establishment of the National Donor-Conceived Person Register and the appointment of authorised persons for the purpose of the 2015 Act. Once these administrative matters are addressed, commencement will be possible by way of a statutory instrument.

The 2015 Act had been enacted weeks before Ireland's successful marriage equality referendum.[33] Afterwards, many same-sex couples married and started families through DAHR, expecting that the legislation would be commenced without delay. Unfortunately, the delay in

[31] Children and Family Relationships Act 2015, s 4.

[32] Children and Family Relationships (Amendment) Act 2018.

[33] The Children and Family Relationships Act 2015 was signed into law on 6 April 2015. Voting in the marriage equality referendum took place on 22 May 2015.

fixing the errors in the 2015 Act and the related delay in commencing the legislation meant that these families have had more than a four-year wait for legal recognition and have to rely on mechanisms such as guardianship (for which there is a two-year waiting period[34]) to establish a legal relationship between the second parent and the child. The best interests of children born into these families have effectively been ignored by the Irish legislature during this period as they are deprived of a legal relationship with the second parent during the first years of life. The commencement of Parts 2 and 3 of the 2015 Act must occur as a matter of urgency in order to safeguard the best interests of these children.

This section examines how the provisions of the 2015 Act that relate to DAHR will operate, once commenced, from the perspective of the best interests of the child. First, the allocation of parentage where conception takes place in the clinical setting is considered and it is questioned whether the relevant provisions will operate in the best interests of children. Second, provisions of the Act that will allow for the retrospective allocation of parentage in cases of DAHR are assessed. Third, the approach taken to the regulation of DAHR that takes place outside of the clinical setting is examined.

5.2.2.1 Allocation of Parentage

The 2015 Act provides that the parents of a child who is born following a DAHR procedure shall be the mother[35] and the spouse,[36] civil partner or cohabitant, as the case may be, of the mother.[37] If the mother is single, she alone shall be the parent of the child.[38] In neither case will the donor of genetic material be regarded as a parent of the child nor will they have any parental rights and duties in respect of the child.[39]

In order for parentage to be allocated to these persons, consents and declarations will be required from each of the parties.[40] The donor of genetic material must consent and make a declaration to the use of their

[34] See Chapter 3.
[35] Children and Family Relationships Act 2015, s 5(1)(a).
[36] Children and Family Relationships Act 2015, s 5(1)(b), as inserted by Marriage Act 2015, s 23.
[37] Children and Family Relationships Act 2015, s 5(1)(b).
[38] Children and Family Relationships Act 2015, s 5(2).
[39] Children and Family Relationships Act 2015, s 5(5).
[40] The legislation provides that the declarations of consent referred to in sections 6, 9 and 11 of the 2015 Act must be in 'such form as may be prescribed'. Regulations have not yet been introduced pursuant to section 41(1) of the 2015 Act prescribing the form of the consent to be used by fertility clinics.

gamete in a DAHR procedure and must declare that they understand that they will not be a parent of any child born through the use of such material following a DAHR procedure.[41] The intending mother is also required to consent and make a declaration to the effect that she agrees to her recognition as the legal mother of the child and that she agrees that the donor of genetic material will not be recognised as a legal parent.[42] In addition, where applicable, the intending mother must consent to the recognition of her spouse, civil partner or cohabitant, as the case may be, as the second legal parent of the child.[43] The spouse, civil partner or cohabitant must also consent and make a declaration to the effect that they agree to their recognition as the child's second legal parent and also that they understand that the donor of genetic material will not be regarded as a parent.[44]

Before these consents can be given, each of the parties must be provided with specific information about the implications of their role in the process.[45] Thereafter, the consents and declarations must be collected and retained by the operator of the DAHR facility, and they are required to transmit this information to the Minister for Health as required.[46] The operator is also obliged to inform the Minister of whether a pregnancy was achieved and also whether this pregnancy resulted in the birth of a child.[47]

Similar to the English provisions, the Irish legislation, once fully commenced, will allocate parentage to the second intending parent on the basis of their intention to be recognised as parent, which is demonstrated by providing consent in advance of the conception. Where the statutory parentage provisions apply, both intending parents will be recognised as legal parents from the moment of the child's birth and both parents will 'have all parental rights and duties in respect of the child' at birth.[48]

At first glance, one might assume that the concept of 'parental rights and duties' is equivalent to the rights and duties of guardianship that were examined in Chapter 3. There is no definition of 'parental rights and

[41] Children and Family Relationships Act 2015, s 6.
[42] Children and Family Relationships Act 2015, s 9.
[43] Children and Family Relationships Act 2015, s 9(3)(d), as amended by Marriage Act 2015, s 23.
[44] Children and Family Relationships Act 2015, s 11, as amended by Marriage Act 2015, s 23.
[45] Children and Family Relationships Act 2015, s 7 and s 13.
[46] Children and Family Relationships Act 2015, s 28.
[47] Children and Family Relationships Act 2015, s 28(4).
[48] Children and Family Relationships Act 2015, s 5(3).

duties' in the 2015 Act, but it is clear that it is not equivalent to guardianship since the allocation of guardianship in cases of DAHR is dealt with separately in the legislation. The guardianship provisions provide that the parent of a child born via DAHR who is married to the mother of the child shall be a guardian of the child;[49] a parent of a child born via DAHR who is a civil partner of the mother shall be a guardian;[50] and a parent who has been a cohabitant of the mother for not less than twelve consecutive months, including at least three months after the birth, shall be deemed to be a guardian.[51] Thus, given that a cohabitant parent will acquire 'all parental rights and duties' upon the birth of the child, but will not acquire guardianship until the specific time periods have been met, it is clear that 'parental rights and duties' and 'guardianship' are not synonymous. This point reinforces the argument made in Chapter 3 as to the importance of adopting appropriate definitions and terminology in child and family law.

5.2.2.2 Retrospective Parentage in Ireland

The Irish legislation governing the allocation of parentage in cases of DAHR was enacted in 2015, but the DAHR provisions have not yet been commenced at the time of writing. Children born through donor conception prior to commencement of Parts 2 and 3 of the 2015 Act are subject to the same rules of parentage that apply in situations where a child is conceived through sexual intercourse: the woman who gives birth to the child is regarded as the child's legal mother;[52] if she is married, her husband (but not her wife) is presumed to be the child's legal father;[53] and if she is not married, the man listed on the birth certificate is presumed to be the legal father.[54] Both presumptions can be rebutted where it is shown, on the balance of probabilities, that the man is not the father of the child. In this situation, the genetic father is regarded as the legal father. As noted earlier, this situation fails to accommodate lesbian couples who engage in DAHR

[49] Guardianship of Infants Act 1964, s 6B(1), as inserted by Children and Family Relationships Act 1964, s 49 and as amended by Marriage Act 2015, s 16(b).

[50] Guardianship of Infants Act 1964, s 6B(2)(a), as inserted by Children and Family Relationships Act 1964, s 49.

[51] Guardianship of Infants Act 1964, s 6B(2)(b), as inserted by Children and Family Relationships Act 1964, s 49.

[52] *MR* v. *An tArd Chláraitheoir* [2014] 3 IR 533.

[53] Status of Children Act 1987, s 46(1).

[54] Status of Children Act 1987, s 46(3), amended by Children and Family Relationships Act 2015, s 88.

as the non-birth mother has no opportunity to be recognised as a legal parent upon the birth of the child.

Following commencement of the DAHR provisions of the 2015 Act, it will be possible for parentage to be retrospectively allocated to an intended parent not previously recognised as a legal parent. Where certain criteria are met, an application can be made to either the District Court[55] or the Circuit Court[56] for a declaration of parentage setting out that the intending parents are the legal parents of a child conceived through DAHR and born before the provisions came into operation.[57] In order to qualify for a declaration, the second intending parent must have been an intending parent at the time when the DAHR procedure was performed.[58] The parents must swear an affidavit[59] or provide other evidence[60] confirming that the second intending parent was an intending parent at the relevant time. Hence, if the birth mother was single (or in a relationship with someone else) at the time that the child was conceived, her new partner cannot be recognised as a legal parent using this section. Moreover, if another person was registered as the child's father or second legal parent at the time of the birth, the application cannot be made.[61] The legislation also requires that the gamete donor must have been unknown to the intending parents and must not him/herself have been an intending parent at the time of the procedure,[62] and the donor must remain unknown to the intending parents at the time of the application.[63] Therefore, where a known donor was used, the declaration cannot be granted.

There is no definition of 'unknown' donor in the legislation. The Special Rapporteur on Child Protection for Ireland has suggested that the provisions could apply where an identifiable donor has been used so long as the mother does not know their identity.[64] It remains to be seen whether the Irish courts will interpret the section in the same way. It is submitted that the best interests of the child require that 'unknown' is

[55] Children and Family Relationships Act 2015, s 21.

[56] Children and Family Relationships Act 2015, s 22.

[57] Children and Family Relationships Act 2015, s 20(1).

[58] Children and Family Relationships Act 2015, s 20(1)(c).

[59] Children and Family Relationships Act 2015, s 21(4).

[60] Children and Family Relationships Act 2015, s 22(5).

[61] Children and Family Relationships Act 2015, s 20(1)(f).

[62] Children and Family Relationships Act 2015, s 20(1)(d).

[63] Children and Family Relationships Act 2015, s 20(1)(e).

[64] Geoffrey Shannon, *Tenth Report of the Special Rapporteur on Child Protection* (Dublin: Special Rapporteur on Child Protection, 2016), p. 149.

interpreted as broadly as possibly. A broad definition is required to ensure that children born through the use of gametes from an identifiable, but not yet identified, donor have the opportunity of acquiring a legal relationship with their second intended parent. This respects the reality of the child's upbringing and does not disadvantage the child due to a choice made by the adults before the child's conception.

If the requirement that the donor must have been unknown is interpreted to mean that the donor must be unidentifiable, this would be at odds with the prohibition on anonymous gamete donation that will apply to all DAHR procedures performed after commencement of the DAHR provisions.[65] Whereas the identity of the donor must be known and officially recorded in respect of DAHR that takes place after the legislation is commenced, his identity must be unknown where the procedure was undertaken before that date. As is discussed in later sections, the prohibition on anonymous gamete donation is regarded as vital to provide the child with important information about their identity. Indeed, it is likely that some couples who engaged in DAHR prior to the commencement of the 2015 Act deliberately chose to use a known donor for this reason.[66] If unknown means unidentifiable, these couples would now be penalised for prioritising the child's right to identity as the second intending parent would be prevented from being recognised as a legal parent under the 2015 Act as a result.

The inclusion of the requirement that the donor must have been, and remain, unknown to the intending parents in order for the retrospective declaration of parentage to be granted was queried during both the Dáil Éireann (Lower House of Parliament) Debates[67] and Seanad Éireann (Upper House of Parliament) Debates[68] on the Children and Family Relationships Bill 2015. Senator Katherine Zappone (as she was then), for example, stated that she did 'not understand the logic' of the provision and called upon the Minister for Justice to clarify same.[69] The Minister, however, did not address this issue in either of the debates.

[65] Children and Family Relationships Act 2015, s 24.

[66] This premise is supported by research which has been conducted in this area in both England and Wales and Ireland. See: Petra Nordqvist, '"Dealing with sperm": comparing lesbians' clinical and non-clinical donor conception processes' (2011) 33 *Sociology of Health & Illness* 114; Jane Pillinger and Paula Fagan, *LGBT Parents in Ireland. Report from a study into the experiences of Lesbian, Gay, Bisexual and Transgender People in Ireland who are parents or who are planning parenthood* (Dublin: LGBT Diversity, 2013), p. 36.

[67] Dáil Éireann Debates, 25 February 2015.

[68] Seanad Éireann Debates, 24 March 2015.

[69] Above.

The Special Rapporteur on Child Protection has opined that the requirement for the donor to be unknown was 'clearly included with the intention of excluding known donor situations such as that in *JMcD* v. *PL*'.[70] In *JMcD* v. *PL*,[71] a sperm donor was found to be the legal father of a child in the absence of any laws stating the contrary. Hence, it is likely that the proviso was included so as to avoid a situation whereby a donor who was originally recorded as the child's second legal parent would subsequently lose his status as such. Where a child is conceived by DAHR before commencement of Parts 2 and 3 of the 2015 Act, the sperm donor is regarded as the legal father. He may only have agreed to act as such on the basis that he would acquire this status. Consequently, it would be unjust to subsequently remove his status against his wishes. Furthermore, where the child has developed a relationship with the gamete donor, regarding that person as a parent, it would run contrary to that child's best interests to then sever the legal relationship between them.

It must also be recalled that currently (prior to the commencement of Parts 2 and 3 of the 2015 Act) there is no requirement for fertility clinics to record the consent of a donor *not* to be regarded as a legal parent – a man cannot waive his legal parental status where he is the genetic father. Therefore, where this man is recorded as the legal father, it would be difficult to prove that he was not an intending parent at the date of the procedure. If the donor is allowed to relinquish his status as a legal parent in circumstances where there is no evidence as to his original consent, this could lead to abuse of the system. For example, it might allow a man who had originally intended to be recognised and act as a legal father to subsequently change his mind and seek a declaration that he is not a legal parent so as to avoid his maintenance obligations towards the child. This example would support the decision to require that the donor must have been unknown and not registered as a legal parent upon the birth of the child.

Notwithstanding the rationale above, it must be noted that the result of the proviso is to create a distinction between children conceived prior to the coming into force of the legislation and children who will be conceived after the relevant provisions of the 2015 Act are commenced. Whereas the latter will be able to benefit from a legal relationship with the second intending parent *and* have an express right to access information about the donor, the former are only afforded one of these rights: the

[70] Shannon, above n. 64, 149.

[71] *JMcD* v. *PL* [2010] 2 IR 199. This case is discussed in Chapter 3.

donor must either be unknown, allowing for the second intending parent to be recognised, or this parent is prevented from being recognised as a legal parent. Regardless of the interpretation of 'unknown', the identity rights of children born prior to full commencement of the legislation are jeopardised as they will either be denied access to identifying information about the donor or this information will be very difficult to access due to the lack of record keeping in place before commencement.

5.2.2.3 Non-clinical Procedures

In introducing the Children and Family Relationships Act 2015, the Irish Government emphasised that the DAHR parentage provisions would not apply to children conceived as a result of DAHR that takes place in a non-clinical setting. The former Minister for Justice, Francis Fitzgerald, clearly stated that it would 'not be possible for the partner [of the birth mother] to become the child's second parent . . . if the AHR treatment has been carried out in a non-clinical setting'.[72] According to the Minister, such exclusion is justified due to 'the need to be able to have clear consents as to the status of all parties'.[73]

The 2015 Act does not expressly provide that the DAHR procedure *must* be performed in a DAHR facility, but this requirement can be implied from various provisions. For example, the legislation requires that the consents and declarations given by the donor(s) and intending parents must be obtained and retained by 'the operator of the DAHR facility'.[74] The operator of the DAHR facility must also provide the Minister for Health with certain information after the procedure has taken place. Therefore, in order for the parentage provisions set out above to apply, the conception must take place under the oversight of the 'operator' and hence in a DAHR facility.

The definition of 'DAHR facility' is, however, rather vague. It is simply defined as 'a place at which a DAHR procedure is performed'.[75] The term 'place' is not defined, and it is notable that the definition of 'DAHR procedure' does not include any reference to the DAHR facility. The phrase 'operator of the DAHR facility' is also broadly defined as 'the person who owns or manages the facility or is otherwise responsible for

[72] Frances Fitzgerald, 'Address by the Minister for Justice and Equality, Frances Fitzgerald TD at the Children's Rights Alliance Seminar' (Children's Rights Alliance Seminar on the Children and Family Relationships Bill 2015, Dublin Castle, 2 March 2015).

[73] Above.

[74] Children and Family Relationships Act 2015, s 28.

[75] Children and Family Relationships Act 2015, s 4.

the running of the facility'.[76] These vague definitions allow for a wide interpretation as to what would constitute a DAHR facility. As there is no reference to a hospital or medical facility, it could be argued that any non-clinical setting, including a person's home, could fall within this definition and whoever owns or runs that property could be regarded as the 'operator' thereof. Therefore, if donor insemination was to take place in a person's home and that person was to acquire, retain and transmit the relevant consents and declarations, as is required of the operator of a DAHR facility, there would appear to be nothing in the 2015 Act to prevent the child born of this arrangement from benefitting from the parentage provisions set out above.

The only caveat to this interpretation is that the parentage provisions contained in the 2015 Act do not apply in cases of self-insemination. Self-insemination, as the term suggests, occurs where the intending mother inseminates herself through artificial means. The 2015 Act expressly sets out that a person shall not perform a DAHR procedure unless that person is either a registered medical practitioner or a registered nurse.[77] As such, self-insemination would only be possible where a doctor or registered nurse seeks to self-inseminate. In all other cases, the assistance of one of these persons would be required so as to bring the non-clinical insemination within the ambit of the 2015 Act's parentage provisions. Nonetheless, once this requirement is adhered to, it would seem that an individual or couple would not necessarily have to engage a hospital or a fertility clinic so as to benefit from the specific rules of parentage that are set out in the 2015 Act.

In light of the stated intention of the Government to exclude non-clinical DAHR from the parentage provisions contained in the 2015 Act,[78] the possibility of the broad interpretation suggested was clearly unintended. The interpretation could have been avoided with tighter definitions of the relevant terms. It is worth noting that section 41 of the 2015 Act provides that the Minister for Health 'may make regulations prescribing any matter or thing' in respect of the parentage provisions. The Minister could, therefore, introduce a regulation requiring every DAHR facility to obtain a specific licence before any procedures could be carried out. The fact that the introduction of such a clause would be at the discretion of the Minister (as indicated by use of the word 'may'),

[76] Children and Family Relationships Act 2015, s 4.

[77] Children and Family Relationships Act 2015, s 25(1).

[78] Fiach Kelly, 'Fitzgerald's children Bill outlines new steps on parentage', *Irish Times*, 12 February 2015.

however, suggests that introduction of a licensing system was not a priority for the drafters of the Act. If this had been their intention, it would have been sensible to include such a proviso in the definition of 'DAHR facility' itself. Furthermore, even if a licensing or similar system was to be introduced, this does not necessarily mean that a non-clinical DAHR facility should be refused a license. That facility, after all, seemingly meets all of the relevant criteria (unless additional criteria were added in the regulations under the ambit of 'any matter or thing').

The discretion that is delegated to the Minister for Health under section 41 is extremely broad, and it could be argued that the section gives the Minister too much power and is, therefore, unconstitutional. Article 15.2.1 of the Irish Constitution gives the Oireachtas (Irish Parliament) exclusive powers to make law. The 'principles and policies test' allows the Oireachtas to delegate law-making power to others but only where the delegation amounts to a 'mere giving-effect to of principles and policies contained in the statute itself'.[79] A statutory instrument cannot establish new principles which are not already found in the parent Act or some other Act of Parliament.

Pursuant to the principles and policies test, the Minister for Health would only be able to use the power vested in them by section 41 of the 2015 Act so as to make regulations which fill in details of a policy already contained in the legislation. The 2015 Act does not, however, contain any mention of the word 'license'. As such, any subsequent attempt by the Minister for Health to introduce a licensing scheme for DAHR facilities under this section may fall foul of Article 15.2.1 of the Irish Constitution as an excessive delegation of power. If the drafters of the 2015 Act had intended that a licensing scheme would operate, this should have been set out in the Act itself.

In light of the above, it is arguable that where a child is conceived through DAHR in a non-clinical setting (after commencement of Parts 2 and 3 of the 2015 Act), the parentage provisions in the 2015 Act should apply so long as a person is identified as the 'operator' of that setting and that person acquires, retains and transmits the relevant consents and declarations, as is required, and provided that a registered medical practitioner or a registered nurse performs the DAHR procedure. Where these criteria are not adhered to, the parentage provisions would not apply.

[79] *City View Press Ltd* v. *An CO* [1980] IR 381.

Although it is unlikely that many non-clinical procedures would meet the criteria above, it is argued that the broad interpretation is required to respect the best interests of the child. If children conceived via DAHR in a non-clinical setting are excluded from the parentage provisions, they will be treated differently to children conceived in virtually identical circumstances in the clinical setting. Yet, this was the intention of the legislature. The implications for the best interests principle of excluding non-clinical procedures from the parentage provisions that apply to clinical procedures are examined in further detail later in the chapter.

5.2.3 *South Africa: Children's Act 2005*

In South Africa, assisted reproduction is regulated by the National Health Act 2003, the Regulations Relating to Artificial Fertilization of Persons 2012 and the Children's Act 2005. Sections 40 and 41 of the Children's Act 2005 refer to 'artificial fertilisation', and so that terminology is used in this section. This section outlines the allocation of parentage where this procedure is used. It is apparent from this analysis that the South African parentage provisions are more restrictive than those that operate in Ireland and in England and Wales. This section questions whether the restrictive parentage provisions adhere to South Africa's constitutional mandate that '[a] child's best interests are of paramount importance in every matter concerning the child'.[80]

5.2.3.1 Allocation of Parentage

In South Africa, only married couples (opposite sex or same sex) can be jointly recognised as legal parents following artificial fertilisation.[81] The unmarried partner, whether male or female, of the birth mother of a child who is conceived by way of artificial fertilisation is not regarded as a legal parent – the legislation simply does not provide for such recognition. Consequently, where an unmarried woman receives fertility treatment, she alone shall be the legal parent.

At first glance, the South African position would appear to run contrary to the judgment of the Constitutional Court in *J and B* v. *Director-General, Department of Home Affairs*.[82] In that case, two women in a permanent same-sex life partnership challenged the refusal of the

[80] Constitution of the Republic of South Africa, s 28(2).

[81] Children's Act 38 of 2005, s 40.

[82] *J and B* v. *Director-General, Department of Home Affairs* [2003] ZACC 3; (2003) (5) BCLR 463.

Department of Home Affairs to register them as the joint parents of twins born to one of the partners as a result of IVF. The oocytes of one of the partners (the genetic mother) had been used in the fertilisation process (along with sperm donated by an anonymous donor), and the resulting embryos were carried by the other partner (the gestational mother). The relevant legislation,[83] however, provided that only the married parents of children born by way of artificial insemination could be recognised as legal parents.

The Constitutional Court held that preventing the registration of both women as parents unfairly discriminated between married parents and parents in same-sex relationships. The relevant provisions were found to be inconsistent with section 9(3) of the South African Constitution which prohibits the State from discriminating directly or indirectly against anyone on the ground of sexual orientation.[84] The Court further held that precluding recognition of the second partner as a legal parent amounted to discrimination against the children who were born to same-sex couples. The Court noted that the effect of the legislation was to legitimise children born to married parents by way of artificial insemination, whereas it denied the children of same-sex relationships this same benefit.[85] Accordingly, the Court ordered that the words 'or permanent same-sex life partner' be read into the legislation after all references to 'married woman or husband'.

J and B v. *Director-General* was decided prior to the coming into force of the Civil Union Act 2006.[86] At the time of the judgment, the applicants could not marry so as to benefit from the parentage provisions. As such, they were unfairly discriminated against when compared to married opposite-sex couples. Same-sex couples can now marry under South African law, and section 40 of the Children's Act 2005 applies equally to prevent *all* unmarried couples from being recognised as joint legal parents following donor insemination. No distinction is made between

[83] Children's Status Act 82 of 1987, s 5. This legislation used the term 'artificial insemination'.

[84] *J and B* v. *Director-General, Department of Home Affairs* [2003] ZACC 3; (2003) (5) BCLR 463, paras. 13–14.

[85] Above, paras 15–16.

[86] The Civil Union Act 17 of 2006 allows for civil unions to take place between persons of the same sex. Civil unions are a type of marriage, but they are separate to civil marriage – only same-sex couples may enter into civil unions and only opposite-sex couples may enter into civil marriages. Apart from this distinction, the two types of marriage are the same. Nomthandazo Ntlama, 'A brief overview of the civil union act' (2010) *13 Potchefstroom Electronic Law Journal* 191.

couples on the basis of sexual orientation. Therefore, it could be argued that any unmarried couple, whether of the opposite or same sex, could simply choose to get married in order to avail of the parentage provisions. By not getting married and nonetheless engaging in donor insemination, the couple could be said to have consented to the non-recognition of the mother's partner as the second legal parent.

This reasoning, of course, ignores the fact that some couples simply do not wish to get married. It also overlooks the fact that the intending parents in a surrogacy agreement do not have to be married so as to benefit from automatic joint parentage.[87] It is submitted that the South African provisions that exclude the unmarried partner of the birth mother from recognition as a legal parent in situations where artificial fertilisation is used are contrary to the demands of the South African Constitution. Section 9 of the Constitution prohibits discrimination on the grounds of marital status while section 28(2) provides that '[a] child's best interests are of paramount importance in every matter concerning the child'. Preventing the child from enjoying a legal relationship with their second intending parent is arguably in breach of both of these provisions. Firstly, the unmarried couple is clearly subject to different treatment when compared to a married couple as the second intending parent is not recognised as a legal parent.[88] Secondly, as a consequence of the provision, the child of the unmarried couple is deprived of a legal relationship with the second intending parent. This runs contrary to that child's best interests, in circumstances where the second intending parent cares for the child from birth. The child of the unmarried couple born via artificial fertilisation is clearly at a disadvantage when compared to the child of a married couple which cannot be in compliance with the best interests principle.

5.2.3.2 Non-clinical Procedures

In South Africa, pursuant to Regulation 9 of the National Health Act 2003, artificial fertilisation or embryo transfer must only take place at an authorised institution and only a competent person may perform artificial fertilisation. A 'competent person' is defined in the Regulations as 'a person registered as such in terms of the Health Professions Act, 1974' who is either 'a medical practitioner specialising in gynaecology with

87 Children's Act 38 of 2005, s 293.

88 Pursuant to section 9(5) of the Constitution of the Republic of South Africa, discrimination on any of the prohibited grounds (which includes marital status) 'is unfair unless it is established that the discrimination is fair'.

training in reproductive medicine' or 'a medical scientist, medical technologist, clinical technologist, with training in reproductive biology and related laboratory procedures'.[89] Therefore, in order for the parentage provisions set out in section 40 the Children's Act 2005 to apply, the artificial fertilisation must have been carried out by a competent person at an authorised institution. This suggests that where a child is conceived by way of artificial fertilisation that occurs outside of the authorised setting, the common law rules of parentage will apply. The implications of excluding non-clinical procedures from the parentage provisions are discussed in detail later in this chapter.

5.3 Donor Conception and the Best Interests of the Child

Donor conception is a process that gives rise to many ethical and legal considerations. This chapter seeks to identify a framework for the regulation of donor conception by same-sex couples that respects and promotes the best interests of the child. This objective requires that a range of issues are examined, including the child's right to identity, non-clinical procedures and access to donor conception services for same-sex couples.

5.3.1 The Child's Right to Identity

The child's right to identity is recognised in Articles 7 and 8 of the United Nations Convention on the Rights of the Child (UNCRC). Article 7 UNCRC provides that '[t]he child shall be registered immediately after birth and shall have the right from birth to a name, the right to acquire a nationality and, as far as possible, the right to know and be cared for by his or her parents'. Article 8 UNCRC imposes a duty on States to 'undertake to respect the right of the child to preserve his or her identity, including nationality, name and family relations as recognized by law without unlawful interference'.

It is argued that the right to identity includes a right for donor-conceived persons to access information pertaining to their genetic origins.[90] The UNCRC does not define the term 'parents', and so it can be taken to mean genetic, gestational, legal or social parents. The

[89] National Health Act 61 of 2003, Reg 1.

[90] Lucy Frith, 'Beneath the rhetoric: The role of rights in the practice of non-anonymous gamete donation' (2001) 15 *Bioethics* 473.

Committee on the Rights of the Child has recommended in its concluding observations to various State Parties that action should be taken to ensure that adopted children and children born through assisted reproduction have access to information about their biological origins.[91] The Committee has noted that these actions are required to ensure compliance with Articles 3 (the best interests principle) and 7 (the right to identity) of the UNCRC.[92] Thus, the child's right to identity and best interests require that children should have access, as far as possible, to knowledge about their genetic progenitors.

Information about genetic origins can have a profoundly positive effect on children's identity formation and sense of self. As Joanna Rose, a donor-conceived woman, said of her donor during her evidence in *Rose* v. *Secretary of State*:

> I feel that these genetic connections are very important to me, socially, emotionally, medically, and even spiritually. I believe it to be no exaggeration that non-identifying information will assist me in forming a fuller sense of self or identity and answer questions that I have been asking for a long time.[93]

Information about a person's genetic background may also be required for medical reasons, although medical necessity would not require that the identity of the donor is made available. The possibility that a donor-conceived person would enter into a sexual relationship with a donor-sibling, without knowing that they are related, represents another argument in favour of providing the person with information pertaining to their genetic background so that accidental incest can be avoided.

Children who are told about the nature of their conception early in life generally react neutrally or positively to the information. By contrast, children who find out about their conception later in life and/or in unplanned ways report feeling deceived by their parents, and late disclosure is associated with negative psychological outcomes.[94] Early

[91] See, for example, Committee on the Rights of the Child, *Concluding Observations: United Kingdom of Great Britain and Northern Ireland*, CRC/C/15/ Add 188 (9 October 2002), paras. 31–32; Committee on the Rights of the Child, *Concluding observations on the combined third and fourth periodic reports of Ireland* (March 2016), paras. 34 and 45.

[92] Above.

[93] *Rose* v. *Secretary of State* [2002] EWHC 1593, para. 7.

[94] Eric Blyth, Marilyn Crawshaw, Lucy Frith and Caroline Jones, 'Donor conceived people's views and experiences of their genetic origins: A critical analysis of the research evidence' (2012) 19 *Journal of Law and Medicine* 769–789; AJ Turner and Adrian Coyle, 'What does it mean to be a donor offspring? The identity experiences of adults conceived by donor

disclosure is therefore beneficial for children and can be regarded as being in their best interests. This acknowledgement is reflected internationally as a growing number of jurisdictions prohibit anonymous gamete donation and allow children to gain access to information about their origins. Given that the best interests principle is to be determined by reference to the child's rights,[95] the child's right to identity is regarded as an important aspect of the principle. As such, this principle demands that sufficient safeguards are put in place to protect the right to identity of donor-conceived children.

5.3.2 *Safeguarding the Right to Identity*

5.3.2.1 England and Wales

In England and Wales, the Human Fertilisation and Embryology Authority is required to keep a register of information relating to persons born by way of donor insemination, and donor-conceived persons may apply to the Authority for information.[96] Non-identifying information about a gamete donor, as well as certain information about donor-conceived siblings,[97] may be requested once the child has reached the age of 16 years, while access to identifying information about the donor may only be requested at 18 years.[98] Only children conceived after 31 March 2005 can access identifying information about the donor, as the law was changed in that year to allow such access.[99] Identifying information includes details as to the following:

- The surname and each forename of the donor;
- The donor's date of birth;

insemination and the implications for counselling and therapy' (2000) 15 *Human Reproduction* 2041–2051.

95 Committee on the Rights of the Child, *General comment No. 14 (2013) on the right of the child to have his or her best interests taken as a primary consideration (art. 3, para. 1)* CRC/C/GC/14, para. 32.

96 Human Fertilisation and Embryology Act 1990, s 31 as amended by Human Fertilisation and Embryology Act 2008, s 24.

97 Information may be provided about the number of persons conceived using material from that donor, the sex of each of them and their year(s) of birth. Human Fertilisation and Embryology Act 1990, s 31ZA(2)(b) as inserted by Human Fertilisation and Embryology Act 2008, s 24.

98 Human Fertilisation and Embryology Act 1990, s 31ZA, as inserted by Human Fertilisation and Embryology Act 2008, s 24.

99 Human Fertilisation and Embryology Authority (Disclosure of Donor Information Regulations) 2004, SI 2004/1511, Reg 2(3).

- The appearance of the donor;
- The last known address of the donor.[100]

Before 2005, donor-conceived children could not access identifying information about the donor. They could apply for certain information about the donor, such as sex, height, weight, ethnic group, eye colour, hair colour, skin colour, year of birth, country of birth and marital status, but the information would only be provided where it could not be used to identify the donor.[101] Moreover, where the donation was made before 2005, the donor may not have provided all of this information, and so the request for information would be limited.

The English laws were changed in 2005 to require the provision of identifying donor information in respect of all children conceived after 31 March of that year. This reform was designed to protect the interests of donor-conceived children. In 2001, the UK Department of Health initiated a public consultation on the provision of donor information.[102] The consultation sought the views of the public and professionals as to whether, and to what extent, information about people who donated sperm, eggs or embryos should be given to children born as the result of those donations. Of the responses, 237 were received to the consultation questionnaire. Of these, 132 respondents were in favour of the provision of identifying information about donors to donor-conceived children, 70 people were against this proposition and 23 were undecided. The most common reasons cited in favour of the provision of identifying information were as follows:

- The provision of information was regarded as a basic human right for children;
- The information would allow children to place themselves in a genetic context, to satisfy curiosity and would allow them to know their identity;
- Secrecy was regarded as damaging to the family and to society;
- Greater openness was seen to reduce the stigma attached to alternative forms of conception.[103]

[100] Human Fertilisation and Embryology Authority (Disclosure of Donor Information Regulations) 2004, SI 2004/1511, Reg 2(3).

[101] Human Fertilisation and Embryology Authority (Disclosure of Donor Information Regulations) 2004, SI 2004/1511, Reg 2.

[102] Department of Health, *Donor Information Consultation: Providing Information about Gamete or Embryo Donors* (London: Department of Health, 2001).

[103] Department of Health, *Summary of Responses Received to the Donor Information Consultation – Providing Information about Sperm, Egg and Embryo Donors* (London: Department of Health, 2002), para. 16.

The most frequent reasons provided by those who were opposed to the provision of identifying information related to the rights of donors and their families and a concern that the removal of donor anonymity would result in a reduction in the number of donations.[104]

Around the same time that the Department of Health consultation was taking place, the case of *Rose* v. *Secretary of State*[105] was heard by the High Court. This case concerned two donor-conceived children (one of whom, Ms Rose, was an adult at the date of the application) who argued that they had a right under Article 8 of the European Convention on Human Rights (ECHR) to information about their anonymous donors. They argued that Articles 8 and 14 ECHR imposed a positive obligation on the State to collect non-identifying information about donors and to make this information available to donor-conceived children and their parents.[106] Having reviewed the relevant jurisprudence of the European Court of Human Rights (ECtHR),[107] Scott Baker J held that Article 8 ECHR was engaged with regard to both identifying and non-identifying information about a donor. It was noted that respect for private and family life requires that everyone should be able to establish details of their identity as individual human beings.

The *Rose* judgment and the results of the Department of Health's consultation process prompted the Department to make recommendations to end donor anonymity in England and Wales.[108] The new regulations apply to donations made after 31 March 2005. Persons who donated gametes anonymously between 1 August 1991 and 31 March 2005 may also choose to retrospectively remove their anonymity.[109] In addition, the Human Fertilisation and Embryology Act 2008 provided for the

104 Above, para. 17.

105 *Rose* v. *Secretary of State* [2002] EWHC 1593.

106 Above, para. 15.

107 The cases considered by the Court included, among others, *Marckx* v. *Belgium*, app. no. 6833/74, 13 June 1979; *Johnston* v. *Ireland*, app. no. 9697/92, 18 December 1986; *Gaskin* v. *United Kingdom*, app. no. 10454/83, 7 July 1989; and *X, Y and Z* v. *United Kingdom*, app. no. 21830/93, 22 April 1997.

108 John Appleby, 'Regulating the provision of donor information to donor-conceived children' in Susan Golombok, Rosamund Scott, John Appleby, Martin Richards and Stephen Wilkinson, *Regulating Reproductive Donation* (Cambridge: Cambridge University Press, 2016), p. 342.

109 Human Fertilisation and Embryology Authority, 'Remove your donor anonymity' www.hfea.gov.uk/donation/donors/remove-your-donor-anonymity/. A more radical approach was adopted in the Australian state of Victoria, which amended the Assisted Reproductive Treatment Act 2008 to retrospectively remove donor anonymity irrespective of the donor's consent.

establishment of a voluntary contact register to facilitate persons who wish to receive information about any person to whom they are genetically related as a result of fertility services.[110] Thus, provisions are in place to facilitate the donor-conceived child's right to identity in England and Wales.

Although donor-conceived children may apply for information about their donor, it should be noted that there is no obligation on parents to tell the children that they are donor-conceived in the first place.[111] This is significant because children will only seek out information if they know they have a reason to do so. As will be seen below, the Irish legislature has attempted to address this issue through the inclusion of a notification procedure in the relevant legislation. The question of notification was considered in England and Wales by the Joint Committee on the Human Tissue and Embryos (Draft) Bill prior to the introduction of the Human Fertilisation and Embryology Act 2008.[112] Proposals were put forward to allow for the mode of conception of donor-conceived children to be stated on their birth certificates. The Committee was of the opinion that including this information on the birth certificate would be a positive step in that it 'would create the incentive to tell the child of the fact of his or her donor conception and would go some way to address the value of knowledge of genetic history for medical purposes'.[113] Ultimately, the English Government chose to reject this proposal, regarding it as preferable to educate parents as to the benefits of disclosure rather than forcing it on them through the annotation of birth certificates.[114]

Hence, the right to identity of many English donor-conceived children is dependent on their parents telling them that they are donor-conceived. Children raised by gay and lesbian couples obviously do not have the same experience: they will naturally realise at some stage, if not told

[110] Human Fertilisation and Embryology Act 1990, s 31ZF, as inserted by Human Fertilisation and Embryology Act 2008, s 24.

[111] The HFEA Code of Practice requires fertility clinics to provide patients with 'implications counselling' in advance of treatment which typically includes discussion of the importance of disclosure and how to commute this to children. Lee, Macvarish and Sheldon, above n. 20, 512.

[112] *Joint Committee on the Human Tissue and Embryos (Draft) Bill, Volume 1: Report*, HL Paper 169-I, HC Paper 630-I (2007).

[113] Above, para. 276.

[114] The UK Government did, however, pledge to keep this matter under review. *Government Response to the Report from the Joint Committee on the Human Tissue and Embryos (Draft) Bill*, Cm. 7209 (October 2007), paras. 69–70.

sooner, that they cannot be genetically related to two parents of the same sex. The children of same-sex parents are thus in a stronger position than the donor-conceived children of opposite-sex couples in terms of establishing details of their identity because, as Bainham puts it, they 'will be on notice that a third person must have been involved in their conception'.[115] Furthermore, numerous studies have demonstrated that lesbian parents who have children through donor insemination are more likely to tell their children of the circumstances of their conception than opposite-sex couples are.[116] Indeed, a study conducted by Beeson and others suggests that lesbian parents are not only more likely to disclose the fact of donor insemination to their children but they are also more likely to do so at an earlier age.[117]

Even if the child is aware that they are donor-conceived, they face a barrier to vindicating the right to identity in that they cannot access identifying information about the donor until the age of 18 years. The right to identity cannot be realised while the child is still a child. Appleby notes that this restrictive approach is premised on the idea that allowing donor-conceived children to access identifying information at an earlier age would disrupt the primary family unit.[118] This, however, is a misplaced premise. As noted above, research shows that the earlier donor-conceived children learn about the nature of their conception, the better their outcomes are in terms of identity formation and development of family relationships.[119] Furthermore, a study by Schieb and others found that many adolescents who had been told that they are donor-conceived (using donor sperm) wanted to know more about the donor and expressed a desire to access identifying information about the

[115] Andrew Bainham, 'Arguments about parentage' (2008) 67 *Cambridge Law Journal* 322, p. 336.

[116] See, for example: A. Brewaeys, I. Ponjaert, E. Van Hall and S. Golombok, 'Donor insemination: Child Development and Family Functioning in Lesbian Mother Families' (1997) 12 *Human Reproduction* 1349; S. Leiblum, M. Palmer, I. Spector, 'Non-traditional mothers: single heterosexual, lesbian women and lesbian couples electing motherhood via donor insemination' (1995) 16 *Journal of Psychosomatic Obstetrics and Gynecology* 11; M. Jacob, S. Klock, D. Maier, 'Lesbian couples as therapeutic donor insemination recipients: Do they differ from other patients?' (1999) 20 *Journal of Psychosomatic Obstetrics and Gynecology* 203.

[117] D. Beeson, P. Jennings and W. Kramer, 'Offspring searching for their sperm donors: how family type shapes the process' (2011) 26 *Human Reproduction* 2415.

[118] Appleby, above n. 108, 344.

[119] Susan Golombok, 'Disclosure and donor-conceived children' (2017) 32 *Human Reproduction* 1532; Marilyn Crawshaw and others, 'Disclosure and donor-conceived children' (2017) 32 *Human Reproduction* 1535.

donor.[120] Although this is not the experience of every donor-conceived person, there is a general (though not absolute[121]) scientific consensus that openness in donor-conception is beneficial for children. As such, it is argued that children should have access to identifying information about a donor before adulthood in order to vindicate their right to identity and hence to comply with the best interests principle.

In Sweden, there is no age limit on access to information about the donor. Instead, the legislation provides for children who are deemed to be 'sufficiently mature' to receive the information,[122] though formal guidance from the National Board of Health and Welfare indicates that this refers to children in their 'upper teens'.[123] In 2015, the Supreme Court of Germany held that donor-conceived children should have access to information about the donor at any age. The Court found that certain conditions would apply to such access but reasoned that the child's right to information about their genetic background would usually carry greater weight than the donor's right to remain anonymous.[124]

There might be a concern that very young children would react negatively to obtaining information about their donor or that they will not know how to respond to this information.[125] In this context, Appleby argues that the parents should be able to access identifying information about the donor at any time so that they can control how and when their children receive the information.[126] There is certainly merit in Appleby's proposal. By providing the parents with the relevant information, they can assess when the child is ready to receive it and then help the child to process and act on the information in an age-appropriate way. Under Article 5 UNCRC States Parties must respect the responsibilities, rights and duties of parents to provide direction and guidance to the child. This Article supports the idea that parents should be able to educate their children about their genetic background when they feel that the child is ready to know about their donor. Having additional information about

[120] Joanna Schieb, Mary O'Riordan and Susan Rubin, 'Adolescents with open-identity sperm donors: reports from 12–17 year olds' (2005) 20 *Human Reproduction* 239–252.

[121] Guido Pennings, 'Disclosure of donor conception, age of disclosure and the well-being of donor offspring' (2017) 32 *Human Reproduction* 969.

[122] Swedish Law of Artificial Insemination 1984 (SFS 1984 1140).

[123] The National Board of Health and Welfare (SOSFS, 1987)

[124] Supreme Court of Germany decision XII ZR 201/13, BGH, Urteil vom 28. January 2015 – XII ZR 201/13.

[125] Appleby, above n. 108, 345.

[126] Appleby, above n. 108, 346.

the donor may also help when the parents first tell the child that he or she is donor-conceived as they are then able to answer any questions the child may have. This may alleviate feelings of frustration that might otherwise arise where the child does not have the additional information.[127]

Once the child has adequate emotional and practical support, there appears to be no reason why they should not acquire identifying information about the donor during childhood. As Blake and others note, 'donor conception needn't be a difficult issue for parents or for children if it has been discussed with children from an early age'.[128] In this light, it is argued that identifying information relating to the donor should be provided to children during childhood once the child is deemed capable of receiving the information, in order to vindicate the child's right to identity and to ensure that the regulation of donor conception operates in the best interests of the child.

5.3.2.2 Ireland

In Ireland, the Children and Family Relationships Act 2015 contains a range of provisions that are designed to protect the child's right to identity in DAHR. Section 24 of the 2015 Act provides that a donated gamete or embryo cannot be acquired by a DAHR facility for use in a DAHR procedure unless identifying information about the donor is also acquired.[129] Therefore, after commencement of Parts 2 and 3 of the 2015 Act, DAHR can only take place where the identity of the donor is known and recorded. In addition, section 33 of the 2015 Act provides that the Minister for Health shall cause to be established and maintained a National Donor-Conceived Person Register ('the Register'). The purpose of this Register is to record information relating to donor-conceived children, including personal details, donor information and recipient parent information.[130] Where a DAHR procedure takes place, an obligation is imposed on the operator of the DAHR facility to keep a record of donor information and recipient parent information. This information must subsequently be transmitted to the Minister for Health for inclusion in the Register.[131]

[127] Schieb, O'Riordan and Rubin, above n. 120.

[128] Lucy Blake, Elena Ilioi and Susan Golombok, 'Thoughts and feelings about the donor: A family perspective' in Golombok and others, above n. 108, 293.

[129] Children and Family Relationships Act 2015, s 24.

[130] Children and Family Relationships Act 2015, s 33(3).

[131] Children and Family Relationships Act 2015, ss 28(3)–28(5).

Donor-conceived children will have the opportunity to request information from the Register once they reach the age of 18 years.[132] This information will include both identifying[133] and non-identifying information about the donor as well as certain limited details about donor siblings.[134] As the provisions of the 2015 Act concerning DAHR have not been commenced at the time of writing, the first requests for information will not be made until at least 2037.

Where the donor-conceived child requests identifying information about the donor, the donor will be notified and will be given the opportunity to request that the Minister does not issue the information in circumstances where 'the safety of the relevant donor or the donor-conceived child, or both, requires that the information not be released'.[135] Where the Minister is satisfied that sufficient reasons exist to withhold the information concerned, they shall refuse to issue same.[136] As such, the child's ability to access important information pertaining to their identity may be impeded in certain circumstances. The best interests of the child must, however, be paramount and so, in light of the importance which is placed upon the child's need to have access to their genetic information, it seems likely that the provisions allowing the Minister to refuse to issue the relevant information will only be used in exceptional circumstances.

The provisions of the 2015 Act that allow the child to access information about the donor broadly mirror those in place in England and Wales, and they have the potential to protect and vindicate the child's right to identity. Similar to England and Wales, a difficulty with the Irish provisions is that the child will not be able to access identifying information about the donor until the child is 18 years old. For the reasons advanced earlier, it is argued that this information should be available at an earlier age.

A significant difference between the Irish and English provisions is the inclusion of unique notification procedures in the Irish legislation that offer additional protection to the child's right to identity. Section 39(1) of the Children and Family Relationship Act 2015 provides that where the Minister for Health records information relating to the birth of a donor-conceived person in the Register, they are obliged to notify an tArd

[132] Children and Family Relationships Act 2015, s 34(1).
[133] Children and Family Relationships Act 2015, s 35(1).
[134] Children and Family Relationships Act 2015, s 34.
[135] Children and Family Relationships Act 2015, s 35(2)(b).
[136] Children and Family Relationships Act 2015, s 35(3)(a).

Chláraitheoir (the Registrar General) of this record.[137] Upon receiving this notification, an tArd Chláraitheoir is then obliged to 'note in the entry in the register of births that the child is a donor-conceived child and that additional information is available from the Register in relation to the child'.[138] Subsequently, where a person over the age of 18 years applies for a copy of their birth certificate, and a note exists in relation to them, an tArd-Chláraitheoir shall, when issuing a copy of the birth certificate requested, inform the person that further information relating to them is available from the Register.[139] The additional information will contain details of the person's donor conception.

The notification process is designed to secure the donor-conceived person's right to identity. However, the issue of notification is controversial due to its intrusive nature. If the child has not previously been told that they are donor-conceived, it may be distressing to discover this upon application for a birth certificate. Of course, as discussed above, this difficulty will realistically only arise in respect of the donor-conceived children of opposite-sex intending parents as the children of same-sex couples will already know that they were donor-conceived.

For the donor-conceived children of opposite-sex parents, the Irish notification provisions have the potential to negatively affect those who have not previously been told of the nature of their conception. Research shows that children who find out about their donor conception later in life or through accidental disclosure typically react negatively and experience psychological distress.[140] Learning about one's donor conception at the Registry Office is therefore likely to lead to psychological distress. On the other hand, the donor-conceived person might never have a reason to apply for their birth certificate, for example if the parents provide them with a copy. In this instance, the notification procedure would never take effect. Overall, although the appropriateness of learning about one's donor conception at the Registry Office may be questioned, it is to be hoped that the notification procedures will encourage more openness among parents and persuade them to tell their children of their donor conception at an earlier age. The provisions demonstrate that, in the eyes of the State, disclosure is regarded as best practice and that secrecy as to the child's origins is to be avoided. Nowadays, the chances of inadvertently finding out about one's donor conception are at a record high as

[137] Children and Family Relationships Act 2015, s 39(1).
[138] Children and Family Relationships Act 2015, s 39(2).
[139] Children and Family Relationships Act 2015, s 39(4).
[140] Blyth and others, above n. 94; Turner and Coyle, above n. 94.

the sale of at-home ancestry DNA kits has become increasingly popular.[141] This demonstrates that the reality of donor conception cannot be kept secret forever, and openness by parents is in the child's best interests. The Irish provisions have the potential to safeguard the child's right to identity by encouraging openness, but it remains to be seen how they will impact on society in practice.

The prohibition on the use of anonymously donated genetic material is a vital safeguard for the child's right to identity. This prohibition may however give rise to difficulties in Ireland due to the fact that the majority of donated genetic material used by Irish fertility clinics is imported from other jurisdictions, some of which adhere to the concept of donor anonymity. Most of Ireland's donated sperm is imported from Denmark.[142] In Denmark, donors may provide samples either anonymously or non-anonymously, and the payment for (and consequently the sale price of) such donations varies according to the level of anonymity of the donor.[143] Donation prices are up to 30 per cent more expensive where the donor profile includes details such as height or eye and hair colour and up to 60 per cent more expensive for a fully identified donor.[144] As such, concerns might be raised that the prohibition on the use of anonymously donated genetic material will lead to a decrease, or indeed a shortage, in the availability of such material in Ireland.[145]

International experience has shown that prohibitions on donor anonymity do not generally have a lasting impact on the rate of donations. Sweden, for example, is frequently cited as an example of the transient effects of the removal of donor anonymity. In that jurisdiction, there was an initial decrease in donations following the removal of donor anonymity, but this was followed by a subsequent increase.[146] Similarly, in England and Wales, although there was initially a decrease in domestic sperm and egg donations following the removal of donor anonymity in

[141] Ellie Hunt, 'Your father's not your father: when DNA tests reveal more than you bargained for' *The Guardian*, 18 September 2018.

[142] Michelle McDonagh, 'What's the reality of going it alone through sperm donation?' *Irish Times*, 6 September 2016.

[143] Cryos Denmark, 'Prices and Payment' www.dk.cryosinternational.com/donor-sperm/prices-and-payment/.

[144] Above.

[145] Former Irish Minister for Justice, Alan Shatter, raised such concerns: Ruadhán MacCormaic, 'Shatter warns Family Bill will end donor-assisted reproduction' Irish Times, 5 March 2015.

[146] Gaia Bernstein, 'Regulating reproductive technologies: Timing, uncertainty, and donor anonymity' (2010) 90 *Boston University Law Review* 1189, pp. 1207–1208.

2005, the numbers of donations made in the years following have continued to surpass the pre-2005 figures.[147]

The problem in Ireland is not that the domestic population may be dissuaded from donating genetic material where they cannot be guaranteed anonymity[148] but, rather, that only a portion of material (sperm, in particular) already available would be permitted for use in Ireland. The removal of donor anonymity in Ireland does not stop men from donating anonymously in Denmark. It simply means that the amount of material available for purchase by Irish DAHR facilities would be curtailed.[149] Whether or not this would ultimately lead to a shortage of available material in Ireland remains to be seen.[150]

Overall, the 2015 Act contains robust provisions that allow for the child's right to identity to be protected. Indeed, the Irish provisions go further than those currently in place in England and Wales and in South Africa. The inclusion of the notification procedure following an application for a birth certificate provides an additional, albeit controversial, safeguard for the child's right to identity. The effect of prohibiting donor anonymity is not yet apparent, but it is submitted that this reform is required so as to protect the child's right to identity and thus to respect their best interests.

5.3.2.3 South Africa

In South Africa, the law provides some protection for the right to identity of donor-conceived persons, but there is no provision enabling access to identifying information about the gamete donor. Section 41 of the Children's Act 2005 provides that the child born as a result of artificial fertilisation is entitled to access medical information and 'any other information' regarding the 'genetic parents' when the child reaches the

[147] Human Fertilisation and Embryology Authority, *Egg and sperm donation in the UK: 2012–2013* (London: Human Fertilisation and Embryology Authority, 2014).

[148] This concern has, however, been raised by some Irish doctors: Paul Cullen, 'Proposed sperm and egg donor register "unacceptable" says doctor' *Irish Times*, 25 February 2015.

[149] The laboratory director of Galway Fertility Clinic stated in 2015 that less than a quarter of donor sperm available for purchase in Ireland at that time was non-anonymous. Claire McCormack, 'Naming sperm donors will hit treatment here' *Irish Independent*, 8 March 2015.

[150] Some Irish clinicians have expressed concern that the potential shortage in available non-anonymous sperm may encourage patients to avail of non-clinical procedures or treatment abroad which would fall outside of the ambit of the Children and Family Relationships Act 2015. McCormack, above.

age of 18 years.[151] However, section 41(2) provides that the information that may be disclosed 'may not reveal the identity of the person whose gamete was or gametes were used for such artificial fertilisation or the identity of the surrogate mother'.[152] In addition, regulation 19 of the Regulations Relating to Artificial Fertilisation of Persons 2012 provides as follows:

> No person shall disclose the identity of any person who donated a gamete or received a gamete, or any matter related to the artificial fertilisation of such gametes, or reproduction resulting from such artificial fertilisation except where a law provides otherwise or a court so orders.[153]

Failure to comply with this regulation is a criminal offence.[154] As such, South African donor-conceived children are denied access to an important aspect of their identities: identifying information about the gamete donor.

The policy reasons for preventing children from knowing the identity of a gamete donor in South Africa are unclear, particularly in light of the fact that adopted children are expressly given the right to access identifying information about their genetic parents.[155] The South African Law Reform Commission (SALRC) notes that, traditionally, there was a culture of secrecy regarding donor conception in South Africa wherein parents were encouraged to keep the donation a secret. Infertility carried social stigma, and so parents would conceal their use of donor gametes to avoid scrutiny from the outside world.[156] This attitude may have contributed to the restrictions on disclosing the identity of a gamete donor. Attitudes towards assisted reproduction have changed in recent years and rates of disclosure by parents of the method of their child's conception are increasing. Yet, the South African legislation continues to prohibit the disclosure of identifying information about the donor to the child or parents.

It is arguable that preventing a child from accessing identifying information about their gamete donor is contrary to section 28(2) of the South African Constitution. This provision provides that '[a] child's best interests are of paramount importance in every matter concerning the child'.

[151] Children's Act 38 of 2005, s 41(1).

[152] Children's Act 38 of 2005, s 41(2).

[153] Regulations Relating to Artificial Fertilisation of Persons 2012, Reg 19.

[154] Regulations Relating to Artificial Fertilisation of Persons 2012, Reg 21.

[155] Children's Act 38 of 2005, ss 247–248.

[156] South African Law Reform Commission, *The Right to Know One's own Biological Origins*, Issue Paper 32 (Pretoria: South African Law Reform Commission, 2017).

In light of the importance that knowledge of one's genetic heritage can have for children's identity formation and psychological development, it is argued that the legislation does not comply with the best interests principle.

The Centre for Child Law, a law clinic that works to promote the rights of the child in South Africa, has argued that withholding information from children regarding their genetic origins is contrary to the best interests of the child for three reasons:

(a) Knowing one's genetic origins is essential to human wellbeing.
(b) People have a right to the truth about their origins.
(c) Children who are aware that they are donor-conceived suffer psychologically when they are denied information about their origins and identity.[157]

The Centre notes that there is a 'developing global trend' towards openness and further that there is a duty on the State 'to use legislative power to ensure that donor-conceived children are aware of their status and the nature of their conception'.[158]

In addition to potentially violating section 28(2) of the Constitution, the current restrictions may also violate section 32 of the Constitution. This section provides that everyone has a right of access to 'any information held by the state' and 'any information that is held by another person and that is required for the exercise or protection of any rights'.[159] It could be argued that identifying donor information is necessary to allow a person to exercise their right to identity. It is thus 'required for the exercise or protection' of that right. Of course, the fact that non-identifying information may be obtained dilutes this argument to a certain extent. Nonetheless, for some individuals, only identifying information will satisfy their curiosity about the donor. As such, a claim could be made that section 41(2) of the Children's Act 2005 is unconstitutional on the basis that it violates both section 28(2) and section 32 of the Constitution.

It is clear from the above that the English and Irish laws offer greater protection to the child's right to identity as donor-conceived children in those jurisdictions can access identifying information about gamete donors. The English and Irish regulation is unsatisfactory in that the

[157] *AB and Surrogacy Advisory Group* v. *the Minister of Social Development (Centre for Child Law as Amicus Curiae)* [2016] ZACC 43, para. 30.
[158] Above, para. 31.
[159] Constitution of the Republic of South Africa, s 32.

child can only access identifying information when they reach the age of 18 years. Yet, it is argued that the English and Irish regulation is still more in keeping with the best interests principle than the South African laws, notwithstanding that the best interests principle is constitutionally enshrined in South Africa. Given that the content of the best interests principle is to be determined by reference to the child's rights,[160] it is submitted that the South African law falls short of the requirements of the principle as it does not respect the right to identity of donor-conceived children. It is in the best interests of children to have access to as much information about their genetic origins as is possible.

5.3.3 *Identity and the 'Fatherless' Child*

Donor insemination is a common pathway to parentage for lesbian couples. Consequently, concern is sometimes raised in relation to the fact that the children born via donor insemination to lesbian intending parents will be legally fatherless from birth. Opponents of lesbian parenting argue that the child's sense of identity will be confused where there are two mothers at birth, while others simply assert that the child needs a paternal influence.[161] This section assesses the legitimacy of these concerns.

Callus has argued that the child's right to identity is jeopardised where two women are recognised as legal parents.[162] For Callus, naming two women as joint parents negatively affects the child's sense of identity because such recognition 'conceals the necessary heterosexual element of human existence'.[163] Callus acknowledges that opposite-sex couples may engage in deception in that they may conceal their use of donor gametes, but, for her, the provisions extending parentage to lesbian partners 'double that deception'.[164]

The problem with Callus' argument is that, as was discussed above, the children of same-sex couples will naturally realise at some stage, if not told sooner, that they cannot be genetically related to two mothers.

160 Committee on the Rights of the Child, above n. 95, para. 32.

161 Victoria Clarke, 'Sameness and difference in research on lesbian parenting' (2002) 12 *Journal of Community and Applied Social Psychology* 210; Dominic McGrattan, 'No need for a father: The human fertilisation and embryology act 2008' (2009) 12(2) *Irish Journal of Family Law* 33; Golombok, above n. 1, ch 2.

162 Thérèse Callus, 'First Designer Babies, Now á la carte parents' (2008) 38 *Family Law* 143, p. 146.

163 Above.

164 Above.

Furthermore, research has shown that lesbian mothers are more likely to inform the child of their genetic origins in any case.[165] Therefore, it seems difficult to argue that the child will be deceived or confused in relation to this aspect of their identity. The donor-conceived children of opposite-sex couples, on the other hand, are more open to deception. In this way, the children of same-sex couples are actually in a stronger position in terms of establishing their identity than those who are born to opposite-sex couples.

Another concern that arises where two women are allocated parental status over a child is the fact that this child will be legally 'fatherless' from birth. For example, in Ireland, certain groups opposed the current regulation of DAHR on the basis that it allows for 'children who will be deliberately raised' without two parents of the opposite sex.[166] As was discussed in Chapter 2, there is a growing body of research that shows that the absence of a father does not impact negatively upon children in circumstances where they are raised by two loving mothers – children raised by two women generally have the same outcomes as those who are raised by a man and a woman.[167] Therefore, despite the assertion that 'love is not enough' to raise a child,[168] the sociological evidence appears to establish the contrary, namely that love and quality of interactions are more important to parent–child relationships than genetics. This point is addressed in further detail below.

Previously in England and Wales, section 13(5) of the Human Fertilisation and Embryology Act 1990 required that the child's 'need for a father' was considered when assessing whether a couple or an individual should be permitted to make use of reproductive treatment.[169] This provision was later removed by the Human Fertilisation and Embryology Act 2008 and replaced by a requirement

[165] Beeson, Jennings and Kramer, above n. 117.

[166] David Quinn, 'Government's rush to embrace the "new normal" downgrades the natural family' *Irish Independent*, 20 February 2015.

[167] Ellen Perrin, Benjamin Siegel and the Committee on Psychosocial Aspects of Child and Family Health, 'Promoting the well-being of children whose parents are gay or lesbian' (2013) 131 *Pediatrics* 1374; Simon Crouch, Elizabeth Waters, Ruth McNair, Jennifer Power and Elise Davis, 'Parent reported measures of child health and wellbeing in same-sex parent families: A cross-sectional study' (2014) 14 *BMC Public Health* 635; Timothy Biblarz and Judith Stacey, 'How does the gender of parents matter?' (2010) 72 *Journal of Marriage and Family* 3.

[168] Breda O'Brien, 'Love is not enough when it comes to children's rights' *Irish Times*, 24 January 2015.

[169] Human Fertilisation and Embryology Act 1990, s 13(5).

to take account of the child's need for 'supportive parenting'.[170] Some commentators were highly critical of the removal of the 'need for a father' consideration. For example, McGratten questioned why children born as a result of assisted reproduction are not in need of a father. He asked, '[a]re such children immune from the profound and wide ranging impact that a lack of father-child relationship evidently causes?'[171] It is not clear what evidence McGratten relied on in making this statement since studies in this area have demonstrated that children who are raised by two mothers are not negatively affected by the absence of a father.[172] Research conducted by Golombok in relation to father presence has found that 'it appears that [it is the father's] role as an additional parent, not as a male parent that is beneficial for the child'.[173] In giving evidence before the Joint Committee on the Human Tissue and Embryos (Draft) Bill, Golombok acknowledged that children raised in single-parent families are more likely to experience developmental problems than those who are raised by two parents, but she noted that 'these greater difficulties ... are very much associated with the circumstances of being in a one parent family rather than just whether or not there is a father present'.[174] According to Golombok, 'in lesbian mother families where two women are heading the family, the presence of two parents seems to be more important than the fact that one parent is male'.[175] She noted that 'it is really the second parent that is most important ... more important than the gender of that parent'.[176]

The English and Welsh legislature was obviously satisfied, on the balance of the evidence presented to it by the Joint Committee on the Human Tissue and Embryos (Draft) Bill Report, that children would not be harmed by removing the 'need for a father' criterion.[177] The shift to 'supportive parenting' evidences a belief that it is the quality rather than the gender of parents that is important.

170 Human Fertilisation and Embryology Act 2008, s 14(2).

171 McGrattan, above n. 161, 33.

172 See Chapter 2.

173 Susan Golombok, *Parenting: What Really Counts?* (London: Routledge, 2000), p. 23.

174 Evidence presented by Professor Susan Golombok to the Joint Committee on the Human Tissue and Embryos (Draft) Bill. *Joint Committee on the Human Tissue and Embryos (Draft) Bill, Volume II: Evidence, HL Paper* 169-II, HC Paper 630-II (2007), p. 231, Q 883.

175 Above, p. 233, Q 893.

176 Above, p. 231, Q 884.

177 *Government Response to the Report from the Joint Committee on the Human Tissue and Embryos (Draft) Bill*, Cm 7209 (October 2007), p. 16.

As was seen in Chapter 2, there is an emerging body of evidence that suggests that children who are raised by same-sex parents have broadly the same psychological and behavioural outcomes as those who are raised by opposite-sex couples. The methodological legitimacy of this research is sometimes questioned,[178] but it is telling that those who oppose the use of donor conception by female couples on the basis that it will 'deprive' children of a relationship with their fathers generally fail to engage with this research in any form.

Nonetheless, such is the concern that children will be deprived of a relationship with two parents of the opposite sex, it has been argued that lesbian couples should not be permitted to access donor conception.[179] In each of the comparator jurisdictions, same-sex couples can avail of donor conception services but some countries continue to restrict access to opposite-sex couples.[180]

Access to donor conception should be provided on a non-discriminatory basis such that patients are not denied access on the basis of marital status or sexual orientation. In *Dickson* v. *United Kingdom*,[181] the ECtHR held that any restriction on access to AHR must be proportionate. As such, any blanket restriction on access to services would have to carefully balance competing individual and public interests in the particular case in order to avoid conflict with the ECHR.

In *Charron and Merle-Montet* v. *France*,[182] the ECtHR considered a complaint brought by a married female couple against French authorities after they were refused access to assisted reproductive treatment under French law. The applicants argued that the refusal was contrary to Articles 8 and 14 ECHR. The ECtHR deemed this complaint to be inadmissible on the basis that the refusal of the applicant's request for assisted reproductive treatment was an individual administrative decision that could have been set aside on appeal for abuse of authority before the administrative courts, but the applicants had not sought such a remedy. Thus, the applicants had not exhausted their domestic remedies and the complaint was inadmissible. As such, this case does not

[178] This research is often criticised on the basis that the studies are not sufficiently longitudinal to present persuasive results or that the sample sizes used are too small. These methodological issues are discussed in Chapter 2.

[179] Golombok, above n. 1; Marie O'Halloran, 'Senator calls for donor-assisted reproduction to be restricted' *Irish Times*, 27 March 2015.

[180] For example, in Italy, Article 5 of law no. 40/2004 restricts access to assisted reproductive technology to opposite-sex couples.

[181] *Dickson* v. *United Kingdom*, app. no. 44362/04, 4 December 2007.

[182] *Charron and Merle-Montet* v. *France*, app. no. 22612/15, 16 January 2018.

provide guidance as to the compatibility or otherwise of provisions excluding same-sex couples from accessing assisted reproduction with Articles 8 and 14 ECHR. On the other hand, as discussed in Chapter 4, the ECtHR's jurisprudence concerning adoption by same-sex couples emphasises that the State cannot differentiate between persons in directly comparable positions in terms of accessing services. Thus, if unmarried opposite-sex couples are permitted to avail of AHR treatment, it is likely that the ECtHR would find that the same opportunity must be available to unmarried same-sex couples to avoid a violation of the ECHR.[183]

5.4 Should Non-clinical Procedures Be Subject to Different Rules of Parentage than Clinical Procedures?

As has been seen, the donor conception laws of the three comparator jurisdictions discussed in this chapter exclude children who are conceived via donor insemination in a non-clinical setting from the statutory parentage provisions governing such procedures (though it is open to debate whether this is the case for all non-clinical procedures in Ireland). Non-clinical donor insemination remains a popular choice for some couples. A study by Nordqvist found that many lesbian couples pursue 'self-arranged conception' because it is cheaper than attending a clinic.[184] Nordqvist concludes:

> It is likely that women will have to negotiate the difficulties, complications and risks embedded in self-arranged conception also in the future as many cannot negotiate access to reproductive health clinics. For example, women of lower socio-economic backgrounds find it hard to negotiate access to clinical treatment due to its high costs.[185]

Prospective parents may also prefer at-home conception for reasons of privacy. After all, if neither member of the couple experiences infertility difficulties, why should they be required to involve a medical team in an act that is private for so many other couples and to pay for the inconvenience of doing so?

It is necessary, therefore, to examine the legitimacy of excluding non-clinical donor conception from the legislative parentage provisions. This exclusion creates a number of difficulties that have the potential to impair

[183] By analogy, see *X and Others* v. *Austria*, app. no. 19010/07, 19 February 2013. This case is discussed in Chapter 4.
[184] Nordqvist, above n. 66, 125.
[185] Nordqvist, above n. 66, 126.

the best interests of the child. In particular, the lack of recognition for non-clinical procedures means that children conceived via this process are subject to different rules of parentage than those conceived through donor insemination in a clinical setting. Children conceived in the clinical setting automatically acquire a legal relationship with both intending parents at birth, whereas those conceived in the non-clinical setting may be deprived of a legal relationship with the non-genetic or non-gestational intending parent for a period of time. These children are denied the same security and stability that is afforded to children conceived in the hospital or clinic. Arguably, this amounts to discrimination against children and cannot be said to be in their best interests. Imposing a different standard of parentage where donor insemination takes place outside of the clinic, for example in the home, will not stop couples from engaging in this practice.[186] It simply means that the children born will be denied the same level of family security that is afforded to children conceived in the clinic.

It is difficult to argue that children should be denied a certain status on the basis of a choice that their parents have made. Article 2(2) of the UNCRC prohibits any discrimination against children on the basis of the 'status, *activities*, expressed opinions, or beliefs of the child's parents, legal guardians, or family members'.[187] Therefore, it may run contrary to the State's obligations under the UNCRC, and thus contrary to the best interests principle, to treat children differently based on the actions of their parents.

On the other hand, there are valid reasons for the State to prefer that the procedure is performed in a hospital or fertility clinic. In the clinical setting, formal procedures are in place to record the donor's identity and consent. There is no oversight of same where the insemination takes place outside of the clinical setting, which means that the donor's identity and/or consent might not be accurately and consistently recorded. This, in turn, may impact negatively upon the child's right to identity. As was discussed earlier, the child's right to identity encompasses a right to access information pertaining to their genetic background. This right would be impeded where only limited information is available about the donor. Therefore, it may be legitimate for the State to limit the parentage rights available following non-clinical donor insemination so as to encourage intending parents to make use of the clinical route and thus help to safeguard the child's right to identity.

[186] Nordqvist, above n. 66.

[187] UN Convention on the Rights of the Child, Art 2(2) [emphasis added].

There is also a lack of medical oversight where the insemination takes place in the non-clinical setting. Fertility clinics screen donated genetic material for transmittable diseases such as HIV, but this may not occur where the donor insemination takes place in a non-clinical setting. That is not to say that the parties that engage in non-clinical donor insemination would not choose to undergo screening, but this is simply more likely to consistently occur where the procedure is performed in the clinical setting. Therefore, the State may validly prefer use of the clinical process for reasons of health and safety.

The best interests of the child must be to the fore in balancing these issues to determine how the legislation should operate. As was discussed in Chapter 1, the best interests of the child should be informed by reference to their rights. The task is, therefore, to assess the competing rights that are engaged in respect of the regulation of non-clinical donor conception so as to identify the implications of the best interests principle. On the one hand, it must be observed that applying different rules where the conception takes place inside and outside of the clinical setting may constitute discrimination against children. This may therefore run contrary to Article 2 UNCRC, which demands that the child is protected against all forms of discrimination. Furthermore, by excluding non-clinical donor conception from the legislative parentage provisions, the child is deprived of a legal relationship with the second intending parent at birth. This may fall foul of Article 7 UNCRC as that intending parent is prevented from properly caring for the child. On the other hand, use of the clinical process seems to offer greater protection to the child's right to identity which is protected by Articles 7 and 8 UNCRC. Furthermore, the clinical process better protects the health and safety of the child. As such, that process may be preferred by reference to Article 24 UNCRC, which provides that the child has the right to 'the enjoyment of the highest attainable standard of health'.

In this light, there is a tension between the child's right to non-discrimination and right to be cared for by their parents on the one hand and the child's rights to identity and health on the other. It is submitted that this tension does not justify excluding non-clinical procedures from the statutory provisions relating to clinical procedures. In fact, it provides an opportunity to incentive couples who avail of non-clinical procedures to protect the rights of the child by linking such efforts to statutory recognition of their legal parentage. It is argued that a mechanism should be put in place to recognise the intended parents as legal parents where non-clinical donor insemination is used so long as certain steps are taken to safeguard the child's rights, in particular the right to identity. A suggested framework for such a mechanism is discussed later.

An accommodating approach is required because the prioritisation of clinical donor conception does not prevent couples from engaging in the non-clinical process. Children will continue to be conceived through non-clinical procedures and will therefore continue to be subject to different rules of parentage to those who are conceived via clinical procedures. An exception arises for the children of married opposite-sex couples. In each of the comparator jurisdictions discussed in this chapter, a presumption of paternity arises in favour of the husband of the woman who gives birth. Therefore, where these couples engage in non-clinical donor insemination, the second parent can be recognised as a legal parent notwithstanding that the procedure falls outside of the statutory provisions governing donor insemination. In England and Wales, a statutory presumption of parentage also operates in favour of same-sex married couples and civil partners in cases of donor insemination.[188] As such, the spouse or civil partner of the birth mother is automatically regarded as the child's second legal parent regardless of whether the procedure takes place in a clinical or non-clinical setting. In these situations, there is no legal disadvantage for the couples in engaging in non-clinical donor insemination (as both intended parents can be recognised as legal parents), yet the threat to the child's right to identity and to their health and safety remains.[189]

In this situation, the rationale for excluding non-clinical procedures from the statute so as to encourage couples to use the clinical process is undermined and only effective in some cases: only certain couples[190] are at a legal disadvantage if they avail of non-clinical donor insemination and will therefore be encouraged to use the clinical process. Therefore, the provisions that are designed to incentivise couples to use clinical donor conception simply serve to disadvantage specific categories of children based on their parents' marital status or sexual orientation. It is submitted that all children should have the same opportunity to be

[188] Human Fertilisation and Embryology Act 2008, ss 35 and 42.

[189] Lydia Bracken, 'In the best interests of the child? The regulation of DAHR in Ireland' (2016) 23 *European Journal of Health Law* 391.

[190] In England and Wales, where the couple are not married or not in a civil partnership, no presumption of parentage arises. In Ireland, neither married nor unmarried same-sex couples benefit from a presumption of parentage. In South Africa, the presumption of parentage is confined to married opposite-sex couples.

legally integrated into their families. Yet, two wrongs do not make a right: just because some parents can circumvent the disadvantage associated with the exclusion of non-clinical procedures from the statutory parentage provisions does not mean that all adults should be allowed to do so. There is a danger that the child's rights would be overlooked in such a system as there would be no incentive for the adults to take steps to protect the child's rights.

Some jurisdictions have extended a presumption of parentage to *all* committed couples to ensure that all children can be legally integrated into their intended families from birth. For example, in British Columbia, section 27 of the Family Law Act 2011 provides that where a child is conceived through assisted reproduction:

> in addition to the child's birth mother, a person who was married to, or in a marriage-like relationship with, the child's birth mother when the child was conceived is also the child's parent unless there is proof that, before the child was conceived, the person
> (a) did not consent to be the child's parent, or
> (b) withdrew the consent to be the child's parent.[191]

This provision essentially creates a presumption of parentage for all committed couples who conceive a child by way of assisted reproduction. The presumption certainly looks advantageous as it ensures that all children conceived by assisted reproduction have a legal relationship with both intended parents at birth. Moreover, as noted above, the exclusion of non-clinical procedures from the statutory parentage provisions governing AHR is essentially meaningless in practice as many couples can already circumvent the rules. Creating options to recognise the second parent in the few cases that are not already covered by the various presumptions merely creates equality for rule evasion. A difficulty with applying a presumption of parentage to all committed couples is that it does not specifically address the rights of the child and there is a danger that the child's right to identity and ability to access information about their genetic origins could be compromised in this system as there is no incentive for the parents to take steps to protect those rights. As such, it is submitted that a more nuanced approach is required to accommodate non-clinical procedures.

An alternative option is to allow the intended parents of a child conceived through non-clinical donor insemination to register the birth of the child and to be jointly listed as parents on the child's birth

[191] Family Law Act 2011, s 27.

certificate provided that certain conditions have been met, for example that they provide a statutory declaration attesting that they are the parents and attesting that they have accurately recorded the donor's identity along with a statutory declaration provided by the donor agreeing that he waives his parental status and did not intend to be recognised as a legal parent at the time of the procedure. This approach would allow the intended parents to be recognised as legal parents shortly after the child's birth but would also ensure that they take steps to safeguard the child's rights prior to conception and to protect the rights of the donor after conception (to ensure that he is not deprived of his parental status against his wishes). A different solution would be to allow the intended parents to apply to court for a declaration of parentage after the birth of the child to establish legal parentage. Safeguards could be built into this mechanism to protect the child's rights. For example, the application could be grounded on evidence establishing the donor's consent to the use of their gamete and evidence demonstrating that details of the donor's identity have been recorded.[192] This would allow the second parent to be legally recognised but would also encourage intended parents to take precautions to protect the child's rights and best interests at the time of the conception. Overall, it is argued that *some* mechanism must be put in place to ensure that all children conceived by non-clinical donor insemination can acquire a legal relationship with the second parent and are not legally disadvantaged by the circumstances of their birth when compared to other children.

5.5 Conclusion

The best interests of the child demand that specific laws are introduced to determine legal parentage in the context of donor conception and to ensure that the child's intended parents are recognised as legal parents, with full responsibilities and rights to care for the child, from birth. The child's right to identity must also be safeguarded in the regulation of donor conception. In both England and Wales and Ireland, donor-conceived children have access to information about their genetic origins, but this access is restricted until the age of 18 years. It has been argued that children should have access to this information during childhood. This is required to vindicate the child's right to identity and to

[192] These solutions are endorsed by LGBT Ireland, *Pathways to Parenting: Proposals for Reform* (Dublin: LGBT Ireland, 2018). Available at www.lgbt.ie.

ensure that the regulation of donor conception operates in the best interests of the child. In South Africa, children do not have access to identifying information about their gamete donor. It is submitted that this approach runs contrary to the child's right to identity as they are deprived of important information about their identity and may be unconstitutional in the South African context as it appears to be contrary to the child's best interests.

In relation to the right to identity of 'fatherless' children, there is a wealth of sociological and psychological evidence that suggests that children who are raised by same-sex parents do just as well as those who are raised by opposite-sex couples, and there is nothing to suggest that children born to lesbian couples are confused in terms of their identity. As such, it is argued that access to fertility services should be available on a non-discriminatory basis, although it may be appropriate to consider the best interests of the child before treatment is provided. This assessment should be a minimal one and applied to all couples who seek access to fertility treatment. The purpose of the assessment is to ensure that the child is not exposed to immediate harm once born.[193]

In each of the comparator jurisdictions discussed in this chapter, children who are conceived via donor insemination in a non-clinical setting are excluded from the statutory parentage provisions governing such procedures. It is argued that the exclusion of non-clinical donor conception from the statutory parentage provisions that apply in cases of clinical conceptions has a legitimate basis but is meaningless in practice as many couples can already circumvent the difficulties associated with exclusion. As such, it is argued that reforms are required to ensure that children conceived via non-clinical procedures are not disadvantaged by the circumstances of their birth when compared to other children conceived in virtually identical circumstances. Such reform is required to promote the best interests of children conceived in the non-clinical setting.

[193] See further Lydia Bracken, 'The pre-conception best interests assessment – part 1: Suitability and feasibility' (2019) 22 *Irish Journal of Family Law* 16; Lydia Bracken, 'The pre-conception best interests assessment – part 2: Implications for the Irish legal framework' (2019) 22 *Irish Journal of Family Law* 2.

6

Surrogacy

6.1 Introduction

Surrogacy is a process where a person agrees to carry a child on behalf of another person or couple. This pathway to parentage is most commonly used by married opposite-sex couples, but it is also popular amongst gay male couples and it tends to be used more by them than by lesbian couples, although data on the provision of services are somewhat unreliable.[1] The process is fraught with legal and ethical issues. In some countries, such as Ireland, these issues are compounded by the fact that there is no legislation governing the allocation of parentage in situations where surrogacy is undertaken. In line with the arguments advanced in the previous chapter, it is argued that the absence of legislation regulating surrogacy is contrary to the best interests of children who are born through this process as they are left in a vulnerable position due to the lack of regulation. As such, the central premise of this chapter is that surrogacy must be subject to specific legal regulation in order to comply with the best interests principle. The central question is precisely *how* surrogacy should be regulated to ensure that this objective is met.

This chapter examines common arguments raised against the use and regulation of surrogacy. It is submitted that the arguments presented do not justify prohibiting the process. The chapter also considers the effect of prohibition in this regard, through analysis of the case law of the European Court of Human Rights (ECtHR). Based on this analysis, it is argued that surrogacy must be regulated to secure the best interests of children who are born through the process. The chapter then considers the regulation of surrogacy in each of the comparator jurisdictions to

[1] Marilyn Crawshaw, Eric Blyth and Olga van den Akker, 'The changing profile of surrogacy in the UK – Implications for national and international policy and practice' (2012) 34 *Journal of Social Welfare and Family Law* 265.

identify a means of regulating surrogacy that adheres to the best interests principle and that balances the interests and needs of all stakeholders in the process.

6.2 The Regulation of Surrogacy

Surrogacy is a contentious area that raises many legal and ethical issues. As a result, attitudes towards surrogacy vary considerably between countries: some jurisdictions prohibit surrogacy completely;[2] some permit surrogacy but do not specifically regulate it;[3] other jurisdictions offer limited recognition of altruistic surrogacy only;[4] while others fully regulate the process.[5] Indeed, such are the diverse views on surrogacy, it has been noted that 'even those who argue for legalizing and regulating surrogacy may completely disagree about the appropriate forms of regulation'.[6]

There are many different types of surrogacy. Gestational or 'full' surrogacy occurs where the surrogate does not provide her own eggs to enable the conception of the child and is therefore not genetically related to the child. The genetic material will instead come from the intended mother or it may be donated by a third party. Traditional or 'partial' surrogacy occurs where the surrogate mother provides her own eggs to enable the conception, and so she is both the gestational carrier and the genetic mother of the child. Surrogacy may also be altruistic (where the surrogate is paid only reasonable expenses) or commercial (where the surrogate is paid for her services).

Some people are opposed to the idea of surrogacy on the basis that it is harmful to the children who are born through the process. The outcomes for children born through surrogacy are discussed in detail later in this section, but a more immediate concern is that the practice of surrogacy, in particular where payment is involved, can amount to the sale and trafficking of children contrary to the United Nations Convention on the

[2] For example, in France, Germany and Italy, all forms of surrogacy are prohibited.

[3] Currently in Belgium, the Czech Republic and Hungary there is no specific legislation to address surrogacy.

[4] The United Kingdom and Greece only allow altruistic surrogacy.

[5] Some US states, such as California, fully regulate both altruistic and commercial surrogacy arrangements.

[6] UN Special Rapporteur on the Sale and Sexual Exploitation of Children, *Report to the Human Rights Council*, A/HRC/37/60, 15 January 2018 at para. 21.

Rights of the Child (UNCRC)[7] and the Optional Protocol to the Convention on the Rights of the Child on the Sale of Children, Child Prostitution and Child Pornography (OPSC).[8] The Committee on the Rights of the Child has confirmed that commercial surrogacy, which is not properly regulated, may amount to the sale of children contrary to international law.[9] Similarly, the United Nations Special Rapporteur on the Sale and Sexual Exploitation of Children has noted that surrogacy, whether commercial or altruistic, can amount to the sale of children, and so States must prohibit, and create safeguards to prevent, the abduction of, sale of, or traffic in children in the context of all forms of surrogacy.[10] The Special Rapporteur has noted that commercial surrogacy does not always amount to the sale of children, namely where 'it is closely regulated in compliance with international human rights norms and standards'.[11] However, the Special Rapporteur has found that, at present, many commercial surrogacy regimes are not regulated in this manner.[12] This demonstrates that any regulation of surrogacy must adhere to international human rights norms, and so the approach adopted in this chapter, which seeks to identify a way to regulate surrogacy that is in line with the child's best interests under the UNCRC, is necessary to ensure that undesirable practices are not normalised through the growth in the use of surrogacy worldwide.

Concern has also been expressed for the interests of those who act as surrogate mothers. For example, in 1984, the Warnock Committee noted that a significant argument against the use of surrogacy is that 'it is inconsistent with human dignity that a woman should use her uterus

[7] Article 35 of the United Nations Convention on the Rights of the Child (UNCRC) provides that 'States Parties shall take all appropriate national, bilateral and multilateral measures to prevent the abduction of, the sale of or traffic in children for any purpose or in any form'.

[8] Article 1 of OPSC prohibits the sale of children, which is defined in Art 2(a) as 'any act or transaction whereby a child is transferred by any person or group of persons to another for remuneration or any other consideration'.

[9] Committee on the Rights of the Child, *Concluding observations on the combined third and fourth periodic reports of India* CRC/C/IND/CO/3–4; Committee on the Rights of the Child, *Concluding observations on the second periodic report of the United States of America submitted under article 12 of the Optional Protocol to the Convention on the sale of children, child prostitution and child pornography*, adopted by the Committee at its sixty-second session (14 January–1 February 2013) CRC/C/OPSC/USA/CO/2; Committee on the Rights of the Child, *Concluding observations on the combined fourth and fifth periodic reports of Mexico* CRC/C/MEX/CO/4–5.

[10] UN Special Rapporteur, above n. 6, para. 41.

[11] UN Special Rapporteur, above n. 6, para. 41.

[12] UN Special Rapporteur, above n. 6, para. 41.

for financial profit and treat it as an incubator for someone else's child'.[13] More recently, a resolution passed by the European Parliament of the European Union in December 2015 condemned all forms of surrogacy on the basis that it 'undermines the human dignity of the woman since her body and its reproductive functions are used as a commodity'.[14] Even where there is no financial gain for the woman who acts as a surrogate, the fact that she is required to 'hand over' the child to the intended parents is regarded as abhorrent to some and contrary to the maternal instincts that she is expected to feel as a gestational mother.[15]

The use of surrogacy by male couples has also been the focus of much, often negative, attention. For example, surrogacy was continually raised as an issue in the build up to the Irish marriage equality referendum in 2015. The potential for surrogacy to be used by male couples was used to argue (ultimately unsuccessfully) against amending the Constitution to allow for same-sex marriage. It was claimed that surrogacy would mean that children would be 'deliberately robbed of a mother' and should not be permitted.[16] More recently, in October 2016, thousands of people marched in Paris against same-sex marriage and against the use of surrogacy to help same-sex couples conceive,[17] while in January 2016, Italy's interior minister called for surrogate parents to be treated as sex offenders in response to moves by the Italian Government to extend the legal recognition of gay and lesbian families.[18]

The arguments raised against the use of surrogacy by male couples range from abstract generalisation ('children will be harmed') to more specific points, such as that children will be 'deliberately robbed' of their mother in situations where both intended parents are male. Lesbian couples may, of course, also avail of surrogacy, but this is a less common scenario,[19] and so the impact on the child of having two mothers is more commonly raised as an issue in the context of donor insemination, as

[13] Committee of Inquiry into Human Fertilisation and Embryology, *Report of the Committee of Inquiry into Human Fertilisation and Embryology* (Cmnd 9314, 1984), para 8.11.

[14] European Parliament. *Annual report on Human Rights and Democracy in the World 2014 and the European Union's policy on the matter (2015/2229(INI))*, para. 115.

[15] Committee of Inquiry into Human Fertilisation and Embryology, above n. 13, para. 8.11.

[16] Juno McEnroe, 'Tánaiste: No posters "sad and demeaning"', *Irish Examiner*, 5 May 2015.

[17] Reuters, 'Thousands March in Paris to repeal same-sex marriage law' NBC News, 16 October 2016.

[18] Rosie Scammell, 'Treat surrogate parents as sex offenders, says Italian minister' *The Guardian*, 6 January 2016.

[19] Crawshaw, Blyth and van den Akker, above n. 1.

discussed in Chapter 5. It should also be noted that, despite the fears raised in relation to the use of surrogacy by male couples, this pathway to parentage is most commonly used by married opposite-sex couples.[20]

This section explores the validity or otherwise of arguments raised against the use of surrogacy, in particular the concerns raised against the use of surrogacy by male couples. Ultimately, it is argued that these concerns are not supported by existing sociological and psychological research. It is further argued that, even if this was not the case, surrogacy must still be appropriately regulated as children will continue to be born through the process irrespective of the legal response. Prohibiting surrogacy in one country will not stop its use in another. Therefore, the children who are born, and who will continue to be born, in this way must be legally recognised and protected. The most appropriate way to regulate surrogacy is considered later in the chapter.

6.2.1 *'[A] Surrogacy Agreement Is Degrading to the Child Who Is to Be the Outcome of It'*

In 1984, the Warnock Committee[21] noted that one of the central arguments against the use of surrogacy is that it distorts the relationship between mother and child because 'in such an arrangement a woman deliberately allows herself to become pregnant with the intention of giving up the child to which she will give birth'.[22] This was seen to be 'potentially damaging to the child, whose bonds with the carrying mother, regardless of genetic connections, are held to be strong, and whose welfare must be considered to be of paramount importance'.[23]

The argument that surrogacy is harmful to children is still made today, over thirty years after the Warnock Report was published, but now we have the benefit of scientific research to assess the validity of the claim. The existing research does not support the idea that children are harmed by surrogacy alone. As the New Zealand Law Reform Commission has noted, 'there appears to be a reliable body of research that suggests that good or bad outcomes for the children born by donor insemination or

20 Crawshaw, Blyth and van den Akker, above n. 1.

21 The title of this subsection is taken from a statement made by members of the Warnock Committee.

22 Committee of Inquiry into Human Fertilisation and Embryology, above n. 13, para. 8.11.

23 Committee of Inquiry into Human Fertilisation and Embryology, above n. 13, para. 8.11.

surrogacy cannot be linked to the method of conception or family form itself'.[24]

The outcomes for children born through surrogacy have been studied as part of longitudinal study conducted by Golombok and others since the year 2000.[25] This study has compared the functioning of surrogacy families with egg donation families and natural conception families and has followed up with the same families when the children reached age 1,[26] age 2,[27] age 3,[28] age 7,[29] age 10[30] and age 14.[31] In the latter phases of the longitudinal study, donor insemination families were also included as a comparison group.[32] This research has found that children born through surrogacy have positive family relationships and psychological well-being when assessed at all ages and are not negatively affected by the fact of being born through surrogacy. In the pre-school years, the children born through surrogacy were found to have more positive parent–child relationships than children in the comparison group of natural conception families.[33] The positive family relationships prevailed when the children reached the middle-school years, although by that time the surrogacy families no longer showed *more* positive parent–child

[24] New Zealand Law Commission, *New Issues in Legal Parenthood*, Report 88 (Wellington: New Zealand Law Commission, 2005), p. 13.

[25] Susan Golombok, Elena Ilioi, Lucy Blake, Gabriela Roman and Vasanti Jadva, 'A longitudinal study of families formed through reproductive donation: Parent-adolescent relationships and adolescent adjustment at age 14' (2017) 53 *Developmental Psychology* 1966–1977.

[26] Susan Golombok, Clare Murray, Vasanti Jadva, Fiona MacCallum and Emma Lycett, 'Families created through surrogacy arrangements: Parent–child relationships in the 1st year of life' (2004) 40 *Developmental Psychology* 400–411.

[27] Susan Golombok, Fiona MacCallum, Clare Murray, Emma Lycett and Vasanti Jadva, 'Surrogacy families: Parental functioning, parent-child relationships and children's psychological development at age 2' (2006) 47 *Journal of Child Psychology & Psychiatry* 213–222.

[28] Susan Golombok, Clare Murray, Vasanti Jadva, Emma Lycett, Fiona MacCallum and John Rust, 'Non-genetic and non-gestational parenthood: Consequences for parent-child relationships and the psychological well-being of mothers, fathers and children at age 3' (2006) 21 *Human Reproduction* 1918–1924.

[29] Susan Golombok, Jennifer Readings, Lucy Blake, Polly Casey, Laura Mellish, Alex Marks and Vasanti Jadva, 'Families created through surrogacy: Mother-child relationships and children's psychological adjustment at age 7' (2011) 47 *Developmental Psychology* 1579–1588.

[30] Susan Golombok, Lucy Blake, Polly Casey, Gabriela Roman and Vasanti Jadva, 'Children born through reproductive donation: A longitudinal study of psychological adjustment' (2013) 54 *Journal of Child Psychology and Psychiatry* 653–660.

[31] Golombok and others (2017), above n. 25.

[32] Golombok and others (2013), above n. 30; Golombok and others (2017), above n. 25.

[33] Golombok and others (2017), above n. 25, 1967.

relationships. At age 7, the children born through surrogacy exhibited higher levels of adjustment difficulties than the naturally conceived children, but this difference disappeared by age 10.[34] The researchers note that transnationally adopted children have been found to experience the same difficulties at this age, and this 'has been attributed to these children's need to confront identity-related issues at a young age'.[35] Similarly, 'children born through surrogacy may be concerned with issues relating to identity at an early age'.[36]

When the children reached adolescence, a period where difficulties in mother–adolescent relationships and adolescent adjustment problems may be anticipated, positive mother–adolescent relationships and well-adjusted adolescents were found in all of the families who participated in the study. The researchers speculate that this finding may be attributed to the fact that the mothers in egg donation, donor insemination and surrogacy families are highly motivated to have children and '[c]hildren born through reproductive donation are, by necessity, planned and there is evidence to show that planned pregnancies are associated with more positive psychological outcomes for mothers and children'.[37] The research found that where differences in the quality of mother–adolescent relationships were identified between family types, 'these reflected *more positive* relationships in the surrogacy families compared with the gamete donation families'.[38] The researchers note that 'mothers in surrogacy families were found to show less negative parenting and reported greater acceptance of their adolescent children and fewer problems in family relationships as a whole'.[39]

The researchers did not expect to find such positive family functioning within the surrogacy families. They note that surrogacy is a controversial pathway to parentage and that negative social attitudes towards surrogacy prevail. Thus, at the outset of the study, surrogacy had been 'assumed to carry the greatest psychological risks'.[40] Ultimately, this hypothesis was not supported by the research findings. The researchers note that the motivations that drive adults to engage in surrogacy may have contributed to the positive family relationships. Those who embark

[34] Golombok and others (2017), above n. 25, 1967.
[35] Golombok and others (2017), above n. 25, 1967.
[36] Golombok and others (2017), above n. 25, 1967.
[37] Golombok and others (2017), above n. 25, 1974.
[38] Golombok and others (2017), above n. 25, 1974 [emphasis added].
[39] Golombok and others (2017), above n. 25, 1974.
[40] Golombok and others (2017), above n. 25, 1974.

on surrogacy typically develop trusting relationships with the surrogate and the majority of couples who become parents in this way maintain some element of contact with the surrogate. The intended parents are highly motivated to become parents; they do not enter into the process lightly and have come to accept that a third party will be involved in the process of creating their family. All of these factors were seen to contribute to the more positive parenting in the surrogacy families when compared to the other family types.[41]

Overall, the findings of the research to date indicate that there is positive family functioning and child development in the surrogacy families. As the researchers noted following the assessment of the families at age 10, the findings 'add to the growing body of research suggesting that biological relatedness between parents and children is not essential for positive child adjustment'.[42] It would seem, therefore, that any fears expressed in respect of the outcomes for children born via surrogacy are based on speculation, not fact.

6.2.2 *The 'Motherless Child'*

Another argument made against the use of surrogacy by male couples is that children born through this process are 'deliberately robbed' of their mother because parentage is transferred from the surrogate to the intended parents upon the child's birth. Some commentators raise concerns that the legally motherless children will be negatively affected. For example, Callus has stated that '[u]nlike a child born to a lesbian couple who knows who his birth mother is, a child born to a surrogate who is then the subject of a parental order in favour of a male same-sex couple, will not have the same point of reference'.[43] Other commentators have simply argued that the child needs a maternal influence. During the Irish marriage equality referendum, for example, O'Brien argued in a national Irish newspaper that not being raised by both a mother and a father 'constitutes a loss' and that children need two parents of the opposite sex in order to thrive.[44] According to O'Brien, '[t]wo men can love each other and two men can love a child. But neither of them can provide a child

[41] Golombok and others (2017), above n. 25, 1974.

[42] Golombok and others (2013), above n. 30.

[43] Thérèse Callus, 'First "Designer Babies", Now *Á la Carte* Parents' (2008) 38 *Family Law* 143, p. 145.

[44] Breda O'Brien, 'Love is not enough when it comes to children's rights' *Irish Times*, 24 January 2015.

with a mother'.[45] In a similar vein, McGratten has contended that the traditional family of a married mother and a married father provides the best environment in which to raise a child. In support of this, he points to research conducted by Morgan which emphasises that the roles of mothers and fathers 'are not interchangeable'.[46] Likewise, Duncan has opined that

> [h]istorical experience and common sense suggest that mothers and fathers are not fungible, but the new parenthood assumes the exact opposite. And the children who are subject to these adult transactions, of course, cannot be consulted until it is too late.[47]

Social science literature pertaining to the outcomes for children who are raised by same-sex couples was discussed in Chapter 2. As was noted in that chapter, studies of gay father families are somewhat limited. This is understandable due to the fact that there are simply fewer gay men who are raising children together than there are lesbian couples. Furthermore, in many countries, criminal prohibitions were imposed on sexual relations between men until relatively recently.[48] As such, the dearth of longitudinal studies can be appreciated.

Golombok and others note that 'it is widely assumed that fathers are less suited to parenting than are mothers' and further that children raised by gay fathers will be exposed to greater stigmatization than children with lesbian mothers because there are fewer families headed solely by men than by women.[49] However, these hypotheses are not supported by the existing research on gay father families. Many studies demonstrate that the children of gay fathers are no different to other children in terms of their development.[50] While less is known about children who are raised by gay fathers than children who are raised by lesbian mothers, the available evidence does not suggest that children raised by male parents

45 Above.

46 P. Morgan, 'How do fathers fit in?' *Civitas: The Institute for the Study of Civil Society* in Dominic McGratten, 'No need for a father: The human fertilisation and embryology act 2008' (2009) 12(2) *Irish Journal of Family Law* 33, p. 34.

47 William Duncan, 'Deconstructing parenthood' (2008) 22(6) *The Family in America* 1.

48 Ireland, for example, only decriminalised consensual sexual relations between adult men in 1993.

49 Susan Golombok, Lucy Blake, Jenna Slutsky, Elizabeth Raffanello, Gabriela Roman, Anke Ehrhardt, 'Parenting and the adjustment of children born to gay fathers through surrogacy' (2018) 89 *Child Development* 1223–1233, p. 1223.

50 Susan Golombok and Fiona Tasker, 'Children in lesbian and gay families: theories and evidence' (1994) 5 *Annual Review of Sex Research* 73 in Susan Golombok, *Parenting: What Really Counts?* (London: Routledge, 2000), p. 58.

differ in terms of their psychological well-being than those children who are raised either by opposite-sex parents or lesbian parents.[51]

A 2014 study conducted by Golombok and others on gay father adoptive families found that '[w]here differences were identified between the gay father adoptive families and the heterosexual parent adoptive families, these reflected more positive functioning in the gay father families'.[52] Thus, the authors concluded that '[t]he findings of this study suggest that men can be just as competent at parenting as women, and that the absence of a female parent does not necessarily have adverse consequences for child adjustment'.[53] Therefore, although the research is limited, it indicates that children can flourish in gay father adoptive families.[54]

Surrogacy raises many issues that do not arise in adoptive families, and so the findings from research conducted on adoptive families cannot automatically be assumed to apply to surrogacy families. Gay father families created through surrogacy encounter unique issues as the children have both a genetic and a non-genetic father and a genetic mother and a gestational mother who may or may not be involved in their upbringing. In 2018, Golombok and others published the findings of the first-ever, controlled, in-depth study of parenting and child adjustment in gay father families created through surrogacy.[55] This study involved forty gay father families created through surrogacy and a comparison group of fifty-five lesbian mother families created through donor insemination with a child aged 3–9 years living in the United States. The research found that there were no differences between gay father families and lesbian mother families in terms of perceived stigma, quality of parenting, parent–child interaction or children's externalizing problems. Indeed, the children of gay fathers had significantly lower levels of parent-reported internalizing problems than the children of lesbian mothers.[56] Overall, the study found that the children of both gay fathers and lesbian mothers showed high levels of psychological adjustment and positive relationships with their parents. The authors

[51] Above, 59.

[52] Susan Golombok, Laura Mellish, Sarah Jennings, Polly Casey, Fiona Tasker and Michael Lamb, 'Adoptive gay father families: Parent–child relationships and children's psychological adjustment' (2014) 85 *Child Development* 456, p. 463.

[53] Above, 465.

[54] Golombok and others (2018), above n. 49, 1224.

[55] Golombok and others (2018), above n. 49.

[56] Golombok and others (2018), above n. 49, 1229–1230.

acknowledge that there were limitations in the study such as the moderate sample size and the use of volunteer samples. Nonetheless, it is notable that the findings are consistent with the earlier research on gay father families. Thus, the available research suggests that children raised in gay father families created through surrogacy are not adversely affected and that the absence of a female parent does not have negative consequences for children.

The South African courts have shown considerable insight in this area. In the case of *Van der Linde* v. *Van der Linde*,[57] for example, the Court was not convinced that the quality of the parental role is determined by gender. Rather the Court opined:

> These days mothering is also part of a man's being. The concept of mothering is indicative of a function rather than a 'persona' and this function is not necessarily situated in the biological mother. It includes the sensitive attachment which flows from the attention devoted from day to day to the child's needs of love, physical care, nutrition, comfort, peace, security, encouragement and support . . . Today the man has the freedom to reveal and live out the mothering feeling.[58]

In the subsequent case of *WH and Others*, the Pretoria High Court was satisfied that the 'mothering of the child is a function that very often does not have anything to do with the gender of a parent'.[59]

The available research suggests that the quality of parenting is the most important feature for the child's well-being. Children raised by gay fathers do not seem to differ in terms of their outcomes than those who are raised by married opposite-sex parents (or indeed those raised by lesbian mothers), and so it would seem that men are quite capable of providing the requisite maternal influence (if indeed a maternal influence is required).[60] As Golombok has concluded, '[f]or children who live with gay fathers, the main difficulty they are likely to face is prejudice from the outside world'.[61]

It is argued that this conclusion provides a strong argument in favour of legally recognising the parentage of male couples who have children through surrogacy, as doing so provides legislative approval of the suitability of gay men as parents. This, in turn, may help to remove any

[57] *Van der Linde* v. *Van der Linde* 1996(3) SA 509 (O).
[58] Above.
[59] *WH and Others* [2011] ZAGPPHC 185, para. 54.2.
[60] See Chapter 2.
[61] Golombok and Tasker, above n. 50, 59.

remaining prejudices that society may hold towards such parents, which can only serve to enhance the best interests of children raised by them.

The discussion above suggests that surrogacy, in and of itself, is not harmful to children. Moreover, it must be acknowledged that the practice of surrogacy will endure regardless of whether or not it is regulated. To prohibit surrogacy in the face of its continued use would be to disregard the interests of children who will continue to be born into an unregulated world of legal uncertainty. Prohibition would lead to difficulties such as have been seen in Italy where a child born through surrogacy was taken into State care on the basis that the intended parents had breached the Italian prohibition on surrogacy.[62] In France, children born through surrogacy have been rendered stateless and legally parentless due to the prohibition on surrogacy in that country.[63] These effects cannot be said to be in the children's best interests, suggesting that prohibiting surrogacy is simply not an option if the best interests of the child are to be a primary consideration.

The ECtHR has dealt with a number of cases concerning surrogacy where issues have arisen due to restrictive domestic laws. These cases demonstrate that there is no consensus on the regulation of surrogacy in Europe which creates difficulties for parents and children. The cases also reveal that, according to the ECtHR, the best interests of the child must be *paramount* in addressing the legal family relationships created through this process. Using this focus, the ECtHR has held that some amount of tolerance and recognition of surrogacy is required in order to respect the best interests of the child. As a result of recent judgments (and the first-ever advisory opinion[64]) from the ECtHR, many European states with restrictive surrogacy laws have been forced to re-evaluate their approach to international surrogacy as they are required to recognise the parentage of children born through surrogacy where there is a genetic connection with the intended father. As a result, domestic prohibitions on surrogacy become increasingly meaningless in practice as intended parents can circumvent the domestic laws in many cases by availing of surrogacy abroad.[65]

[62] *Paradiso and Campanelli* v. *Italy*, app. no. 25358/12, 27 January 2015.

[63] *Mennesson* v. *France*, app. no. 65192/11, 26 September 2014; *Labassee* v. *France*, app. no. 65941/11, 26 September 2014.

[64] European Court of Human Rights, *Advisory Opinion concerning the recognition in domestic law of a legal parent-child relationship between a child born through a gestational surrogacy arrangement abroad and the intended mother*, Request no. P16-2018-001, 10 April 2019.

[65] Claire Fenton-Glynn, 'International surrogacy before the European Court of Human Rights' (2017) 13 *Journal of Private International Law* 546.

6.3 The European Convention on Human Rights

The cases of *Mennesson* v. *France*[66] and *Labassee* v. *France*[67] concerned the refusal of French authorities to grant legal recognition to parent–child relationships that had been legally established in the United States between children born as a result of surrogacy and their intended parents. Surrogacy is prohibited in France and, as a result, the French authorities refused to recognise the US birth certificates that listed the intended parents as the legal parents. Mr and Mrs Mennesson and Mr and Mrs Labassee unsuccessfully applied to the French courts to have the birth certificates entered into the French register of births. The Court of Cassation dismissed the request on the grounds that recording such entries in the register would give effect to surrogacy agreements that were void on public policy grounds under the French Civil Code. The applicants subsequently brought a claim to the ECtHR arguing that their inability to obtain recognition in France of the parent–child relationships legally established abroad amounted to a violation of Article 8 ECHR (the right to private and family life). They further argued that there was a violation of Article 14 ECHR (prohibition of discrimination) taken in conjunction with Article 8 ECHR as the children were subject to differential treatment when compared to other children. The cases were heard simultaneously by a Chamber of the Fifth Section of the ECtHR and the same result was reached in both cases.

In both *Mennesson* and *Labassee*, the ECtHR found that there was no violation of the applicant's right to family life under Article 8 ECHR. Although the family experienced practical difficulties because of the lack of legal recognition of the parent–child relationships, the issues were not insurmountable, nor did they impede the applicants' exercise of their right to respect for their family life on a day-to-day basis.[68]

By contrast, the ECtHR found that there had been a violation of the applicants' right to private life under Article 8 ECHR. The Court noted that the children were unrecognised under French law. They could not acquire French nationality, and they were denied inheritance rights by virtue of the non-recognition. The issues took on a 'special dimension' because the children were genetically related to their intended father. The

[66] *Mennesson* v. *France*, app. no. 65192/11, 26 September 2014.
[67] *Labassee* v. *France*, app. no. 65941/11, 26 September 2014.
[68] *Mennesson* v. *France*, app. no. 65192/11, 26 September 2014, paras. 92–94.

ECtHR noted that biological parentage is an important component of each individual's identity and found that it was contrary to the best interests of the child to deprive them of a legal relationship with a biological parent where the biological reality of that tie was established, and the child and the parent concerned sought its full recognition.[69] The Court held that the children's right to respect for their private life under Article 8 ECHR had been violated.

In both cases, the ECtHR noted that States enjoy a wide margin of appreciation in determining the regulation of surrogacy, but the judgments make it clear that the margin will be reduced where an important component of the child's identity is at stake. Moreover, the decisions emphasise that the best interests of the child must be paramount in cases of surrogacy when balancing the competing interests that arise.

Following the *Mennesson* and *Labassee* cases, the ECtHR issued its first-ever advisory opinion following a request from the French Court of Cassation under Article 1 of Protocol No 16 to the ECHR. The request was made to clarify the implications of the *Mennesson* and *Labassee* judgments. The French Court noted that, in line with those judgments, the State was required to register the details of a birth certificate that designated the intended father as the child's legal father following a surrogacy arrangement in cases where he was also the genetic father. It was not possible to register the details of the intended mother. As such, the Court of Cassation submitted two questions to the ECtHR worded as follows:

1. By refusing to enter in the register of births, marriages and deaths the details of the birth certificate of a child born abroad as the result of a gestational surrogacy arrangement, in so far as the certificate designates the 'intended mother' as the 'legal mother', while accepting registration in so far as the certificate designates the 'intended father', who is the child's biological father, is a State Party overstepping its margin of appreciation under Article 8 of the European Convention for the Protection of Human Rights and Fundamental Freedoms? In this connection should a distinction be drawn according to whether or not the child was conceived using the eggs of the 'intended mother'?
2. In the event of an answer in the affirmative to either of the two questions above, would the possibility for the intended mother to

[69] Above, para. 100.

adopt the child of her spouse, the biological father, this being a means of establishing the legal mother-child relationship, ensure compliance with the requirements of Article 8 of the Convention?[70]

In addressing the first question, the ECtHR restricted its examination to 'a situation where the child was conceived using the eggs of a third-party donor and where the legal parent-child relationship with the intended father has been recognised in domestic law'.[71] Hence, the Advisory Opinion did not consider a situation where traditional surrogacy (using the eggs of the surrogate) was used, nor did it consider a situation where a male couple engaged in surrogacy. The Court noted that the 'general and absolute impossibility of obtaining recognition of the relationship between a child born through a surrogacy arrangement entered into abroad and the intended mother is incompatible with the child's best interests'.[72] At a minimum, each situation has to be examined in the light of the particular circumstances of the case, which is not feasible where a blanket prohibition on recognition applies. The Court found that, in the surrogacy situations referred to:

> the right to respect for private life, within the meaning of Article 8 of the Convention, of a child born abroad through a gestational surrogacy arrangement requires that domestic law provide a possibility of recognition of a legal parent-child relationship with the intended mother, designated in the birth certificate legally established abroad as the 'legal mother'.[73]

In relation to the mechanism required to recognise the relationship with the intended mother, the ECtHR found that there was no obligation on States to register the details of the birth certificate legally established abroad. Rather, 'the choice of means by which to permit recognition of the legal relationship between the child and the intended parents falls within the States' margin of appreciation'.[74] The Court was satisfied that Article 8 ECHR does not impose a general obligation on States to recognise *ab initio* the parent–child relationship between the child and the intended mother. However, the relationship had to be recognised once 'it has become a practical reality'.[75] Adoption by the intended

[70] European Court of Human Rights, above n. 64, para. 9.
[71] European Court of Human Rights, above n. 64, para. 32.
[72] European Court of Human Rights, above n. 64, para. 42.
[73] European Court of Human Rights, above n. 64, para. 46.
[74] European Court of Human Rights, above n. 64, para. 51.
[75] European Court of Human Rights, above n. 64, para. 52.

mother or another mechanism could be used for this purpose, so long as the procedure can be 'implemented promptly and effectively'[76] to ensure that the child is 'not kept for a lengthy period in a position of legal uncertainty as regards the relationship'.[77]

Although the Advisory Opinion was focused on the legal recognition of the intended mother, the same principles could be applied to a situation where two men engage in surrogacy abroad, one of whom is the genetic father of the child, where they are both listed as parents on the child's birth certificate. Even in countries that do not currently recognise same-sex parenting, it is argued that the Advisory Opinion could be used to demand that a mechanism is made available to recognise the legal parental status of the second father. After all, in *Mennesson* and *Labassee*, recognition was deemed necessary notwithstanding the French prohibition on surrogacy.

The effect of the *Mennesson* and *Labassee* cases, combined with the Advisory Opinion, is that 'intended parents can effectively circumvent local prohibitions on surrogacy by accessing services abroad'.[78] So long as one intended father has a genetic relationship with the child, both that relationship and the relationship with the other intended parent listed on the birth certificate must be recognised. The genetic link is significant here – a point which is underlined by the later judgment in *Paradiso and Campanelli* v. *Italy*.[79] In that case, the lack of any genetic link between the child and the intended parents meant that there was no violation of Article 8 ECHR in circumstances where the Italian authorities refused to recognise the parental relationship legally established in Russia between a child born through surrogacy and the intended parents.

In *Paradiso*, an Italian couple had a child through surrogacy in Russia. Upon their return to Italy, the Italian authorities refused to recognise the parent–child relationship between the child and the intended parents. Criminal proceedings were brought against the parents for 'misrepresentation of civil status' (as the child's birth certificate was found to contain false information) and the child was removed from the intended parents and placed in State care.

[76] European Court of Human Rights, above n. 64, para. 55.

[77] European Court of Human Rights, above n. 64, para. 54.

[78] Lydia Bracken, 'Assessing the best interests of the child in cases of cross-border surrogacy: Inconsistency in the Strasbourg approach?' (2017) 39 *Journal of Social Welfare and Family Law* 368, p. 373.

[79] *Paradiso and Campanelli* v. *Italy*, app. no. 25358/12, 24 January 2017.

The case was initially heard by a Chamber of the ECtHR, which found that the removal of the child by the Italian authorities constituted a violation of the applicants' right to family life contrary to Article 8 ECHR. The Italian Government subsequently requested that the case be referred to the Grand Chamber of the ECtHR. At the outset, the Grand Chamber distinguished the case from the earlier judgments in *Mennesson* and *Labassee* on the basis that the issue in those cases was the refusal to register the particulars of a birth certificate and the children's right to obtain recognition of the legal parent–child relationship, whereas the present case concerned the measures taken by the Italian authorities that resulted in the permanent separation of the child and the applicants.[80]

The Grand Chamber was not satisfied that family life existed between the applicants but found that the private life aspect of Article 8 ECHR had been engaged. Although the removal of the child was found to constitute an interference with the private life of the applicants, the Court held that the removal was in accordance with law and struck a fair balance between the public interest pursued through the prohibition of surrogacy and the best interests of the child.[81] As a result, there was no violation of Article 8 ECHR.

The *Paradiso* judgment makes it clear that there is no obligation on States to recognise a foreign surrogacy arrangement where there is no genetic link between the intended parents and the child. The decision emphasises the importance of the genetic link and, in doing so, reinforces the decision in *Mennesson* and *Labassee* such that States are required to legally recognise parent–child relationships created through international surrogacy where there is a genetic link.[82] The *Mennesson* and *Labassee* judgments have had a significant effect on the recognition of international surrogacy arrangements in Europe. For example, in a case heard by the French Court of Cassation in 2015, it was held that the *Mennesson* ruling had to be followed such that the birth certificate of a French citizen, issued in a foreign country, had to be transcribed into the French Birth Register, unless it is found that the birth certificate is unlawful or forged or that the facts stated on it do not correspond to reality.[83] Similarly, the German Federal Court of Justice has found that, following the ECtHR jurisprudence, a foreign birth certificate issued in

[80] Above, para. 131.
[81] Above, para. 202–211.
[82] Fenton-Glynn, above n. 65, 561.
[83] Cour de Cassation, Ruling no. 619 (3 July 2015).

a case of surrogacy had to be recognised.[84] The judgments emphasise that the children who are born through surrogacy should not be disadvantaged by virtue of the circumstances of their birth – but only where there is a genetic connection.

Fenton-Glynn notes that the ECtHR jurisprudence has created a situation where there is 'dual treatment' of surrogacy in countries where it is prohibited under the domestic law. Notwithstanding the prohibition, the domestic courts are required to recognise the parentage of children born through surrogacy abroad, at least where there is a genetic connection between the child and the parents. Fenton-Glynn notes that

> [a]s a result, those with financial means can choose another regulatory scheme, and thus avoid the restrictions put in place by domestic authorities, in effect buying their way out of the ethical decisions given legislative force in their own jurisdiction.[85]

International surrogacy is discussed in more detail later in the chapter, but it is relevant to note at this point that the Hague Conference on Private International Law is working to develop an international response to surrogacy.[86] Until this is in place, individual States will have to grapple with the complex issues arising where a child has been born through surrogacy conducted abroad. Whatever response is adopted, it is important that the child is not penalised due to the circumstances of their conception. It is argued that this is required under Article 2 UNCRC, which provides that the child should not experience discrimination based on the activities or status of the parents, among other things. Once the child has developed a relationship with the intended parents, it is almost always in their best interests to transfer parentage to the intended parents or to recognise them as legal parents in another way. As the English High Court acknowledged in *Re X and Y (Foreign Surrogacy)*, it

> is almost impossible to imagine a set of circumstances in which by the time the case comes to court, the welfare of any child (particularly a foreign child) would not be gravely compromised (at the very least) by a refusal to make an order [transferring parentage to the intended parents].[87]

[84] Case XII ZB 463/13 (10 December 2014).

[85] Fenton-Glynn, above n. 65, 564.

[86] Hague Conference on Private International Law, *Report of the Experts' Group on the Parentage/Surrogacy Project* (Report February 2017).

[87] *Re X and Y (Foreign Surrogacy)* [2008] EWHC 3030 (Fam).

Due to the complexities of international surrogacy, it is suggested that the home nation of the intended parents should not automatically recognise the parentage of children born through surrogacy abroad but nor should it automatically refuse to recognise parentage. Instead, the courts should carefully review the situation, taking the best interests of the child as the paramount consideration. As the Special Rapporteur on the Sale and Sexual Exploitation of Children has noted:

> The State of the intending parents should only grant parentage and parental responsibility to intending parents after such evaluations, based on the best interests of the child. The child must not be punished or discriminated against due to the circumstances of his or her birth, and the rights of surrogate-born children must be protected. The States concerned, namely the State(s) of the intending parents and the State in which the child is born, are responsible for ensuring that statelessness does not occur.[88]

The regulation of surrogacy in England and Wales, Ireland and South Africa is discussed in the following sections. That discussion focuses on the domestic regulation of surrogacy in each jurisdiction. England and South Africa adopt very different approaches to the regulation of parentage in surrogacy, while there is currently no specific legislation concerning surrogacy in Ireland. The following sections assess the various approaches to consider which, if any, best protects the interests of the child. Concerns about the potential exploitation of surrogates and the commodification of surrogate-born children are also addressed throughout.

6.4 Surrogacy in England and Wales

Surrogacy has been regulated in England and Wales for over thirty years. The first statute to regulate the area, the Surrogacy Arrangements Act 1985, was restrictive in nature and sought to limit surrogacy by prohibiting advertising in respect of this process and restricting the arrangement of surrogacy by third parties. The intention was to make it more difficult for intended parents and potential surrogates to make connections with one another. Legislators expected that this would impede the use of surrogacy and reduce the number of surrogacy arrangements taking place in the United Kingdom.[89]

[88] UN Special Rapporteur, above n. 6, para. 70.

[89] Natalie Gamble, 'A better legal framework for United Kingdom surrogacy' in Susan Golombok, Rosamund Scott, John Appleby, Martin Richards and

Various amendments have been made to the regulation of surrogacy over the years. The Human Fertilisation and Embryology Act 1990 introduced provisions to address the legal parentage of children born through surrogacy and these were subsequently updated by the Human Fertilisation and Embryology Act 2008. In addition, the Human Fertilisation and Embryology Act 2008 amended the Surrogacy Arrangements Act 1985 to allow for non-profit organisations to introduce intended parents and potential surrogates and to advertise their services.

The English legislation now establishes that, in cases of surrogacy, the surrogate will be regarded as the legal mother when the child is born.[90] The intended parents may then apply for a parental order so as to transfer legal parentage from the surrogate (and her husband if applicable) to them. This order cannot be made for the first six weeks after the child's birth, but it must be made within six months of the birth.[91]

The application for the parental order can be made by a married couple, civil partners or two people of the same or opposite sex who are living as partners in an enduring family relationship and are not within the prohibited degrees of relationship in relation to each other.[92] As of 2018, single applicants may also apply for a parental order.[93] In order for the application to be made, at least one member of the couple must be genetically related to the child.[94]

The allocation of parentage in cases of surrogacy is based on a post-birth or 'delayed' model of recognition: the surrogate is regarded as the legal mother at birth and parentage is later transferred to the intended parents by way of a parental order. The application for the parental order cannot be made for the first six weeks after the child's birth but it must be made within six months of the birth.[95] Traditionally, the statutory time limits were strictly applied by the English courts but, more recently, the

Stephen Wilkinson (eds.), *Regulating Reproductive Donation* (Cambridge: Cambridge University Press, 2016), p. 141.

90 Human Fertilisation and Embryology Act 2008, s 33.

91 Human Fertilisation and Embryology Act 2008, ss 54-54A.

92 Human Fertilisation and Embryology Act 2008, s 54(2).

93 Human Fertilisation and Embryology Act 2008, s 54A, as inserted by Human Fertilisation and Embryology Act 2008 (Remedial) Order 2018, SI 1413/2018. Prior to 2018, single applicants were not eligible to apply for a parental order. The Family Division of the High Court held that this approach was incompatible with Articles 8 and 14 ECHR in the case of *In the matter of Z (A Child) (No 2)* [2016] EWHC 1191 (Fam).

94 Human Fertilisation and Embryology Act 2008, s 54(1)(b).

95 Human Fertilisation and Embryology Act 2008, s 54(3) and s 54(7).

courts have shown flexibility. In *Re X (A Child) (Surrogacy: Time limit)*,[96] the President of the High Court (Munby P) described a strict application of the time limit as 'the very antithesis of sensible' and he held that the Court had discretion to accept an application for a parental order made more than six months after the child's birth.[97] Munby P noted that the parental order has a profound impact on the child: the order was said to have a 'transformative effect, not just in its effect on the child's legal relationships with the surrogate and intended parents but also . . . in relation to the practical and psychological realities of [the child's] identity'.[98] Given the 'transcendental importance' of the parental order, Munby P could not accept that the legislature intended that 'the gate should be barred forever if the application for a parental order is lodged even one day late'.[99] The President was satisfied that to construe the time limit strictly would be 'almost nonsensical'. The judge concluded that the parental order could be made notwithstanding the expiration of the six-month period.[100] The judge emphasised, however, '[e]very case will, to a greater or lesser degree, be fact specific'.[101] Thus, the six-month deadline is not an absolute cut-off date but neither will it be extended in every case. This allows for the child's best interests to be paramount in the application and it means that the best solution for the child is not automatically disregarded where the time limit has elapsed.[102]

The English courts have adopted a more stringent approach to the legislative requirement that the surrogate must consent to the transfer of parentage. The case law makes it clear that the surrogate's consent can only be dispensed with where she is deceased or cannot be located.[103] In all other cases, the surrogate's consent is required, even if it is unreasonably withheld. This approach can be seen in the case of *AB (Surrogacy: Consent)*.[104] In this case, two children born through surrogacy had been in the care of their intended parents (who were also the genetic parents) since the day following their birth. The intended parents subsequently applied for a parental order to transfer legal parentage to them. The

96 *Re X (A Child) (Surrogacy: Time limit)* [2014] EWHC 3135 (Fam).

97 Above, para. 55.

98 Above, para. 54.

99 Above, para. 55.

100 In this case, the child was over two years of age at the time of the application.

101 *Re X (A Child) (Surrogacy: Time limit)* [2014] EWHC 3135 (Fam) at paras 57 and 65.

102 Lydia Bracken, 'The role of the best interests principle in regulating parentage in surrogacy in Ireland' [2017] *International Family Law* 115.

103 *D and L (Surrogacy)* [2012] EWHC 2631 (Fam).

104 *AB (Surrogacy: Consent)* [2016] EWHC 2643 (Fam).

surrogate and her husband refused their consent to the parental order. The surrogate felt that the intended parents did not show sufficient concern for her well-being whilst pregnant, and so the refusal was based on her 'own feelings of injustice, rather than what is in the children's best interests'.[105]

With the exception of the provision of the consent of the respondents, all other legislative criteria for the making of a parental order had been met. Nonetheless, without the consent of the surrogate and her husband, the parental order could not be granted. As a result, the children at the centre of this case are left in an undesirable position where the surrogate and her husband remain the legal parents but have no desire to play any part in their upbringing.[106] Meanwhile, the children are cared for by the intended parents who are not recognised as legal parents.

While the courts cannot award parentage to the intended parents where the surrogate does not consent, they may transfer care of the child to the intended parents where it is in the best interests of the child to do so. For example, in *Re N*,[107] a surrogate had refused to transfer parentage to the intended parents. The Court had to determine whether the surrogate or the intended parents should have responsibility to care for the child for the remainder of his childhood. The Court of Appeal noted that the surrogate had deceived the intended parents from the outset as 'she had never had any other objective than to obtain insemination by surrogacy, with the single purpose of acquiring for herself, and her family, another child'.[108] The trial judge awarded care of the child to the intended parents on the basis of evidence presented by two expert witnesses that this was in the best interests of the child. This finding was upheld by the Court of Appeal. Thus, there is some flexibility in cases where the surrogate refuses to consent to the transfer of parentage, and it is clear that her lack of consent does not necessarily mean that she will be permitted to continue caring for the child – though she will still be regarded as the legal mother.

The requirement that the surrogate must consent to the parental order was designed to protect the surrogate so that she has the opportunity to change her mind about the arrangement after the birth of the child. The requirement is based on the assumption that the surrogate will bond with the baby during the pregnancy and seeks to avoid a situation where she

[105] Above, para. 8.
[106] Above, para. 9.
[107] *Re N* (2007) EWCA Civ 1053.
[108] Above, para. 4.

would be forced to give the child to the intended parents after birth against her wishes. It is argued, however, that this focus on 'protecting' the surrogate by allowing her to change her mind is not supported by existing evidence. Research shows that women who act as surrogates typically do not view the child as their own and are able to distance themselves from the child, making it easier to hand the child over to the intended parents at birth.[109] Indeed, it is notable that there have only been three reported cases in the United Kingdom where surrogates have refused to consent to the transfer of parentage.[110] While there may be other situations that do not come before the courts, it is clear that the vast majority of surrogates are content to fulfil their original undertaking and that it is very rare for a surrogate to refuse to hand over the baby at birth. Thus, the legislative focus on 'protecting' the surrogate against any unforeseen emotional bond that she might develop with the child appears to be misplaced. This point is discussed further below.

6.4.1 The Delayed Model of Parentage

One of the main disadvantages of the UK regulation of surrogacy is the fact that parentage cannot be transferred to the intended parents until at least six weeks after the birth of the child. As noted above, the vast majority of surrogacy arrangements proceed as intended and very few surrogates seek to keep the child. Nonetheless, the post-birth or delayed model of parentage creates difficulties that arguably do not operate in the best interests of the child or indeed in the best interests of any of the stakeholders in the agreement.

The delayed model of parentage fails to reflect the reality of surrogacy: the child will be transferred to the care of the intended parents soon after birth, but they cannot be recognised as legal parents until the time that the parental order is made. Instead, the surrogate (and her husband, if she has one) is regarded as the legal parent. The model deprives the child of the security and protections that would flow from automatic legal recognition of the role of the intended parents.

The post-birth recognition of parentage also causes concern for intended parents. They will not know whether they will be recognised as legal parents until such time as the surrogate gives her consent to the

[109] Vasanti Jadva, 'Surrogacy: Issues, concerns and complexities' in Golombok and others, above n. 89, 128.

[110] Gamble, above n. 89, 148.

transfer of parentage. Until this consent is given, there is uncertainty as to whether the child will remain as the legal child of the surrogate or whether parentage will be transferred to the intended parents. As such, the child is left in a sort of 'parental limbo' as their ultimate parental status is unclear.[111] This operates to the detriment of both the child and the intended parents.

The UK regulation disproportionately favours the surrogate by giving her an absolute veto to change her mind about the process. Gamble opines that the imbalance of power created by the surrogacy legislation 'sought to discourage surrogacy, to make it a perilous undertaking that few would brave'.[112] As discussed above, the regulation is also based on the idea that the post-birth model of parentage best protects the surrogate's interests. This focus ignores the fact most surrogacy arrangements proceed as planned and that most surrogates do not view the child as their own.

In 2018, Surrogacy UK, a leading not-for-profit surrogacy organisation, published the results of the largest survey to date on the experiences of UK surrogates, intended parents and other interested parties.[113] There were a total of 510 responses representing 103 surrogates, 8 partners of surrogates, 209 intended parents (58 of whom were in same-sex couples) and 190 'others'. Among other things, the survey asked surrogates about their motivations for engaging in surrogacy. While the surrogates' responses naturally differed, all were positive. The stated motivations included

> the love of being a parent themselves and wanting to help others have a family and experience the same; having easy pregnancies and births; knowing or having known people with fertility problems; having had fertility problems themselves and/or having seen or read something about surrogacy that inspired them.[114]

Of the surrogates, 95% who responded to the survey felt that the current UK law on surrogacy is in need of reform;[115] 68.6% of the surrogates expressed the view that the intended parents should be recognised as the

[111] Bracken, above n. 102, 121.

[112] Natalie Gamble, 'Should surrogate mothers still have an absolute right to change their minds?' *Bionews*, 22 October 2012.

[113] Surrogacy UK, *Surrogacy in the UK: Further Evidence for Reform. Second Report of the Surrogacy UK Working Group on Surrogacy Law Reform* (London: Surrogacy UK, 2018), p. 32.

[114] Above, 33.

[115] Above, 42.

legal parents of a child born through surrogacy at birth,[116] while 81.6% of the surrogates did not believe that surrogates should have the option to change their mind about transferring the baby to the intended parents.[117]

These results mirror the findings of the Law Commission for England and Wales and the Scottish Law Commission in their consultation on surrogacy conducted in 2019. In this consultation, many respondents expressed concern about the current UK surrogacy laws on the basis that 'the current law does not reflect the intentions of any of the participants in a surrogacy arrangement'.[118] Among the difficulties noted were that the intended parents may be prevented from making important medical decisions for the child in the days after the birth because they are not legal parents. Women who had acted as surrogates also expressed concern about being legally responsible for the child, who they did not consider to be theirs, unless and until the parental order is granted.[119]

Other studies support the conclusion that women who act as surrogates do not typically feel that the child is 'theirs' or consider that there is a special bond between them and the child.[120] As Horsey notes, 'from the limited empirical evidence that is available on the practice of surrogacy, it is arguable that far from being vulnerable, surrogates feel empowered by their ability to exercise control over their bodies and the altruism that underpins surrogacy arrangements'.[121] Thus, the paternalistic approach created by the current regulation, which is based on the idea that the surrogate will want to keep the child, has little foundation in reality.

Recognising the surrogate as the legal mother upon the birth of the child means that she is bestowed with rights *and responsibilities* to care for the child. As the legal mother, her consent may be required before the child can undergo medical treatment. Given that most surrogates do not

116 Above, 34.

117 Above, 35.

118 Law Commission and Scottish Law Commission, *Building families through surrogacy: A new law A joint consultation paper* (Law Commission Consultation Paper 244; Scottish Law Commission Discussion Paper 167, 2019).

119 Above, para. 1.45.

120 Vasanti Jadva, Clare Murray, Emma Lycett, Fiona MacCallum, Susan Golombok, 'Surrogacy and the experiences of surrogate mothers' [2003] *Human Reproduction* 2196; Fiona MacCallum, Emma Lycett, Clare Murray, Vasanti Jadva, Susan Golombok, 'Surrogacy: The experience of commissioning couples' (2003) *Human Reproduction* 133.

121 Kirsty Horsey, 'Challenging presumptions: Legal parenthood and surrogacy arrangements' (2010) 22 *Child and Family Law Quarterly* 449, p. 451. See also: Eric Blyth, 'Interviews with surrogate mothers in Britain' (1994) 12 *Journal of Reproductive and Infant Psychology* 189.

view the child as their own, this can be an onerous burden to carry. Furthermore, if the surrogate has existing children, their rights and interests may be threatened through her automatic recognition as the legal mother of the surrogate child. If the surrogate was to die during childbirth, for example, the child born through surrogacy, as the legal child of the surrogate, would be entitled to succeed from her estate under succession law. This would have the effect of reducing the legal right share of the surrogate's existing children. As such, their financial security may be jeopardised by virtue of the fact that the surrogate has been recognised as the legal mother of the child born through surrogacy.

The current regulation of surrogacy in the United Kingdom might also create concern for the surrogate as she may legitimately fear that the intended parents will change *their minds* about the arrangement and will not seek the parental order after the birth of the child leaving her, quite literally, holding the baby.[122] The much-publicised case of Baby Gammy adds weight to this concern. This case came to public attention when Gammy, a child who was born with Down's syndrome to a surrogate in Thailand in 2013, was left by the Australian intended parents in Thailand while his twin sister Pipah was taken by them back to Australia. Additional facts came to light in a case before the Family Court of Western Australia in 2016.[123] In this case, Thackray CJ held that the intended parents had not abandoned Gammy in Thailand – a series of rather unfortunate events led to their decision to leave Thailand without the child.[124] Nonetheless, the significant media attention surrounding this case and the initial reporting of it might rightly leave surrogates concerned that the intended parents will not take the child after birth. The current UK regulation imposes no legal responsibility on the intended parents to care for the child, and so the only option for the

[122] This concern was expressed by some surrogates in the consultations conducted by English and Scottish Law Commissions. See: Law Commission and Scottish Law Commission, above n. 118, para. 7.61.

[123] *Farnell and Another* v. *Chanbua* [2016] FCWA 17.

[124] Gammy was critically ill after birth and had been kept in hospital much longer than his sister. When civil unrest broke out in Bangkok, the Australian intended parents were advised by Australian embassy staff to leave the country. They left with Pipah but planned to later return for Gammy. However, the series of events leading to this point made it clear that the surrogate wanted to keep Gammy and would not consent to him living with the intended parents in Australia. The judge felt that the surrogate's actions throughout the pregnancy and after birth demonstrated she had always intended to keep the baby and that this feeling was solidified after the birth when it emerged that the intended father had a prior conviction for child sexual abuse. *Farnell and Another* v. *Chanbua* [2016] FCWA 17.

surrogate who does not wish to keep the child would be to place them for adoption. Therefore, if the focus is on 'protecting' the surrogate, it is arguable that greater protection could be provided under a system that does not automatically regard her as the legal mother of the child.

This author has argued elsewhere that the English regulation of surrogacy is 'out of step with the reality of surrogacy'.[125] Many others have expressed similar views. For example, in the public consultation on surrogacy undertaken by the Law Commission for England and Wales and the Scottish Law Commission, over 340 people and groups responded that the current law 'was not fit for purpose'. These criticisms led the Law Commissions to undertake a review of the current surrogacy laws.[126] In 2019, the Law Commissions published a consultation paper on surrogacy containing a wide range of provisional proposals for reform of the current law.[127] Among the proposals is a recommendation for a 'new parentage pathway' to be introduced. Under this pathway, the intended parents of a surrogate-born child would be the child's legal parents from birth and the surrogate would not be regarded as a legal parent, unless the surrogate objects in which case the arrangement leaves the new pathway and enters the court system.[128] This proposal was made in response to the 'overwhelming view' of both intended parents and surrogates 'that recognising the intended parents as legal parents from birth reflects the wishes and intentions of all the parties to a surrogacy arrangement'.[129] More importantly, the Commissions were of the view that this approach would 'best promote the welfare of the child'.[130] The advantages of a pre-conception approach to legal parentage in surrogacy are discussed in detail later in this chapter.

6.5 Surrogacy in Ireland

Currently in Ireland, surrogacy is permitted, but there is no specific legislation to regulate the process. As a result, parentage is determined by reference to the same provisions that apply where a child is conceived following sexual intercourse: the woman who gives birth to the child is

[125] Lydia Bracken, 'The assisted reproduction bill 2017: An analysis of proposals to regulate surrogacy in Ireland' (2017) 68 *Northern Ireland Legal Quarterly* 577, p. 584.
[126] Law Commission, 'Surrogacy' www.lawcom.gov.uk/project/surrogacy/.
[127] Law Commission and Scottish Law Commission, above n. 118.
[128] Law Commission and Scottish Law Commission, above n. 118, para. 8.13.
[129] Law Commission and Scottish Law Commission, above n. 118, para. 7.3.
[130] Law Commission and Scottish Law Commission, above n. 118, para. 7.3.

always regarded as the child's legal mother;[131] if she is married, her husband (but not her wife) is presumed to be the child's legal father;[132] and if she is not married, the man listed on the birth certificate is presumed to be the legal father.[133] Both presumptions can be rebutted where it is shown, on the balance of probabilities, that the man is not the father of the child.

This approach to the allocation of parentage does not adequately accommodate surrogacy arrangements as it means that at least one of the intended parents in the surrogacy arrangement (the non-gestational intended mother or non-genetic intended father) will not have any legal connection to the child at birth. This was seen in the case of *MR and An tArd Chláraitheoir*[134] where the Irish Supreme Court had to determine whether the genetic mother of twins born to a surrogate mother could be recognised as the legal mother. In this case, the gametes of both of the (opposite-sex) intended parents were used to conceive the children. When the children were born, the surrogate was registered as the legal mother and the intended father was registered as the legal father. The parties subsequently sought to register the intended mother as the legal mother instead of the surrogate. This application was refused by the Registrar for Births (An tArd Chláraitheoir), and so the parties subsequently sought a declaration from the High Court stating that the genetic mother was the legal mother of the twins. The High Court held that the genetic mother should be registered as the legal mother, but this was subsequently appealed to the Supreme Court.

The Supreme Court emphasised that it was not the role of the Court to regulate surrogacy arrangements; this was 'quintessentially a matter for the Oireachtas [Irish Parliament]'.[135] The Court clarified that its remit in this case was to interpret the meaning of existing Irish law as it relates to birth registration and not to create new law to regulate surrogacy arrangements. The Court held that there was no provision in the existing law to allow for a genetic mother, rather than a gestational mother, to be registered as the legal mother. The existing law defined the mother in terms of gestation, and so the Court concluded that the surrogate was to be regarded as the legal mother.

[131] *MR* v. *An tArd Chláraitheoir* [2014] 3 IR 533.
[132] Status of Children Act 1987, s 46(1).
[133] Status of Children Act 1987, s 46(3), amended by Children and Family Relationships Act 2015, s 88.
[134] *MR and An tArd Chláraitheoir* [2014] 3 IR 533.
[135] Above, para. 113.

This case demonstrates the difficulties that arise as a result of the absence of specific surrogacy legislation in Ireland. Indeed, it is notable that each of the seven Supreme Court judges in the appeal remarked on the lack of legal regulation in this area and called on the Irish Parliament to introduce legislation to address the area. The judges also noted the vulnerable position of the children born through surrogacy in the absence of legislation. For example, O'Donnell J expressed the view that it was

> surely most clearly and profoundly wrong from the point of children born through an unregulated process into a world where their status may be determined by happenstance, and where simple events such as registration for schools, attendance at a doctor, consent to medical treatment, acquisition of a passport and even joining sports teams may involve complications, embarrassment and the necessity for prior consultation with lawyers resulting in necessarily inconclusive advice.[136]

Surrogacy legislation has been discussed in Ireland for many years. In 2014, provisions to regulate parentage in surrogacy were included in the Children and Family Relationships Bill. The provisions were subsequently removed from the 2014 Bill, as it was felt that further policy work and consultations were required in relation to surrogacy. As such, the regulation of surrogacy was deferred to the General Scheme of the Assisted Human Reproduction Bill 2017 (the AHR Bill), which was approved for drafting in October 2017. The General Scheme proposes to introduce a comprehensive, but restrictive, framework for the regulation of surrogacy in Ireland.

A major omission from the AHR Bill relates to children born through surrogacy prior to enactment and commencement of the Bill – there is no provision in the Bill to recognise the parentage of such children. By contrast, as was discussed in Chapter 5, the Children and Family Relationships Act 2015 makes provision for the retrospective allocation of parentage to an intended parent not previously recognised as a legal parent in cases of DAHR.[137] As it currently stands, the AHR Bill deprives children who have already been born through surrogacy of a streamlined process to acquire a legal relationship with the second intended parent. Without specific regulation, the only option available will be for the second parent to apply for guardianship or second-parent adoption in respect of the child.

[136] Above, para. 211.

[137] Children and Family Relationships Act 2015, ss 20–23.

The AHR Bill is restrictive in that it only covers certain surrogacy arrangements, namely those that are domestic, gestational and non-commercial.[138] The domestic requirement means that both the surrogate and at least one of the intended parents must be domiciled in Ireland in order for the Bill to apply to the surrogacy. Therefore, surrogacy undertaken in another jurisdiction would not be recognised. This is problematic as recent figures show that Ireland is currently the second-highest user of surrogacy in the world, and the vast majority of Irish couples who engage in surrogacy do so abroad.[139] Of course, the high number of international surrogacies may be due to the fact that there is currently no domestic regulation of surrogacy in Ireland, but the figures also suggest that international surrogacy cannot simply be ignored by the Irish legislature.

The AHR Bill also requires that the surrogacy must be gestational. This means that the surrogate's egg cannot be used in the conception. Instead, the egg must come from the intended mother or from a donor. In addition, commercial surrogacy is prohibited, meaning that the surrogate cannot be offered or given any payment or other reward other than 'reasonable expenses' for her involvement in the process. Many other conditions are stipulated in the Bill, including age limits and criteria that the intended parents and surrogate must meet and stipulations regarding the provision of counselling and legal advice. Surrogacy that does not comply with the provisions of the Bill is prohibited.[140] Under the provisions of Part 9 of the AHR Bill, it would be a criminal offence for any person to engage in a surrogacy arrangement that does not meet these criteria, whether through the provision of treatment or by acting as a surrogate or intending parent.[141] Thus, an intended parent or surrogate who engages in an international surrogacy arrangement would be committing a criminal offence under Irish law if the Bill is enacted. This is problematic for a number of reasons, not least because, if the parents are imprisoned, the child will have to be taken into State care. The difficulties associated with such prohibitions are starkly illustrated by the analysis of the ECtHR case law earlier in the chapter.

138 General Scheme of the Children and Family Relationships Bill 2014, Head 36.

139 A survey conducted by Families Through Surrogacy in 2017 found that 68% of surrogacies carried out by Irish couples took place in the Ukraine. Mark Tighe, 'Irish surrogacy rates are world's second-highest' *The Sunday Times*, 7 October 2018.

140 General Scheme of the Assisted Human Reproduction Bill 2017, Head 36(4).

141 General Scheme, Head 86(3).

The model for allocating parentage in the AHR Bill is far from straightforward as it proposes a two-step process for surrogacy arrangements. Before the surrogacy can be undertaken, the AHR treatment provider is required to apply for written authorisation for the surrogacy agreement from a new body, the Assisted Human Reproduction Regulatory Authority.[142] Where authorisation is granted, it simply means that the surrogacy can be performed; pre-authorisation will not impact on the allocation of parentage. When the child is born, the surrogate will be regarded as the legal mother and, if she is married to a man, her husband will be presumed to be the legal father. The surrogate is subsequently required to consent to the child living with the intended parents.[143] In order for parentage to be transferred to the intended parents, they have to obtain a parental order from the court. The Bill stipulates that the application for the parental order cannot be made earlier than six weeks and not more than six months after the child's birth,[144] but the court may extend the time limit in exceptional circumstances where it is deemed to be in the best interests of the child to do so. The consent of the surrogate (and her husband, if she has one) is required before the parental order can be granted. The court may, however, dispense with the required consents in certain circumstances, such as where the surrogate is deceased or cannot be located or 'for any other reason the court considers to be relevant'.[145]

It seems anomalous that the AHR Bill appears to *require* the surrogate to consent to the child living with the intended parents after birth but allows her discretion as to whether to consent to the transfer of parentage.[146] Moreover, the application for the parental order cannot be made for the first six weeks following the child's birth, while consent to the child living with the intended parents will seemingly be required immediately after the child's birth. The Explanatory Note accompanying the General Scheme explains that the waiting period that applies before the application for the parental order can be made is designed 'to allow the surrogate sufficient time to recover from the rigours of pregnancy and childbirth before participating in proceedings'.[147] Although the transfer

[142] General Scheme, Head 37(2).
[143] General Scheme, Head 46.
[144] General Scheme, Head 47(6).
[145] General Scheme, Head 48(2).
[146] General Scheme, Heads 46 and 48.
[147] Explanatory note accompanying Head 47 of the General Scheme of the Assisted Human Reproduction Bill 2017.

of parentage has far greater legal consequences than the transfer of residence, the requirement for the initial consent creates inconsistency in the approach of the legislation: is the intention to safeguard the surrogate in case she should change her mind about the transfer of parentage or is it designed to give effect to the pre-conception intentions of all parties? The rationale for the delay in the transfer of parentage suggests that the focus is on protecting the surrogate but, if this is so, surely this should apply to all decisions post-birth.

The model of parentage that is proposed in the AHR Bill is a delayed or post-birth model that will operate along the same lines as the current English regulation, discussed earlier, with the added burden of pre-authorisation in Ireland. As such, the same difficulties that were outlined earlier in the chapter will also apply in the Irish context if the Bill is enacted in its current form.[148] The AHR Bill does, however, avoid some of the issues that arise in the English context. For example, any concerns that the surrogate might have that the intended parents will not subsequently seek the parental order are alleviated in the Bill as the application for the parental order can be made by the intended parents, one intended parent or by the surrogate herself.[149] Therefore, if the intended parents do not make the application, the surrogate can do so. The Bill also expressly provides that the time limit for the application for the parental order can be extended by the court where it is in the best interests of the child to do so.[150] Therefore, where the parties erroneously miss the deadline, the court may still hear the application. In addition, where the surrogate unreasonably withholds her consent to the transfer of parentage, that consent could be waived for any reason that the court thinks relevant.[151] Thus, the Irish Bill would avoid a situation like that which arose in the English case of *AB (Surrogacy: Consent)*[152] where parentage could not be transferred to the intended parents because the surrogate refused her consent.

Overall, therefore, the Irish Bill allows for more flexibility than the current English regulation. However, there are still difficulties. The requirement for pre-authorisation is burdensome and adds to the expense of the process. The pre-authorisation does not affect the allocation of parentage. It simply means that the surrogacy agreement must be

148 See further, Bracken, above n. 125.
149 General Scheme, Head 47(2).
150 General Scheme, Head 47(7).
151 General Scheme, Head 48(2).
152 *AB (Surrogacy: Consent)* [2016] EWHC 2643 (Fam).

authorised twice: before conception by the Regulatory Authority and after the birth of the child by the court when the parental order is made. Similar to the arguments made in the English context, it is submitted that the post-birth model of parentage would not operate in the best interests of the child as it means that the child will not have a legal relationship with one or both of the intended parents for at least six weeks after birth even though those parents are caring for the child on a daily basis. This leaves the child in a vulnerable position, which cannot be said to be in the child's best interests. It is argued that a more sensible approach would be to allow for parentage to be determined pre-conception. This point is explored further below when considering the South African approach to surrogacy. In the next section, it is argued that a preconception allocation of parentage is more in keeping with the best interests principle than the post-birth model of recognition, and so the South African approach has advantages over the English model as well as the proposed Irish laws.

6.6 Surrogacy in South Africa

The South African Children's Act 2005 defines a 'surrogate motherhood agreement' as

> an agreement between a surrogate mother and a commissioning parent in which it is agreed that the surrogate mother will be artificially fertilised for the purpose of bearing a child for the commissioning parent and in which the surrogate mother undertakes to hand over such a child to the commissioning parent upon its birth, or within a reasonable time thereafter, with the intention that the child concerned becomes the legitimate child of the commissioning parent.[153]

Where a valid surrogate motherhood agreement is in place, any child born to the surrogate is deemed to be the child of the commissioning (intended) parent(s) from the moment of birth. The commissioning parents can be a married couple, in a permanent relationship or single.[154] Parentage is determined pre-conception. In order for this to operate, the surrogate motherhood agreement must be confirmed by the High Court before the conception of the child.[155] The court will not confirm the agreement without the consent of all parties. This means that

[153] Children's Act 38 of 2005, s 1.
[154] Children's Act 38 of 2005, s 292–293.
[155] Children's Act 38 of 2005, s 292 and 295.

where the surrogate is married or in a permanent relationship, the consent of her spouse or partner is also required, though the court may confirm the agreement in the absence of such consent where it is unreasonably withheld.[156] The agreement is only valid where at least one of the commissioning parents and the surrogate are domiciled in South Africa.[157] In addition, the gametes of at least one of the commissioning parents must be used to enable the conception of the child.[158]

The High Court will only confirm the surrogate motherhood agreement where certain criteria are met including, inter alia, that the intended parents are unable to give birth to a child; are deemed to be 'suitable persons to accept the parenthood of the child that is to be conceived'; and understand and accept the legal consequences of the surrogate motherhood agreement.[159] The surrogate must, inter alia, be deemed to be 'a suitable person to act as a surrogate mother'; understand and accept the legal consequences of the surrogate motherhood agreement; have undertaken the surrogacy for altruistic reasons; have already experienced at least one pregnancy; and have a living child of her own.[160] If these and other conditions are met, and the High Court is satisfied that it is in the best interests of the child to do so, the agreement will be confirmed.[161] The surrogacy procedure cannot take place prior to the confirmation of the agreement and it must take place within eighteen months of the confirmation.[162]

Where the surrogate motherhood agreement is confirmed by the High Court, the intended parents are deemed to be the child's legal parents from the moment of the child's birth.[163] The surrogate mother does not acquire any parental status and she is legally required to 'hand over' the child as soon as is reasonably possible after the birth.[164] In general, the surrogate motherhood agreement cannot be terminated after the conception of the child,[165] but an exception exists where traditional surrogacy is used, that is where the surrogate is also the genetic mother of the child. In this case, the surrogate retains the right to terminate the

[156] Children's Act 38 of 2005, s 293.
[157] Children's Act 38 of 2005, s 292.
[158] Children's Act 38 of 2005, s 294.
[159] Children's Act 38 of 2005, s 295(b).
[160] Children's Act 38 of 2005, s 295(c).
[161] Children's Act 38 of 2005, s 295(e).
[162] Children's Act 38 of 2005, s 296.
[163] Children's Act 38 of 2005, s 297(a).
[164] Children's Act 38 of 2005, s 297(b).
[165] Children's Act 38 of 2005, s 297(e).

surrogate motherhood agreement by filing written notice with the court within sixty days of the birth of the child.[166]

Where the surrogate motherhood agreement is invalid or where pre-authorisation is not sought from the court, any child born will be deemed to be the child of the woman that gave birth. The South African courts have, however, adopted a flexible approach to this issue. For example, in *Ex Parte MS and Others*,[167] confirmation of the surrogate motherhood agreement was not sought until the surrogate was thirty-three weeks pregnant. Nonetheless, the South African Court found that it had the power to retrospectively confirm the agreement and, on the specific facts of the case and in light of the best interests of the child, it was held that confirmation should be granted.[168] In doing so, however, the Court emphasised that confirmation of a surrogacy agreement post-conception should be considered to be an exception to the general rule[169] and the burden was on the parties to explain why the confirmation was not sought before conception and why it is warranted notwithstanding the delay.[170]

In *Ex Parte MS and Others*, the Court emphasised that the best interests of the child are paramount in every matter concerning them. The focus on the best interests of the child is evident throughout the judgment. The Court noted that

> [the child's] future rights and interests are the most important of all the rights and interests involved. To ensure that they are adequately protected, the law requires certainty and judicial scrutiny of the proposed surrogacy arrangement before there is even any prospect of the child coming into being.[171]

According to the Court, pre-authorisation of the surrogacy agreement is required to secure the best interests of the child by 'ensuring that there is

166 Children's Act 38 of 2005, s 298.

167 *Ex Parte MS and Others* 2014 (3) SA 415 (GP).

168 This case was the first to address the issue of the retrospective validation of a surrogate motherhood agreement since the introduction of the Children's Act 38 of 2005.

169 *Ex Parte MS and Others* 2014 (3) SA 415 (GP), para 61.

170 The Court also noted that it remains an offence for any person to artificially inseminate a woman in the execution of a surrogate motherhood agreement in the absence of prior authorisation from a court. As such, the health-care professionals involved in an artificial insemination which takes place prior to confirmation (notwithstanding that the agreement is subsequently confirmed) would remain open to criminal prosecution. Above, para. 58.

171 Above, para. 9.

certainty in the legal relationship between the parties involved'.[172] This certainty was found to advance the child's best interests

> in that there can be no doubt that it is in the prospective child's best interests for his or her legal and parental status to be settled at the earliest possible opportunity. Ideally, this should be before there is any prospect of conception.[173]

On the facts of the case, the Court was satisfied that it was in the best interests of the child that the confirmation should be granted.[174] However, the Court emphasised that '[t]he window period for a post-fertilisation confirmation of a surrogacy agreement exists only during the period before the child is born'.[175] As such, any application for the retrospective confirmation of a surrogacy agreement can only be granted prior to the birth of the child and confirmation cannot be sought after the child has been born. The Court reasoned that this restriction is necessary to maintain the certainty of the child's parental status which confirmation of the agreement is designed to achieve.

This case emphasises the advantages of the preconception model of parentage in surrogacy. This approach allows for certainty in the child's legal relationships as all parties know who the legal parents will be once the child is born and there is no need for post-birth litigation to establish parental status. The advantages of adopting a pre-conception approach to parentage in surrogacy are discussed further below.

6.7 Pre-conception Allocation of Parentage

It is submitted that the pre-conception model of parentage in surrogacy has many advantages when compared to the post-birth model of parentage that operates in England and Wales and that has been proposed in Ireland. Determining parentage prior to conception means that the intended parents have parental responsibilities and rights from the moment of the child's birth and are fully able to care for the child from that point. By contrast, in the post-birth model, both intended parents will not have parental responsibility at the time of the child's birth and there is always an element of uncertainty as to whether the surrogate will consent to the transfer of parentage after birth. Given that the child will

172 Above, para. 38.
173 Above.
174 Above, paras. 75–76.
175 Above, para. 67.

be cared for by the intended parents from birth, the pre-conception model of parentage respects the reality of the child's intended upbringing, and it is argued that the pre-conception model is more in keeping with the best interests principle than the post-birth or 'delayed' model of parentage. The pre-conception allocation of parentage allows the child to be legally integrated into their intended family from the moment of birth. Article 7 UNCRC provides that the child has the right to know and be cared for by their parents. This right provides weight to the argument that recognition of the child's legal relationship with the intended parents from the moment of birth is more in keeping with the best interests principle.

The pre-conception model of parentage in South Africa operates on the basis of court orders, but this is not the only option for allocating parentage prior to conception. The Law Commission for England and Wales and the Scottish Law Commission have provisionally proposed a new model for surrogacy in the United Kingdom based on pre-conception agreements, rather than court orders.[176] In this 'new pathway', the intended parents would be recognised as the legal parents at the time of the surrogate-born child's birth. The surrogate would not be regarded as a legal parent, but she would retain a right to object to the parentage of the intended parents within a certain period. Where the surrogate objects, parentage would revert to her and the intended parents would be required to apply for a parental order from the court. This application would be decided on the basis of the best interests of the child. Thus, the Commissions do not propose that the new pathway would be the only method by which parentage could be transferred in surrogacy cases. Cases that do not meet the criteria for the new pathway would be subject to a revised parental order model.

The Commissions propose that, in order to avail of the new pathway to parentage in surrogacy, the parties would have to enter into a surrogacy agreement prior to the conception of the child. This agreement would record all details pertaining to the surrogacy as well as a statement to the effect that the parties agree that the intended parents will be the child's legal parents when the child is born.[177] The parties would need to expressly consent to this allocation of parentage prior to the conception. Where all of the procedural safeguards and eligibility requirements are

[176] Law Commission for England and Wales and Scottish Law Commission, above n. 118.

[177] Law Commission for England and Wales and Scottish Law Commission, above n. 118, para. 8.8.

met, the intended parents would then be the legal parents of the child at the time of the birth.[178]

The Commissions favour this pre-conception model of parentage whereby legal parentage would be conferred by operation of law, not by court order, because they were 'concerned about the ability of the court to make an order before birth in respect of a child not yet born'.[179] In addition, the Commissions note 'the unwelcome potential for such a law to suggest that a pregnant woman does not, during her pregnancy, retain her right to choose what happens to her own body'.[180]

With respect to the Commissions, it is argued that use of a pre-conception court order would not interfere with the surrogate's bodily integrity during pregnancy provided that the relevant legislation specifies same. In South Africa, for example, where surrogacy operates through pre-conception court orders, the Children's Act 2005 expressly provides that a decision to terminate the pregnancy lies solely with the surrogate, though she is required to consult with the intended parents before the termination takes place.[181] This demonstrates that safeguards to protect the surrogate's bodily integrity during pregnancy can be specified in legislation where pre-conception court orders are used.

A positive aspect of the proposed UK approach is that it removes the need for court intervention in cases that meet the criteria for the new pathway, freeing up court time to deal with more complicated cases. However, in line with the arguments advanced in previous chapters in this work,[182] it is submitted that some independent oversight is preferable to ensure that the best interests of the child remain paramount in the surrogacy process.[183] This could be achieved through judicial validation of the surrogacy agreement or validation by another regulatory body. Oversight is advantageous as it ensures that all legislative criteria are met

[178] The regulated surrogacy organisation (or a clinic) would be required to keep a record of those surrogacy agreements into which it enters. These records should then be available to both the regulator and the birth registrar, so that the latter can confirm, when asked to register the intended parents as parents on the birth certificate, that they are indeed the legal parents of the child at birth. Law Commission for England and Wales and Scottish Law Commission, above n. 118, para. 8.12.

[179] Law Commission for England and Wales and Scottish Law Commission, above n. 118, para. 7.82.

[180] Law Commission for England and Wales and Scottish Law Commission, above n. 118, para. 7.82.

[181] Children's Act 38 of 2005, s 300.

[182] See, for example, Chapter 3, Section 3.4.2.3: 'Extension Mechanisms'.

[183] It is submitted that the fertility clinic has a financial interest in the surrogacy, and so oversight by the clinic alone cannot constitute 'independent' oversight for this purpose.

before the conception takes place. This ensures that the agreement is valid, and that parentage will, in fact, be allocated to the intended parents upon the birth of the child. Moreover, oversight ensures that the child's best interests have been considered in the agreement and that the parties are suitable persons to enter into same. For these reasons, it is suggested that confirmation of the agreement by an independent body or court prior to the conception of the child provides a necessary safeguard to uphold the child's best interests. It is acknowledged that a system of judicial oversight would add to the costs of a surrogacy procedure, with the danger that some prospective parents would be priced out of the system. The focus of this work is on the best interests of the child and how to regulate surrogacy in line with the best interests principle. As such, discussion of costs is outside of the primary focus of this work, but it is an important point to be borne in mind when considering the legal regulation of the area.

Whatever model is adopted, it is argued that the pre-conception approach to surrogacy better respects the rights of all stakeholders, including the surrogate. As noted above, research demonstrates that most surrogates do not consider the surrogate child to be their own but understand that they carry the child for someone else.[184] Jadva opines that '[t]he main factor here appears to be the *intention* for the pregnancy to be a surrogate pregnancy'.[185] The pre-conception agreement can help to ascertain and clarify this intention before the conception has taken place. This, in turn, may reduce the possibility that the surrogate would subsequently seek to keep the child (which is already a rare occurrence).[186]

The UN Special Rapporteur on the Sale and Sexual Exploitation of Children has raised concerns about the use of pre-conception contracts to allocate parentage in cases of surrogacy. The Special Rapporteur has criticised this approach as depriving the surrogate mother of her rights and as amounting to the sale and trafficking of children, which is contrary to the UNCRC and OPSC. According to the Special Rapporteur, '[o]nce the surrogate mother is reduced, during pregnancy, to a never-a-mother gestational carrier acting for the benefit of intending parents, the door is open to enforcing contracts that purport to alienate her rights

[184] Surrogacy UK, above n. 113; Vasanti Jadva, 'Surrogacy: Issues, concerns and complexities' in Golombok and others, above n. 89.

[185] Jadva, above, 128.

[186] Jamie Levitt, 'Biology, technology and genealogy: A proposed uniform surrogacy legislation' (1992) 25 *Columbia Journal of Law and Social Problems* 451.

and freedoms'.[187] To ensure that the surrogacy does not amount to the sale of children, the Special Rapporteur has recommended that the surrogate should be recognised as the legal mother at birth and the transfer of parentage to the intended parents should only be possible after the birth of the child.[188] In this way, the transfer of parentage would be based on the surrogate's post-birth intentions, rather than any legal obligation or contractual duty. Somewhat similarly, the Committee on the Rights of the Child has expressed concerns 'about the situations when parentage issues are decided exclusively on a contractual basis at pre-conception or pre-birth stage'.[189]

It is difficult to accept the Special Rapporteur and Committee's argument that the post-birth transfer of parentage is acceptable, but the pre-conception transfer amounts to the sale of a child. As discussed above, the vast majority of surrogates do not regard the child as their own and do not struggle with the decision to transfer parentage after birth. Thus, they enter the arrangement with the predetermined decision to transfer parentage; they are not 'forced' to hand over the child against their wishes. As such, it seems tenuous to argue that the surrogate's post-birth consent is legitimate but her pre-conception consent amounts to a transaction. Indeed, there is surely more scope for buying and selling after the child has been born as the surrogate could demand more money for a psychically healthy baby or the intended parents may bargain down the payment if the child has 'unwanted' characteristics when born.

In addition, given that the OPSC was designed to prevent the sale of children, it is difficult to see how a purely altruistic surrogacy arrangement would fall foul of its provisions. As the Law Commission for England and Wales and the Scottish Law Commission argue:

> [I]n the context of an arrangement from which the surrogate is not profiting, there may be scope to query the Rapporteur's view that not recognising the surrogate as a legal parent at birth means that there is a breach of the Optional Protocol.[190]

[187] UN Special Rapporteur, above n. 6, para. 57.

[188] UN Special Rapporteur, above n. 6, para. 71.

[189] Committee on the Rights of the Child, *Concluding observations on the combined third and fourth reports submitted by the United States of America under article 12 (1) of the Optional Protocol to the Convention on the Rights of the Child on the sale of children, child prostitution and child pornography* CRC/C/OPSC/USA/CO/3-4, para. 24.

[190] Law Commission for England and Wales and Scottish Law Commission, above n. 118, para. 7.103.

At the same time, the Law Commissions note that surrogacy that is based on a contractual model of parentage may still be considered difficult to reconcile with the welfare of the child. To avoid this, the Commissions propose that their proposed pre-conception allocation of parentage should take place by virtue of the law, rather than as a result of a contract.[191] Although this may appear a tenuous distinction, clarifying that the allocation of parentage occurs by virtue of the law, rather than contract, may assist in making the process more appealing to the general public as the surrogate is not 'forced' to hand over the child because of a contractual obligation. Indeed, the Law Commissions propose a further safeguard for the surrogate whereby she would be able to object to the allocation of parentage to the intended parents for a limited period after the birth of the child. These safeguards protect the surrogate from unwittingly 'contracting away' her claim to motherhood. The same benefits could be derived from an approach that requires judicial oversight of the surrogacy agreement – in this model, parentage is transferred by way of court order, not by contract.

Overall, it is argued that the pre-conception model of parentage does not amount to the 'sale' of children and in fact better respects the interests of *all stakeholders* in the surrogacy process. This model of parentage better respects the reality of the child's life and offers them increased protection. As such, it is submitted that the pre-conception model has the greatest potential to respect the best interests of children who are born through the process.

6.8 International Surrogacy

Although the pre-conception model of parentage is endorsed above, it must be acknowledged that it would be very difficult to apply this model in a situation where the intended parents travel abroad for surrogacy. Earlier in the chapter, it was argued that international surrogacy arrangements must be recognised across borders in order to secure the best interests of surrogate-born children who have already bonded with the intended parents by the time the family returns to the home country. However, it remains to be seen how this practice can be regulated in accordance with the best interests of the child.

[191] Law Commission for England and Wales and Scottish Law Commission, above n. 118, para. 7.80.

In international or 'cross-border' surrogacy, the intended parents travel overseas to engage in surrogacy. In this situation, the country of origin has no oversight of the surrogacy and cannot guarantee that appropriate safeguards have been put in place, for example in relation to the child's right to identity and payments to the surrogate. The potential exploitation of women who act as surrogates is also a concern in relation to international arrangements. These factors add weight to the idea that judicial scrutiny should be required when the family returns to the home country to ensure that appropriate safeguards have been adhered to. These points are highlighted in the UK Law Commissions' consultation paper on surrogacy. The Commissions note:

> Given the wide disparity in surrogacy laws that exist worldwide, we think that the parental order process provides significant safeguards that need to be maintained. In particular, the application ensures that the child has genuinely been born through a surrogacy arrangement. The process also offers some safeguards against concerns of exploitation of women as surrogates and, in particular, the sale of children.[192]

The State could not sanction in advance a process that takes place in another country. This would only be possible where an international convention, akin to the Hague Convention on the Protection of Children and Co-operation in Respect of Intercountry Adoption, or a bilateral agreement is in place setting out common criteria and procedures for international surrogacy. As noted earlier, the Hague Conference on Private International Law is currently evaluating the feasibility of drawing up an international instrument to address the issues arising in cross-border surrogacy, but they are far from reaching a consensus.[193] In the absence of a bilateral or international agreement on surrogacy, it is submitted that the only feasible way to accommodate international surrogacy is to allow the intended parents to be recognised as legal parents through a court procedure that takes place after the birth of the child in the parents' home country.[194] It is argued that an international or bilateral agreement that sets common standards and safeguards for the

[192] Law Commission for England and Wales and Scottish Law Commission, above n. 118, para. 16.89.

[193] Hague Conference on Private International Law, above n. 86.

[194] It is acknowledged that it will almost always be in the best interests of the child to make the parental order in this situation. In the UK, the courts have adopted an approach whereby the parental order will almost always be granted (as it is in the best interests of the child to do so) unless there is the clearest abuse of public policy. See Fenton-Glynn, above n. 65, 551.

surrogacy arrangement would be the most effective mechanism through which to secure the rights and interests of children who are born through international surrogacy. However, it would seem that the creation of such agreement(s) between countries is a long way off at the time of writing due to the polarised views on surrogacy that prevail in different jurisdictions.

6.9 Conclusion

The growth in the use of surrogacy demands that it is appropriately regulated. This chapter has shown that domestic prohibitions on surrogacy do not work and simply impede the best interests of surrogate-born children. Domestic prohibitions do not prevent surrogacy; they simply push intended parents to use surrogacy abroad which then creates significant legal obstacles for the recognition of family life when they return to their home country with the child. This reality must be acknowledged by domestic legislatures. Surrogacy is a positive and valuable pathway to parentage for many individuals and couples who wish to become parents. This too must be recognised, and appropriate legal regulation put in place. Regulation is necessary to avoid children's rights abuses within surrogacy, in particular to ensure that the process does not amount to the buying and selling of children. It has been argued that a pre-conception model of parentage has the greatest potential to vindicate the rights of all stakeholders in the surrogacy process. However, it is suggested that the pre-conception model could only apply to domestic arrangements as the State could not sanction in advance a process that takes place in another country, unless an international or bilateral agreement has been concluded. Nonetheless, it is likely that appropriate domestic regulation would curb the flow of prospective parents to other jurisdictions as they could then avail of surrogacy in their home country. Surrogacy will continue, and so a head-in-the-sand approach at the domestic level is simply not an option. The pre-conception approach to parentage is required to respect the reality of the child's life once born.

Conclusion

7.1 Introduction

As has been seen throughout this book the best interests principle often arises in discussions about same-sex parenting. In this context, the principle has been shown to have both 'a pessimistic and optimistic version'.[1] The pessimistic version argues that children should not be raised by same-sex couples on the basis that this is harmful to them, while the optimistic version contends that 'children are somehow better with married, heterosexual parents'.[2]

The objective of this work was to assess the demands of the best interests principle in the context of same-sex parenting. In order to achieve this aim, it has been necessary to analyse the best interests principle in two contexts to consider *whether* and *how* the law should recognise same-sex parenting arrangements. In order to address the first point, sociological and psychological research was used to assess the validity of the pessimistic and optimistic versions of the best interests principle. Ultimately, it was shown that such arguments lack scientific authority, and it was concluded that the children of same-sex couples have existing needs that must be met through legal recognition of their family relationships. In considering *how* the law should regulate the pathways to parentage that are available to same-sex couples, it was necessary to consider the demands of the best interests principle in terms of its application. In line with the guidance of the Committee on the Rights of the Child, the principle has been applied as a substantive right, a fundamental interpretive legal principle and

1 Jennifer Rosato, 'Children of same-sex parents deserve the security blanket of the parentage presumption' (2006) 44 *Family Court Review* 74, p. 74.
2 Above.

a rule of procedure.[3] This understanding of best interests was adopted in each chapter to identify the most appropriate way to regulate each of the pathways to parentage discussed.

7.2 The Way Forward: Implications of the Best Interests Principle

The arguments advanced in this book demonstrate that the best interests principle, applied using the conceptual framework identified in Chapter 1, constitutes the most favourable method to decide issues relating to the upbringing of children and, in particular, that it is the most appropriate mechanism through which to address the pessimistic and optimistic best interests arguments that are advanced in discussions about same-sex parenting.

In Chapter 1, it was shown that the best interests principle allows for the interests of children to be prioritised in a way that would not be possible under a purely rights-based approach – the principle ensures that those interests are considered and elevated over other considerations. In line with the guidance of the Committee on the Rights of the Child, the best interests principle is taken to be a right, the contents of which are to be determined by reference to the other rights contained in the United Nations Convention on the Rights of the Child (UNCRC). This understanding provides guidance on how the principle is to be applied and can reduce the subjectivity of the best interests determination. Chapter 1 also demonstrated that the criticisms raised against the use of the principle do not dictate that it be abandoned. For example, it was shown that the indeterminacy of the principle may actually be regarded as a strength as it ensures flexibility in the determination of what is best for an individual child.

Chapter 2 built on the analysis in Chapter 1 through examination of sociological and psychological research relating to same-sex parenting. This research was used to further guide the application of the best interests principle. In that chapter, it was noted that there has historically been resistance to the legal recognition of same-sex parenting on the basis of a perception that this would not be 'best' for the children concerned. The research analysed in the chapter demonstrated that the arguments

[3] Committee on the Rights of the Child, *General comment No. 14 (2013) on the right of the child to have his or her best interests taken as a primary consideration (art. 3, para. 1)* CRC/C/GC/14, para. 6.

made against same-sex parenting lack scientific legitimacy. There is a wealth of research that shows positive outcomes for children who are raised by gay and lesbian parents. This research indicates that children do not necessarily need to be raised by both a mother and a father in order to achieve optimal development. Indeed, children raised by gay and lesbian parents have been consistently shown to have the same outcomes as those who are raised by opposite-sex parents. The gender of parents does not seem to affect children's outcomes, but instead outcomes are determined by the quality of parenting. Although it was noted that methodological issues relating to the relevant research mean that the results could not be regarded as definitive, it is notable that no existing study has found that children are harmed by being raised by gay and lesbian parents.

It has been argued that the best interests principle can be used to demand that legal recognition of same-sex parenting should be forthcoming. Same-sex parenting is a reality, and this must be acknowledged. Each chapter in this work has shown that the absence of legal recognition for same-sex parenting places children in a vulnerable position, and it means that the children of same-sex relationships are denied many of the legal protections that are afforded to the children of opposite-sex couples. Children must be given the opportunity to obtain the security of having a legal relationship with both of their parents, whatever the gender of those parents may be. Thus, in order to protect the best interests of children who are raised by same-sex couples, legal recognition of their family relationships must be made available.

Having identified an appropriate theoretical framework for best interests, Chapters 3 to 6 of the work focused on identifying the most appropriate means of regulating various pathways to parentage for same-sex couples. Chapter 3 dealt with the area of parental responsibility. This chapter argued that the existence of a mechanism to extend parental responsibility to social parents is in the best interests of children who are currently being raised by more than two persons. Article 7 UNCRC provides that the child has the right to be cared for by their parents. Using this Article to inform the application of the best interests principle, it was concluded that it is in the child's best interests to have a legal relationship with the social parent who is fulfilling a parental role.

Chapter 4 examined the question of second-parent adoption and joint adoption by same-sex couples. This chapter examined jurisprudence from England and Wales, Northern Ireland and South Africa in which it was found that the best interests principle demanded that same-sex couples should be afforded the opportunity to apply for adoption. The dicta from the cases analysed emphasise the benefits that children can derive from having a secure adoptive relationship with the persons caring for them. Furthermore, the case law demonstrates that there is no logical argument to be made to prevent same-sex couples from accessing joint adoption of 'stranger' children. The approach of the European Court of Human Rights (ECtHR) was also examined in this chapter. The ECtHR has not yet found that same-sex couples enjoy a general right to access adoption under Article 8 of the European Convention on Human Rights (ECHR). It was argued that the central case in this area, *Gas and Dubois* v. *France*,[4] failed to adequately consider the position of the child who was at the centre of the case and did not take the best interests principle into account. It was argued that consideration of the rights of the child would have required a different decision in this case.

Chapter 5 addressed the area of donor conception. The objective of this chapter was to determine how the best interests of the child can be secured in legislating for donor conception. Overall, it was argued that donor conception must be regulated in a manner that allows the child to acquire a legal relationship with both of the intending parents from birth. Nonetheless, it was noted that the child has a number of competing rights in this area that must be taken into account in assessing the demands of the best interests principle. This chapter therefore involved examination of the child's right to be cared for by their parents,[5] the child's right to freedom from discrimination,[6] the child's right to health[7] and the child's right to identity.[8] In certain areas, such as the regulation of non-clinical procedures, it was apparent that the rights of the child clashed with one another and so a value judgment was required. This analysis revealed that the indeterminacy of the best interests principle cannot be overcome through examination of the rights of the child alone. That did not mean that the principle was an inappropriate tool through which to assess the legal regulation of donor conception, however, because a value judgment would also be required if a purely rights-based approach was to be adopted. The child's right to identity was also considered and it was concluded that children who are born through donor conception must have access to information about their genetic origins in order to vindicate this right.

[4] *Gas and Dubois* v. *France*, app no 25951/07, 15 March 2012.

[5] UN Convention on the Rights of the Child, Art. 7.

[6] UN Convention on the Rights of the Child, Art. 2(2).

[7] UN Convention on the Rights of the Child, Art. 24.

[8] UN Convention on the Rights of the Child, Arts. 7 and 8.

Finally, Chapter 6 discussed the area of surrogacy. It was argued that surrogacy must be appropriately regulated because it will continue regardless of the domestic response. An intention-based model of parentage, facilitated through pre-conception agreements, in surrogacy was favoured in this chapter as this approach respects the reality of the child's relationships with the intended parents. It was submitted that an intention-based model has the greatest potential to respect the best interests of children who are born through the process. Specific issues concerning international surrogacy were also addressed and it was argued that, in the absence of a bilateral or international agreement on surrogacy, the only feasible way to accommodate international surrogacy is to allow the intended parents to be recognised as legal parents through a court procedure that takes place after the birth of the child in the parents' home country.

7.3 Conclusion

This book began by considering the overarching question of *whether* the law should recognise same-sex parenting arrangements. The answer to this question is a resounding *YES*. The quality of parenting has been shown to be the most important contributor to positive outcomes for children, and there is no evidence to suggest that children raised by gay and lesbian parents are disadvantaged in any way. The only exception relates to prejudice from the outside world, which is the only potential threat to these children. It is argued that this, in itself, provides a strong argument in favour of legally recognising same-sex parenting as this guarantees legislative, and hence State, approval of these families. This, in turn, may help to remove any remaining prejudices that society may hold towards such parents, which can only serve to enhance the best interests of children raised by them.

Having addressed the question of 'whether', the work then addressed the question of 'how' legal recognition should be provided. The proposals for reform subsequently advanced in each chapter are designed to secure the best interests of the child. However, it is not the intention of this work to identify a 'perfect' legal regime, nor does the work attempt to identify a universal definition of what is best for children in each of the areas discussed. The best interests principle must be applied in accordance with the constitutional, political, social and cultural context in which it is invoked. Moreover, the principle must remain flexible so that it can be adjusted and defined on an individual basis according to the situation of the child or children concerned.[9] Hence, no work can prescribe the 'best' form of legal regulation without considering the specific conditions of the country under scrutiny. This monograph has shown how a universal conceptual framework for best interests can be used to minimise the subjectivity of the principle and achieve consistent, but not identical, results in different countries. In doing so, the conceptual framework provides a tool for advancing the rights and interests of children in many different jurisdictions.

[9] Committee on the Rights of the Child, above n. 3, para. 32.

BIBLIOGRAPHY

Books

Bainham, A., *Children: The Modern Law*, 3rd ed. (London: Family Law, 2005).

Bainham, A. and Gilmore, S., *Children: The Modern Law*, 4th ed. (London: Family Law, 2013).

Ball, C., *Same-Sex Marriage and Children* (Oxford: Oxford University Press, 2014).

Bracken, L., *Child Law in Ireland* (Dublin: Clarus Press, 2018).

Buck, T., *International Child Law* (London: Cavendish Publishing, 2005).

Detrick, S. (ed.), *The United Nations Convention on the Rights of the Child: A Guide to the 'Travaux Preparatoires'* (The Hague: Martinus Nijhoff, 1992).

Eekelaar, J., *Family Law and Personal Life*, 2nd ed. (Oxford: Oxford University Press, 2017).

Fineman, M., *The Neutered Mother, the Sexual Family and Other Twentieth Century Tragedies* (London: Routledge, 1995).

Fortin, J., *Children's Rights and the Developing Law*, 3rd ed. (Cambridge: Cambridge University Press, 2009).

Golombok, S., *Modern Families: Parents and Children in New Family Forms* (Cambridge: Cambridge University Press, 2015).

Golombok, S., *Parenting: What Really Counts?* (London: Routledge, 2000).

Herring, J., *Family Law*, 5th ed. (Harlow: Pearson Education Limited, 2011).

Lowe, N. and Douglas, G., *Bromley's Family Law*, 10th ed. (Oxford: Oxford University Press, 2007).

Mallon, G., *Gay Men Choosing Parenthood* (Columbia: Columbia University Press, 2004).

McLanahan, S. and Sandefur, G., *Growing Up with a Single Parent: What Hurts, What Helps* (Harvard: Harvard University Press, 1994).

Schäfer, I., *The Law of Access to Children* (Cape Town: LexisNexis, 2007).

Shannon, G., *Child Law*, 2nd ed. (Dublin: Thomson Reuters, 2010).

Thomas, N., *Children's Rights: Policy into Practice* (Lismore: Centre for Children and Young People, 2011).

Chapters in Edited Books

Alston, P.,'The best interests principle: Towards a reconciliation of culture and human rights' in Alston, P. (ed.), *The Best Interests Principle: Reconciling Culture and Human Rights* (Oxford: Oxford University Press, 1994).

Amos, T. and Rainer, J.,'Parenthood for same-sex couples in the EU' in Boele-Woelki, K. and Fuchs, A. (eds.), *Same-Sex Relationships and Beyond*, 3rd ed. (Cambridge: Intersentia, 2017).

Appleby, J.,'Regulating the provision of donor information to donor-conceived children' in Golombok, S., Scott, R., Appleby, J., Richards, M. and Wilkinson, S. (eds.), *Regulating Reproductive Donation* (Cambridge: Cambridge University Press, 2016).

Bainham, A.,'Parentage, parenthood and parental responsibility: Subtle, elusive yet important distinctions' in Bainham, A., Day Sclater, S. and Richards, M. (eds.), *What Is a Parent? A Socio-Legal Analysis* (Oxford: Hart Publishing, 1999).

Blake, L., Ilioi, E. and Golombok, S.,'Thoughts and feelings about the donor: A family perspective' in Golombok, S., Scott, R., Appleby, J., Richards, M. and Wilkinson, S. (eds.), *Regulating Reproductive Donation* (Cambridge: Cambridge University Press, 2016).

Bracken, L.,'Gas and Dubois v France' in Stalford, H., Hollingsworth, K. and Gilmore, S. (eds.), *Rewriting Children's Rights Judgments from Academic Vision to New Practice* (Oxford: Hart Publishing, 2017).

Eekelaar, J., 'Families and children: From welfarism to rights' in McCrudden, C. and Chambers, G. (eds.), *Individual Rights and the Law in Britain* (Oxford: Clarendon Press, 1994).

Freeman, M.,'Article 3: The best interests of the child' in Alen, A., Vande Lanotte, J., Verhellen, E., Ang, F., Berghmans, E. and Verheyde, M. (eds.), *A Commentary on the United Nations Convention on the Rights of the Child* (Leiden: Martinus Nijhoff Publishers, 2007).

Friedman, A. and Pantazis, A., 'Children's rights' in Stu Woolman and Michael Bishop (eds.), *Constitutional Law of South Africa*, 2nd ed. (Lansdowne: Juta and Co, Ltd., 2006).

Gamble, N., 'A better legal framework for United Kingdom surrogacy' in Golombok, S., Scott, R., Appleby, J., Richards, M. and Wilkinson, S. (eds.), *Regulating Reproductive Donation* (Cambridge: Cambridge University Press, 2016).

Gonzalez-Beilfuss, C.,'All or nothing: The dilemma of southern jurisdictions' in Boele-Woelki, K. and Fuchs, A. (eds.), *Legal Recognition of Same-Sex Relationships in Europe: National, Cross-Border and European Perspectives*, 2nd ed. (Cambridge: Intersentia, 2012).

Jadva, V., 'Surrogacy: Issues, concerns and complexities' in Golombok, S., Scott, R., Appleby, J., Richards, M. and Wilkinson, S., *Regulating Reproductive Donation* (Cambridge: Cambridge University Press, 2016).

Jänterä-Jareborg, M., 'Parenthood for same-sex Couples: Scandinavian developments' in Boele-Woelki, K. and Fuchs, A. (eds.), *Legal Recognition of Same-Sex Relationships in Europe: National, Cross-Border and European Perspectives*, 2nd ed. (Cambridge: Intersentia, 2012).

Kilkelly, U.,'The best interests of the child: A gateway to children's rights?' in Sutherland, E. and Barnes Mcfarlane, L. A. (eds.), *Implementing Article 3 of the United Nations Convention on the Rights of the Child: Best Interests, Welfare and Well-Being* (Cambridge: Cambridge University Press, 2017).

Skelton, A.,'Parental Responsibilities and Rights' in Boezaart, T. (ed.), *Child Law in South Africa* (Cape Town: Juta and Co. Ltd., 2009).

Sloth-Nielsen, J., 'The contribution of children's rights to the reconstruction of society: Some implications of the constitutionalism of children's rights in South Africa' in Freeman, M. (ed.), *Children's Rights: Volume II* (Dartmouth: Ashgate Publishing Limited, 2005).

Journal Articles

Alston, P., 'Best interests principle: Towards a reconciliation of culture and human rights' (1994) 8 *International Journal of Law, Policy and the Family* 1.

Amato, P., 'The consequences of divorce for adults and children' (2000) 62 *Journal of Marriage and the Family* 1269–1287.

American Academy of Pediatrics, 'Coparent or second-parent adoption by same-sex parents' (2002) 109 *Pediatrics* 339–340.

American Academy of Pediatrics, 'Task force on the family: Family pediatrics' (2003) 111 *Pediatrics* 1541.

Bainham, A., 'Arguments about parentage' (2008) 67 *Cambridge Law Journal* 322.

Bainham, A., 'Can we protect children and protect their rights?' (2002) 32 *Family Law* 279.

Bainham, A., 'Changing families and changing concepts: Reforming the language of family law' (1998) 10 *Child and Family Law Quarterly* 1.

Bainham, A., 'Rowing back from Re G? Natural parents in the supreme court' (2010) 40 *Family Law* 394.

Beeson, D., Jennings, P. and Kramer, W., 'Offspring searching for their sperm donors: How family type shapes the process' (2011) 26 *Human Reproduction* 2415.

Bernstein, G., 'Regulating reproductive technologies: Timing, uncertainty, and donor anonymity' (2010) 90 *Boston University Law Review* 1189.

Biblarz, T. and Stacey, J., 'How does the gender of parents matter?' (2010) 72 *Journal of Marriage and Family* 3.

Blyth, E., 'Interviews with surrogate mothers in Britain' (1994) 12 *Journal of Reproductive and Infant Psychology* 189.

Blyth, E., Burr, V. and Farrand, A., 'Welfare of the child assessments in assisted conception: A social constructionist perspective' (2008) 26 *Journal of Reproductive and Infant Psychology* 31.

Blyth, E., Crawshaw, M., Frith, L. and Jones, C., 'Donor conceived people's views and experiences of their genetic origins: A critical analysis of the research evidence' (2012) 19 *Journal of Law and Medicine* 769–789.

Bonthuys, E., 'The best interests of children in the South African constitution' (2006) 20 *International Journal of Law, Policy and the Family* 23.

Bracken, L., 'Assessing the best interests of the child in cases of cross-border surrogacy: Inconsistency in the Strasbourg approach?' (2017) 39 *Journal of Social Welfare and Family Law* 368.

Bracken, L., 'Challenging normative constructions of parentage in Ireland' (2017) 39 *Journal of Social Welfare and Family Law* 316.

Bracken, L., 'In the best interests of the child? The regulation of DAHR in Ireland' (2016) 23 *European Journal of Health Law* 391.

Bracken, L., 'Strasbourg's response to gay and lesbian parenting: Progress, then plateau?' (2016) 24 *International Journal of Children's Rights* 358.

Bracken, L., 'The Assisted Reproduction Bill 2017: An analysis of proposals to regulate surrogacy in Ireland' (2017) 68 *Northern Ireland Legal Quarterly* 577.

Bracken, L., 'The pre-conception best interests assessment – part 1: Suitability and feasibility' (2019) 22 *Irish Journal of Family Law* 16.

Bracken, L., 'The pre-conception best interests assessment – part 2: Implications for the Irish legal framework' (2019) 22 *Irish Journal of Family Law* 2.

Bracken, L., 'The role of the best interests principle in regulating parentage in surrogacy in Ireland' (2017) 2 *International Family Law* 115.

Brewaeys, A., Ponjaert, I., Van Hall, E. and Golombok, S., 'Donor insemination: Child development and family functioning in lesbian mother families' (1997) 12 *Human Reproduction* 1349.

Brinamen, C., 'On becoming fathers: Issues facing gay men choosing to parent' (2000) 61 *Dissertation Abstracts International* 2794.

Callus, T., 'First Designer Babies, Now á la carte parents' (2008) 38 *Family Law* 143.

Cashmore, J. and Parkinson, P., 'The use and abuse of social science research evidence in children's cases' (2014) 20 *Psychology, Public Policy, and Law* 239–250.

Cheng, S. and Powell, B., 'Measurement, methods, and divergent patterns: Reassessing the effects of same-sex parents' (2015) 52 *Social Science Research* 615.

Clarke, V., 'Sameness and difference in research on lesbian parenting' (2002) 12 *Journal of Community and Applied Social Psychology* 210.

Crawshaw, M. and others, 'Disclosure and donor-conceived children' (2017) 32 *Human Reproduction* 1535.

Crawshaw, M., Blyth, E. and Van den Akker, O., 'The changing profile of surrogacy in the UK: Implications for national and international policy and practice' (2012) 34 *Journal of Social Welfare and Family Law* 265.

Crouch, S., Waters, E., McNair, R., Power, J. and Davis, E., 'Parent reported measures of child health and wellbeing in same-sex parent families: A cross-sectional study' (2014) 14 *BMC Public Health* 635.

Crowl, A., Ahn, S. and Baker, J., 'A meta-analysis of developmental outcomes for children of same-sex and heterosexual parents' (2008) 4 *Journal of GLBT Family Studies* 385–407.

Dambach, M., 'The international legal context governing intercountry adoptions by gay men and lesbians' (2011) 35 *Adoption and Fostering* 65.

Dey, I. and Wassoff, F., 'Mixed messages: Parental responsibilities, public opinion and the reforms of family law' (2006) 20 *International Journal of Law, Policy and the Family* 225.

Duncan, W., 'Deconstructing parenthood' (2008) 22(6) *The Family in America* 1.

Eekelaar, J., 'Beyond the welfare principle' (2002) 14 *Child and Family Law Quarterly* 237.

Eekelaar, J., 'Rethinking parental responsibility' (2001) 31 *Family Law* 426.

Eekelaar, J., 'The role of the best interests principle in decisions affecting children and decisions about children' (2015) 23 *International Journal of Children's Rights* 3.

Fenton-Glynn, C., 'International surrogacy before the European Court of Human Rights' (2017) 13 *Journal of Private International Law* 546.

Frith, L., 'Beneath the rhetoric: The role of rights in the practice of non-anonymous gamete donation' (2001) 15 *Bioethics* 473.

Gamble, N. and Ghevaert, L., 'The human fertilisation and embryology act 2008: Revolution or evolution?' (2009) 39 *Family Law* 730.

Golombok, S., 'Disclosure and donor-conceived children' (2017) 32 *Human Reproduction* 1532.

Golombok S. and Tasker, F., 'Children in lesbian and gay families: Theories and evidence' (1994) 5 *Annual Review of Sex Research* 73.

Golombok, S., Blake, L., Casey, P., Roman, G., and Jadva, V., 'Children born through reproductive donation: A longitudinal study of psychological adjustment' (2013) 54 *Journal of Child Psychology and Psychiatry* 653–660.

Golombok, S., Blake, L., Slutsky, J., Raffanello, E., Roman, G. and Ehrhardt, A., 'Parenting and the adjustment of children born to gay fathers through surrogacy' (2018) 89 *Child Development* 1223–1233.

Golombok, S., Ilioi, E., Blake, L., Roman, G. and Jadva, V., 'A longitudinal study of families formed through reproductive donation: Parent-adolescent relationships and adolescent adjustment at age 14' (2017) 53 *Developmental Psychology* 1966–1977.

Golombok, S., MacCallum, F., Murray, C., Lycett, E. and Jadva, V., 'Surrogacy families: Parental functioning, parent-child relationships and children's psychological development at age 2' (2006) 47 *Journal of Child Psychology & Psychiatry* 213–222.

Golombok, S., Mellish, L., Jennings, S., Casey, P., Tasker, F. and Lamb, M., 'Adoptive gay father families: Parent–child relationships and children's psychological adjustment' (2014) 85 *Child Development* 456.

Golombok, S., Murray, C., Jadva, V., Lycett, E., MacCallum, F. and Rust, J., 'Non-genetic and non-gestational parenthood: Consequences for parent-child relationships and the psychological well-being of mothers, fathers and children at age 3' (2006) 21 *Human Reproduction* 1918–1924.

Golombok, S., Murray, C., Jadva, V., MacCallum, F. and Lycett, E., 'Families Created Through Surrogacy Arrangements: Parent–Child Relationships in the 1st Year of Life' (2004) 40 *Developmental Psychology* 400–411.

Golombok, S., Readings, J., Blake, L., Casey, P., Mellish, L., Marks, A. and Jadva, V., 'Families created through surrogacy: Mother-child relationships and children's psychological adjustment at age 7' (2011) 47 *Developmental Psychology* 1579–1588.

Hammarberg, T., 'The UN convention on the rights of the child: And how to make it work' (1990) 12 *Human Rights Quarterly* 97.

Harris-Short, S., 'Family law and the Human Rights Act 1998: Judicial restraint or revolution?' (2005) 17 *Child and Family Law Quarterly* 329.

Horsey, K., 'Challenging presumptions: Legal parenthood and surrogacy arrangements' (2010) 22 *Child and Family Law Quarterly* 449.

Jacob, M., Klock, S. and Maier, D., 'Lesbian couples as therapeutic donor insemination recipients: Do they differ from other patients?' (1999) 20 *Journal of Psychosomatic Obstetrics and Gynecology* 203.

Jadva, V., Murray, C., Lycett, E., MacCallum, F. and Golombok, S., 'Surrogacy and the experiences of surrogate mothers' (2003) 18 *Human Reproduction* 2196.

Lau, C., 'The stability of same-sex cohabitation, different-sex cohabitation, and marriage' (2012) 74 *Journal of Marriage and Family* 973.

Lee, E., Macvarish, J. and Sheldon, S., 'Assessing child welfare under the Human Fertilisation and Embryology Act 2008: A case study in medicalisation?' (2014) 36 *Sociology of Health and Illness* 500.

Leiblum, S., Palmer, M. and Spector, I., 'Non-traditional mothers: Single heterosexual, lesbian women and lesbian couples electing motherhood via donor insemination' (1995) 16 *Journal of Psychosomatic Obstetrics and Gynecology* 11.

Levitt, J., 'Biology, technology and genealogy: A proposed uniform surrogacy legislation' (1992) 25 *Columbia Journal of Law and Social Problems* 451.

Lowe, N., 'The meaning and allocation of parental responsibility: A common lawyer's perspective' (1997) 11 *International Journal of Law, Policy and the Family* 192.

MacCallum, F. and Golombok, S., 'Children raised in fatherless families from infancy: A follow-up of children of lesbian and single heterosexual mothers at early adolescence' (2004) 45 *Journal of Psychology and Psychiatry* 1407.

MacCallum F., Lycett, E., Murray, C., Jadva, V. and Golombok, S., 'Surrogacy: The experience of commissioning couples' (2003) 18 *Human Reproduction* 1334.

Marshall, A., 'Comedy of adoption: When is a parent not a parent?' (2003) 33 *Family Law* 840.

McCandless, J., 'Status and anomaly: Re D (contact and parental responsibility: Lesbian mothers and known father) [2006] EWHC 2 (Fam), [2006] 1 FCR 556' (2008) 30 *Journal of Social Welfare and Family Law* 63.

McGrattan, D., 'No need for a father: The Human Fertilisation and Embryology Act 2008' (2009) 12(2) *Irish Journal of Family Law* 33.

Messina, R. and D'Amore, S., 'Adoption by lesbians and gay men in Europe: Challenges and barriers on the journey to adoption' (2018) 21 *Adoption Quarterly* 59.

Mnookin, R., 'Child-custody adjudication: Judicial functions in the face of Indeterminacy' (1975) 39 *Law and Contemporary Problems* 226.

Nordqvist, P., '"Dealing with sperm": Comparing lesbians' clinical and non-clinical donor conception processes' (2011) 33 *Sociology of Health & Illness* 114.

Ntlama, N., 'A brief overview of the Civil Union Act' (2010) 13 *Potchefstroom Electronic Law Journal* 191.

Pelka, S., 'Sharing motherhood: Maternal jealousy among lesbian co-mothers' (2009) 56 *Journal of Homosexuality* 195.

Pennings, G., 'Disclosure of donor conception, age of disclosure and the well-being of donor offspring' (2017) 32 *Human Reproduction* 969.

Perrin, E., Siegel, B. and the Committee on Psychosocial Aspects of Child and Family Health, 'Promoting the well-being of children whose parents are gay or lesbian' (2013) 131 *Pediatrics* 1374–1383.

Peterson, J. and Zill, N., 'Marital disruption, parent-child relationships, and behavior problems in children' (1986) 48 *Journal of Marriage and the Family* 295–307.

Price Cohen, C., 'The role of the United States in the drafting of the convention on the rights of the child' (2006) 20 *Emory International Law Review* 185.

Rathus, Z., 'A call for clarity in the use of social science research in family law decision-making' (2012) 26 *Australian Journal of Family Law* 81–115.

Reece, H., 'The paramountcy principle: Consensus or construct?' (1996) 49 *Current Legal Problems* 267.

Regenerus, M., 'How different are the adult children of parents who have same-sex relationships? Findings from the New Family Structures Study' (2012) 41 *Social Science Research* 752.

Ribar, D., 'Why marriage matters for child wellbeing' (2015) 25 *The Future of Children* 11–27.

Rosato, J., 'Children of same-sex parents deserve the security blanket of the parentage presumption' (2006) 44 *Family Court Review* 74.

Rosenfeld, M., 'Couple longevity in the era of same-sex marriage in the United States' (2014) 76 *Journal of Marriage and Family* 905.

Rosenfeld, M., 'Nontraditional families and childhood progress through school' (2010) 47 *Demography* 755.

Ross, H., Gask, K. and Berrington, A., 'Civil partnership five years on' (2011) 145 *Population Trends* 172.

Schieb, J., O'Riordan, M. and Rubin, S., 'Adolescents with open-identity sperm donors: Reports from 12–17 year olds' (2005) 20 *Human Reproduction* 239–252.

Stacey, J., 'Gay male parenthood and the decline of paternity as we knew it' (2006) 9 *Sexualities* 27.

Stewart, N., 'Marriage facts' (2008) 31 *Harvard Journal of Law and Public Policy* 313.

Tasker, F., 'Lesbian mothers, gay fathers, and their children: A review' (2005) 26 *Developmental and Behavioral Pediatrics* 224.

Tobin, J. and McNair, R., 'Public international law and the regulation of private spaces: Does the convention on the rights of the child impose an obligation on states to allow gay and lesbian couples to adopt?' (2009) 23 *International Journal of Law, Policy and the Family* 110.

Turner, A. J. and Coyle, A., 'What does it mean to be a donor offspring? The identity experiences of adults conceived by donor insemination and the implications for counselling and therapy' (2000) 15 *Human Reproduction* 2041–2051.

Vanfraussen, K., Ponjaert-Kristoffersen, I. and Brewaeys, A., 'Family functioning in lesbian families created by donor insemination' (2003) 73 *American Journal of Orthopsychiatry* 78.

Reports/Other Publications

Adoption Authority of Ireland, *Annual Report 2016* (Dublin: Adoption Authority of Ireland, 2016).

American Psychological Association, *Lesbian and Gay Parenting* (Washington, DC: American Psychological Association, 2005).

American Psychological Association, *Lesbian and Gay Parenting* (Washington, DC: American Psychological Association, 1995).

Anderson Moore, K., Jekielek, S. and Emig, C., *Marriage from a Child's Perspective: How Does Family Structure Affect Children, and What Can We Do about It?* (Washington, DC: Child Trends, 2002).

Center for Marriage and Families, *The Scholarly Consensus on Marriage. Fact Sheet No. 2* (New York: Institute for American Values, 2006).

Committee of Inquiry into Human Fertilisation and Embryology, *Report of the Committee of Inquiry into Human Fertilisation and Embryology* (Cmnd 9314, 1984).

Committee on the Rights of the Child, *Concluding Observations on the Combined Third and Fourth Periodic Reports of India* CRC/C/IND/CO/3–4.

Committee on the Rights of the Child, *Concluding Observations on the Combined Third and Fourth Periodic Reports of Ireland* (March 2016).

Committee on the Rights of the Child, *Concluding Observations on the Second Periodic Report of the United States of America Submitted under Article 12 of the Optional Protocol to the Convention on the Sale of Children, Child Prostitution and Child Pornography*, adopted by the Committee at its sixty-second session (14 January–1 February 2013) CRC/C/OPSC/USA/CO/2.

Committee on the Rights of the Child, *Concluding Observations on the Combined Third and Fourth Reports Submitted by the United States of America under Article 12 (1) of the Optional Protocol to the Convention on the Rights of the Child on the Sale of children, Child Prostitution and Child Pornography* CRC/C/OPSC/USA/CO/3–4.

Committee on the Rights of the Child, *Concluding Observations on the Combined Fourth and Fifth Periodic Reports of Mexico* CRC/C/MEX/CO/4–5.

Committee on the Rights of the Child, *Concluding Observations: United Kingdom of Great Britain and Northern Ireland*, CRC/C/15/ Add 188 (9 October 2002).

Committee on the Rights of the Child, *Consideration of Reports Submitted by States Parties under Article 44 of the Convention on the Rights of the Child. Concluding Observations: Ireland* (Committee on the Rights of the Child, 2006).

Committee on the Rights of the Child, *General Comment No. 14 (2013) on the Right of the Child to Have His or Her Best Interests Taken as a Primary Consideration (art. 3, para. 1)* CRC/C/GC/14.

Department of Education, 'Statistical First Release' SFR 27/2010 (September 2010).

Department of Health, *Donor Information Consultation: Providing Information about Gamete or Embryo Donors* (London: Department of Health, 2001).

Department of Health, *Summary of Responses Received to the Donor Information Consultation: Providing Information about Sperm, Egg and Embryo Donors* (London: Department of Health, 2002).

European Court of Human Rights, *Advisory Opinion Concerning the Recognition in Domestic Law of a Legal Parent-Child Relationship between a Child Born through a Gestational Surrogacy Arrangement Abroad and the Intended Mother*, Request no. P16-2018–001, 10 April 2019.

European Parliament, *Adoption of Children in the European Union* (Briefing, June 2016).

European Parliament, *Annual Report on Human Rights and Democracy in the World 2014 and the European Union's Policy on the Matter (2015/2229(INI))*.

Gallagher, M. and Baker, J., *Do Mothers and Fathers Matter? The Social Science Evidence on Marriage and Child Well-Being* (Washington, DC: Institute for Marriage and Public Policy, 2004).

Government Response to the Report from the Joint Committee on the Human Tissue and Embryos (Draft) Bill, Cm 7209 (October 2007).

Hague Conference on Private International Law, *Report of the Experts' Group on the Parentage/Surrogacy Project* (Report February 2017).

Human Fertilisation and Embryology Authority, *Code of Practice*, 9 ed. (London: Human Fertilisation and Embryology Authority, 2019).

Human Fertilisation and Embryology Authority, *Egg and Sperm Donation in the UK: 2012–2013* (London: Human Fertilisation and Embryology Authority, 2014).

Iona Institute, *Made for Children: Why the institution of Marriage Has Special Status* (Dublin: Iona Institute, 2010).

Joint Committee on the Constitutional Amendment on Children, *Final Report* (Dublin: Joint Committee on the Constitutional Amendment on Children, 2010).

Joint Committee on the Human Tissue and Embryos (Draft) Bill Volume 1: Report, HL Paper 169-I, HC Paper 630-I (2007).

Law Commission and Scottish Law Commission, *Building Families through Surrogacy: A New Law* (Law Commission Consultation Paper No 244; Scottish Law Commission Discussion Paper No 167, 2019).

Law Commission, *Family Law, Review of Child Law, Guardianship and Custody*, Law Com No. 172 of 1988 (London: Law Commission, 1988).

Law Reform Commission, *Consultation Paper on Legal Aspects of Family Relationships*, LRC CP55-2009 (Dublin: Law Reform Commission, 2009).

Law Reform Commission, *Report on Legal Aspects of Family Relationships*, LRC 101–2010 (Dublin: Law Reform Commission, 2010).

LGBT Ireland, *Pathways to Parenting: Proposals for Reform* (Dublin: LGBT Ireland, 2018).

New Zealand Law Commission, *New Issues in Legal Parenthood*, Report 88 (Wellington: New Zealand Law Commission, 2005).

Pillinger, J. and Fagan, P., *LGBT Parents in Ireland. Report from a Study into the Experiences of Lesbian, Gay, Bisexual and Transgender People in Ireland Who Are Parents or Who Are Planning Parenthood* (Dublin: LGBT Diversity, 2013).

Rodgers, B., Trinder, L. and Williams, T., *Towards a Family Justice Observatory to Improve the Generation and Application of Research* (London: Nuffield, 2015)

Scottish Law Commission, *Parental Responsibilities and Rights, Guardianship and the Administration of Children's Property*, Discussion Paper No 88 of 1990 (Edinburgh: Scottish Law Commission, 1990).

Shannon, G., *Tenth Report of the Special Rapporteur on Child Protection* (Dublin: Special Rapporteur on Child Protection, 2016).

South African Law Reform Commission, *The Right to Know One's own Biological Origins*, Issue Paper 32 (Pretoria: South African Law Reform Commission, 2017).

Surrogacy UK, *Surrogacy in the UK: Further Evidence for Reform. Second Report of the Surrogacy UK Working Group on Surrogacy Law Reform* (London: Surrogacy UK, 2018).

Task Force on the Guidelines for the Use of Social Science Research in Family Law, *Guidelines for the Use of Social Science Research in Family Law* (Madison: Association of Family and Conciliation Courts, 2018).

UN Special Rapporteur on the Sale and Sexual Exploitation of Children, *Report to the Human Rights Council*, A/HRC/37/60, 15 January 2018.

Witherspoon Institute, *Marriage and the Public Good: Ten Principles* (Princeton: Witherspoon Institute, 2008).

News Articles/ Opinion Pieces

Bracken, L., 'The kids are not alright: Why some children are in a legal bind' *RTÉ Brainstorm*, 25 May 2018.

Carey, A., 'Marriage equality: The young movement that swung the Yes vote', *Irish Times*, 16 November 2015.

Cullen, P., 'Proposed sperm and egg donor register "unacceptable" says doctor' *Irish Times*, 25 February 2015.

Evershed, N., 'Think of the kids: Why marriage equality opponents are wrong on parenting', *The Guardian*, 17 August 2017.

'Family court magistrate suspended after objecting to same-sex parents', *Pink News*, 18 January 2015.

Gamble, N., 'Should surrogate mothers still have an absolute right to change their minds?' *Bionews*, 22 October 2012.

Gartland, F., 'Change sought to anomaly in adoption law' *Irish Times*, 28 June 2014.

Hunt, E., 'Your father's not your father: When DNA tests reveal more than you bargained for' *The Guardian*, 18 September 2018.

Kelly, F., 'Fitzgerald's children Bill outlines new steps on parentage', *Irish Times*, 12 February 2015.

'Lesbian mums can't register baby in Italy' *BBC News*, 19 April 2018.

MacCormaic, R., 'Shatter warns Family Bill will end donor-assisted reproduction' *Irish Times*, 5 March 2015.

McCormack, C., 'Naming sperm donors will hit treatment here' *Irish Independent*, 8 March 2015.

McDonagh, M., 'What's the reality of going it alone through sperm donation?' *Irish Times*, 6 September 2016.

McEnroe, J., 'Tánaiste: No posters "sad and demeaning"' *Irish Examiner*, 5 May 2015.

McQuinn, C., 'Ireland set for award for support of LGBTI community at World Pride event' *Irish Independent*, 15 May 2019.

Minihan, M., 'Who opposes children's referendum?' *Irish Times*, 30 October 2012.

O'Brien, B., 'Love is not enough when it comes to children's rights' *Irish Times*, 24 January 2015.

O'Halloran, M., 'Senator calls for donor-assisted reproduction to be restricted' *Irish Times*, 27 March 2015.

Quinn, D., 'Government's rush to embrace the "new normal" downgrades the natural family' *Irish Independent*, 20 February 2015.

Reuters, 'Thousands march in Paris to repeal same-sex marriage law' *NBC News*, 16 October 2016.

Ronán Mullen, 'Head to head: Ronán Mullen argues against same-sex marriage' *Irish Times*, 22 May 2015.

RTÉ News, 'Lawyer group say Yes vote for same-sex marriage will affect assisted reproduction rights' *RTÉ News*, 15 May 2015.

Scammell, R., 'Treat surrogate parents as sex offenders, says Italian minister' *The Guardian*, 6 January 2016.

The Local, 'First same-sex overseas adoption takes place in Sweden' *The Local*, 5 September 2017.

Tighe, M., 'Irish surrogacy rates are world's second-highest' *The Sunday Times*, 7 October 2018.

Lectures/Talks/Debates

Dáil Éireann Debates, 25 February 2015.

Evidence presented by Professor Susan Golombok to the Joint Committee on the Human Tissue and Embryos (Draft) Bill. *Joint Committee on the Human Tissue and Embryos (Draft) Bill, Volume II: Evidence, HL Paper* 169-II, HC Paper 630-II (2007).

Fitzgerald, F., 'Address by the Minister for Justice and Equality, Frances Fitzgerald TD at the Children's Rights Alliance Seminar' (Children's Rights Alliance Seminar on the Children and Family Relationships Bill 2015, Dublin Castle, 2 March 2015).

Hammarberg, T., 'The Principle of the Best Interests of the Child: What It Means and What It Demands from Adults' (Lecture by Thomas Hammarberg, Commissioner for Human Rights, Council of Europe, Warsaw, 30 May 2008).

Hansard, HL, vol 640, col 601, 5 November 2002.

O'Mahony, C. and Bracken, L., 'The Child's Right to Family Life: Shifting Sands and Social Science' (International Journal of Children's Rights UNCRC 30th Anniversary Conference, 21 June 2019).

Seanad Éireann Debates, 24 March 2015.

Stacey, J., 'What Is Needed to Defend the Bipartisan Defense of Marriage Act of 1996?' Hearing before the Subcomm. on the Constitution, Civil Rights and Property Rights of the Senate Comm. on the Judiciary, 108th Cong., 4 September 2003.

Von Dadelszen, P., 'Rights or Obligations? Review of the Guardianship Act 1968', Triennial New Zealand Law Society Conference and 4th New Zealand Family Law Conference, Christchurch, 6 October 2001.

Internet Resources

CoramBAAF, 'Statistics: England' www.corambaaf.org.uk/fostering-adoption/looked-after-children-adoption-fostering-statistics/statistics-england

Cryos Denmark, 'Prices and Payment' www.dk.cryosinternational.com/donor-sperm/prices-and-payment/

Human Fertilisation and Embryology Authority, 'Remove your donor anonymity' www.hfea.gov.uk/donation/donors/remove-your-donor-anonymity/

Law Commission, 'Surrogacy' www.lawcom.gov.uk/project/surrogacy/

O'Mahony, C., 'The Constitution, the Right to Procreate and the Marriage Referendum' Constitution Project @ UCC, 21 April 2015 www.constitutionproject.ie/?p=503

INDEX